Other Books by Shana Alexander

Happy Days

When She Was Bad

The Pizza Connection

Nutcracker

Very Much a Lady

Anyone's Daughter

Talking Woman

Shana Alexander's State-by-State Guide to Women's Rights

The Feminine Eye

THE ASTONISHING ELEPHANT

THE ASTONISHING ELEPHANT

Shana Alexander

RANDOM HOUSE · NEW YORK

Grateful acknowledgment is made to the following for permission to reprint previously published material:

LIFE MAGAZINE: Excerpt from an article by Romain Gary from the December 22, 1967, issue of *Life* magazine; excerpts from "Belle's Baby" by Shana Alexander from the May 11, 1962, issue of *Life* magazine; excerpts from "For the Love of Elephants" by Shana Alexander, from the March 1980 issue of *Life* magazine. Copyright © 1962, 1967, 1980 by Time, Inc. Reprinted by permission.

WALKER GIBSON: Four lines from "The Circus Ship Euzkera." Originally appeared in *The New Yorker*. Reprinted by permission of Walker Gibson.

PENGUIN PUTNAM, INC.: Excerpts from *Battle for the Elephants* by Iain and Oria Douglas-Hamilton. Copyright © 1992 by Iain Douglas-Hamilton. Reprinted by permission of Viking Penguin, a division of Penguin Putnam, Inc.

PENGUIN PUTNAM, INC., AND LAURENCE POLLINGER LIMITED: "The Elephant Is Slow to Mate," from *The Complete Poems of D. H. Lawrence* by D. H. Lawrence, edited by V. de Sola Pinto and F. W. Roberts. Copyright © 1964, 1971 by Angelo Ravagli and C. M. Weekley, Executors of the Estate of Frieda Lawrence Ravagli. Rights throughout the United Kingdom are controlled by Laurence Pollinger Limited. Reprinted by permission of Penguin Putnam, Inc., and Laurence Pollinger and the Estate of Frieda Lawrence Ravagli.

SABINA W. SANDERSON: Excerpts from *The Dynasty of Abu* by Ivan T. Sanderson. Reprinted by permission of Sabina W. Sanderson.

Library of Congress Cataloging-in-Publication Data

Alexander, Shana.
The astonishing elephant/Shana Alexander.
p. cm.
Includes bibliographical references.
ISBN 0-679-45660-0
1. Elephants—North America. I. Title.
QL737.P98 A43 2000 599.67—dc21 99-050038

Random House website address: www.atrandom.com

Printed in the United States of America on acid-free paper

98765432

First Edition

Book design by Mercedes Everett

For Dr. Matthew Maberry, D.V.M.,
my first teacher

There is a mystery behind that masked gray visage, an ancient life force, delicate and mighty, awesome and enchanted, commanding the silence. . . .

—Peter Matthiessen, *The Tree Where Man Was Born*

CONTENTS

INTRODUCTION

How did I get hooked on elephants—me of all people—a woman born and raised in the middle of Manhattan, someone with zero knowledge or experience of animals, domestic or wild? I was thirty-six years old and had never even owned a pet when I first heard of a young elephant named Belle. She lived at the zoo in Portland, Oregon, and was believed to be in an advanced state of pregnancy. If the zoo's calculations and press releases were correct, Belle's baby would be the first elephant born in the Americas since prehistoric times, when woolly mammoths roamed. Reporters and zoologists from around the world were converging on the zoo, and with scant forethought I hastened to join them. I hung around for a few days, intrigued as much by the colorful gathering of animal experts as by the animals themselves, but nothing happened, and I went home.

Each time the zoo veterinarian convinced himself birth was imminent, he telephoned me, and I leapt onto the next plane, determined to write the story of this major milestone in the annals of mammals.

My fourth mad dash to Portland finally paid off, and early on the morning of Easter Saturday 1962 I arrived in time to observe and eventually to write up for *Life* magazine what the editors billed on *Life*'s cover as BIG BLESSED EVENT: 225 POUNDS AND ALL ELEPHANT.

Playing midwife to an elephant had been fascinating, and more fun than any previous story I'd worked on. Over the succeeding years, between celebrity profiles, political commentary, and, finally, books, I wrote a few other elephant stories. Gradually I learned more about this most compelling of creatures, and always I stored up notes for the book on elephants that I knew from my first days in Portland I would one day find time to write.

Only after I'd begun writing it did I recognize that my empathy for the order Proboscidea had begun long before Portland. As a girl growing up in the 1930s in a series of New York City apartment hotels, most of them shadowed by the complex latticework of the Sixth Avenue El, my surefire sign of spring was the annual arrival in nearby Madison Square Garden of the Ringling Brothers, Barnum & Bailey Circus. My father, my sister, and I regularly attended this event with the fervor of Crusaders, catching two or three matinees every year. Our father, a composer of popular music, was a pal of Merle Evans, the red-coated circus bandmaster, and this assured us not just the best box seats in the arena, but early admission to the preperformance menagerie and freak show set up in the Garden basement.

Usually we got to the basement early enough to watch the elephants being dressed up for the "spec," the big parade that began the show upstairs. We were astonished one year to see immense gold tiaras being attached to the elephants' heads with rhinestone chin straps, and monstrous ballet skirts of pink tulle tied round their middles. The spectacle made me feel squirmy and sad. Our father explained that this season the pachyderms would be lurching and twirling to ballet music commissioned by the circus from Igor Stravinsky, and performing dance routines "choreographed" by George Balanchine. At age eight I'd never heard of Stravinsky or Balanchine, or of choreography for that matter, but I was painfully aware of the humiliation these great beasts must feel at finding themselves in such inappropriate, insensitive circumstances.

A few lines back I used the word "sad." The truth is, performing elephants have always embarrassed me. Let the vainglorious lion be king of beasts. To me the elephant is mandarin, and I do not enjoy watching him on his hind legs.

Given the facts of my animal-free childhood and early life, where does my strong attachment to elephants come from? Musing about this not long ago, I recalled a forgotten treasure of my earliest years, a French Noah's Ark book. It was a gift from my mother's Parisian friend, and she used to read it aloud to three-year-old me seated on her lap. I don't speak French these days, and had not thought of *L'Arc de Noë* for about sixty years, until dawn one morning in the Serengeti, in East Africa, where I had gone on assignment for *National Geographic.* I was being driven across the empty savanna in a Land Rover when far off on the horizon a frieze of wild animals appeared in silhouette against the rising sun. Suddenly I was on my feet waving my arms and shouting, "*Les éléphants! La girafe!*"

Doubtless I also got hooked on elephants because I was already hooked on metaphor. Every writer is, and the elephant is one of the oldest, biggest, and most universal metaphors mankind has ever stumbled against and been wowed by. An awareness that elephants are something very special is found in every civilization. Students of Scripture used to quote the powerful passage in the Book of Job:

> Behold now behemoth, which I made with thee;
> He eateth grass as an ox.

Lo now, his strength is in his loins,
And his force is in the stays of his body.
He straineth his tail like a cedar;
The sinews of his thighs are knit together.
His bones are pipes of brass;
His gristles are like bars of iron.
He is the beginning of the ways of God.

Alas, better scholars now agree that this particular behemoth was, I regret to say, a rhinoceros.

Herodotus, in the fifth century B.C., termed the elephant "of all animals the most akin to man." Writer to writer thereafter, through the centuries, from Aristotle ("the beast that passeth all others in wit and mind . . . and by its intelligence, it makes as near an approach to man as matter can approach spirit") to Cicero, deploring the slaughter of elephants in the Roman Games ("they arouse both pity and a feeling that the elephant is somehow allied with man") to Chaucer ("For mayst thou sormounten thise olifaunts in greatnesse or weight of body?") to passionate John Donne ("Nature's great master-peece, an Elephant, / The onely harmlesse great thing") the elephant has caused poets, playwrights, scholars, aphorists, fabulists, and all other citizens of the world of imagination to bow and marvel, scratch their heads and nibble their quills. This century's poets are no different. They can neither resist the elephant nor agree about him. To D. H. Lawrence he incarnates the world's most oceanic orgasm. Marianne Moore sees the same beast as the very avatar of Buddhist tranquillity: "asleep on an elephant, that is repose!" My own viewpoint is closest to that of Louis MacNeice, who begins his elephant poem: "Tonnage of instinctive / Wisdom in tinsel."

Over the years I have come to understand that human beings and elephants enjoy a unique relationship, different from our connection to every other animal species. Perhaps it is because, as

Ivan T. Sanderson remarks in *The Dynasty of Abu*, "Elephants are just as unlike all other living things as we are."

Romain Gary may have said it best in a well-known love letter, "Dear Elephant, Sir:"

> For a long time now I have had the feeling that our destinies are linked. . . . In my eyes . . . you represent to perfection everything that is threatened today with extinction in the name of progress, efficiency, ideology, materialism, or even reason, for a certain abstract, inhuman use of reason and logic are becoming more and more allies of our murderous folly. It seems clear today that we have been merely doing to other species, and to yours in the first place, what we are on the verge of doing to ourselves.

Above and beyond these correspondences, elephants have always had a special importance to man, a connection unrelated to size or power or skeletal structure. No animal has been more beloved than the elephant by all the peoples and cultures who have known him, and I know of no legends, myths, or folktales of evil elephants. In real life, of course, exceptions always come along to prove the rule, and nothing is perfect, least of all elephants, as we shall see.

Nonetheless, the animal seems to be a universal symbol for good in every part of the world and throughout human history. Elephants and mammoths appear in the prehistoric art of Europe, Africa, Asia, the Arctic, and even of Central America, where elephants ridden by turbaned mahouts carrying traditional Indian elephant hooks have been found carved onto Mayan stele in the jungles of Guatemala.

The elephant, I have learned, is unique among all the creatures of earth and sea. Nothing else is anything like it. At the same time, a mysterious, even metaphysical bond connects our two species, and always has. Humans and elephants are very alike in myriad ways, and this likeness fascinates people everywhere. The elephant fires the human imagination like no other beast. It appears in the art and myth of virtually all the peoples of the world. It turns up in every major religion, and it has been performing chores for mankind and stunts for our enjoyment since history began.

What is one to make of it all? Perhaps this: elephants are not like us entirely, but they are a lot like the very best of us. They are like what we would want to be, the ideal toward which we strive. They have essential nobility, serenity, sagacity, loyalty, and playfulness, a simple goodness, a lack of animosity—unless provoked. They occupy a special place in our consciousness; they convey a sense of perfect beings. In many ways, they represent what Jehovah, Jesus, the Prophet, the Buddha, and the other great teachers of mankind adjure us to be. Yet these same creatures that appear to embody the best in humankind have throughout history brought out the worst: our savagery, greed, and unfeeling cruelty.

And the sadness? Perhaps it stems from a visceral awareness that today both elephant species, Asian and African, tremble on the edge of extinction. Yet if we allow the elephant to vanish from the planet, do we not forfeit some of what is best in ourselves?

PART I

GETTING HOOKED

CHAPTER 1

THE ELEPHANT'S CHILD

I HEARD ABOUT it first on the radio, listening to the twenty-four-hours-a-day news broadcasts to which I had by then become addicted. An elephant in Portland, Oregon, was 1,000 pounds overweight and believed soon to give birth. Very likely the zoo's three other female elephants were pregnant, too. If true, the story was big zoo news. Elephants are notoriously hard to breed in captivity, said the reporter, and all the "newborn" elephants exhibited here, at least in my lifetime, had in fact been babies captured in Asia. A genuine infant elephant had never been seen in America, not even by other elephants.

I got the news in Los Angeles, in my office at *Life* magazine. It was shortly before Christmas 1961, and I had recently been elevated to the exalted rank of staff writer, after having toiled at the magazine for more than a decade as a researcher and bureau correspondent. For the first time I had a byline and some say in choosing my assignments. My editors back in New York City agreed that the zoo was worth a look, and soon I was on a plane to Portland.

I found the city in a delirium of anticipation. Newspapers waved banner headlines: ELEPHANTICIPATING! and ELEPHANTRICIANS ALERT! One local radio station was broadcasting hourly "Belle Bulletins," and another had launched a "Name the Baby" contest. Toy departments were completely sold out of stuffed elephants. As Portlanders came to realize that their zoo's elephant house had become a vast maternity ward, a carnival mood swept the city, and the zoo was being deluged with gifts for the newborn—everything from gigantic, gold-plated diaper pins to hand-knitted baby elephants. Schoolchildren were assigned to draw pictures of what they imagined the baby would look like. Portland is proud to call itself the Rose City, and the morning I arrived the local florists' association had constructed a gigantic papier-mâché baby-bootie, filled it with 300 long-stemmed roses, and delivered the tribute as cameras rolled.

The Washington Park Zoo (now the Oregon Zoo) was shrouded in heavy mists and intermittent rain as I sloshed my way for the first time to its pink-painted elephant house. On this chilly, miserable day, the elephants had retreated from their outdoor patio to their heated indoor quarters. The line of people standing out in the wet, waiting to get in, was sixty or seventy yards long, but the doorkeepers were moving it forward at a steady pace. I got in line and soon found myself staring into a gloomily lit, hay-strewn concrete chamber twenty feet deep and eighty feet long. The long wall nearest us was solid, unbreakable glass. Seven feet inside the glass was a row of stout, concrete-filled, floor-to-ceiling, four-inch steel pipes set just far enough apart for a man in a hurry to slip through sideways. Separating the spectators from the glass was a narrow alleyway that was beginning to fill up with camera crews and equipment. Workmen on ladders were installing a strip of floodlights on the ceiling so that the momentous nativity could be recorded on color film.

I stared through the glass and past the pipes at four looming, gray beasts. Two were slowly rocking back and forth on stout, pillar-like legs, while the other two languidly patrolled their quarters, rhythmically swishing the concrete floor with their trunks as if wielding invisible long-handled dustpans and brooms.

It was difficult at first to determine which one was Belle. In profile, her condition was not especially notable; a thousand or so extra pounds on six thousand pounds of well-fed elephant is not as eye-catching as one might suppose. But viewed head-on, Belle could be seen to bulge amidships as if she had just swallowed a dozen watermelons. Seemingly ignored by her three ponderous ladies-in-waiting, the expectant mother strolled heavily around her quarters, nibbled hay, and occasionally glanced back over her shoulder at the slowly moving line of spectators. Once or twice Belle seemed to focus her mild gaze directly on me, an experience I found disconcerting. Her small eyes had wrinkled lids thickly fringed with long, Betty Boop–style lashes.

Outdoors again, I ducked around behind the elephant house and found a large rear storage room piled high with bales of hay, first-aid supplies, and other zoo paraphernalia. By now Belle's condition had attracted worldwide press attention, and a score of reporters and photographers were perched at varying heights on a twenty-foot-high haystack that filled one corner of the otherwise bare concrete chamber. Facing them stood a handful of zoo officials.

The slim, weary-looking man in work clothes and high-top boots, his gray hair rumpled, was Dr. Matthew Maberry, the zoo's veterinarian, and he was introducing the other members of his team: the zoo's director, two doctors from the University of Oregon Medical School, a professional wild-animal importer, and the zoo's head elephant keeper. As I listened, I thought of the fabled six blind men of India. "Very like a fan," said the man fingering the elephant's ear. "Like a tree," said the man feeling the leg. "Like a serpent," said the man at the trunk. Each one knew something about an elephant, but none had the whole picture.

Maberry himself knew the most. "Doc" favored a hayseed style of speech and dress, and looked like Percy Kilbride in the movies. His abashed demeanor successfully masked the fact that he had trained at the federal Centers for Disease Control in Atlanta, and had extensive, worldwide experience in large animal work. He also had broad obstetrical experience, having delivered lions, tigers, buffaloes, and bears; he had performed cesarean sections on cows and horses. But an elephant is not only much larger, she is differently constructed in certain significant respects than any other animal on earth. And Dr. Maberry had never delivered an elephant.

Doc Maberry's two consulting physicians were Howard Tatum, M.D., professor of obstetrics at the University of Oregon Medical School, and Dr. James Metcalfe, associate cardiologist at the medical school and president of the Oregon Heart Association. Though experts in their own fields, the two doctors knew nothing whatsoever about elephants. Dr. Tatum said he was especially eager to get his hands on—or, more accurately, to get his arms around—an elephant placenta. He wanted to take a biopsy of this eighty-pound organ and make tissue cultures from it to grow in his laboratory for further study. Dr. Metcalfe hoped to do some blood studies. "The metabolic problems of an elephant are positively fantastic," he remarked with relish.

The zoo's director, Jack Marks, was no naturalist, but he knew a lot about how to please the public and the city fathers. When he determined to build "the ultimate modern zoo," Marks first visited zoos all over the nation accompanied by two architects who then designed the present open-plan arrangement. Instead of birds and beasts confined in outdoor cages and smelly, overheated buildings, Portland was one of the first zoos to offer a modern habitat display, each animal exhibited in its natural setting, and separated from the public only by a deep moat.

Marks confessed he was a bit weary, having spent the previous several days arranging for extra security guards and barricades to handle the crowds, dealing with eager VIPs from the Zoological Society and the Parks Commission, and serving the clamoring, ever-growing press corps. By now he'd even assigned Belle her own still photographer and film crew.

Next to Marks stood a stocky, mild-looking man in rimless glasses, wearing a knitted navy watchcap and khaki coveralls. He was Morgan Berry, a Seattle wild-animal importer who had procured two of the zoo's four females, Belle and little seven-year-old Pet; Berry also owned the sire, the mighty fourteen-year-old bull Thonglaw, to whom we had yet to be introduced. Berry knew valuable details of Belle's history, including the vital fact that she had been bred to Thonglaw on July 19, 1960, had not come into season since, and hence was now almost certainly eighteen months pregnant. He offered the opinion that Belle's maternal instincts would kindle naturally when her baby was born. Berry knew a lot about elephants, but next to nothing about obstetrics.

The lean, laconic fellow in coveralls standing at the end of the row, the sixth man, was Head Keeper Alvin Tucker. He had eight years' experience watching, feeding, and cleaning up after the largest animals on earth. Belle's daily diet, he said, included one and a half bales of best timothy hay, three gallons of oats, six pounds of bread, fifty pounds of carrots, half a box of apples, twenty-five pounds of bananas, a quarter-box of oranges, and ten pounds of freshly dug dirt. Like other expectant mothers, Belle had developed special cravings. Her new favorite tidbits were discarded cartons from photographic film and containers of black coffee donated by reporters.

Nobody had yet answered the key questions on everybody's mind: When was it going to happen, and what would it be like? How long does it take an elephant to have an elephant, anyway? It turned out that precious little information was available. In *Patterns of Mammalian Reproduction*, the 437-page standard reference book on the subject by Professor S. A. Asdell of Cornell University, only a page and a half were devoted to elephants. The gestation period was reported to vary from 500 to 720 days, based on twenty-five recorded cases. Furthermore, the book expressed considerable doubt about the animal's age of puberty. It had been variously recorded as age nine to fifteen in the male and eight to sixteen in the female. Thonglaw and Belle, Berry had told us, were ten and fourteen respectively.

Belle's doctors did have one other reference book, *The Care and Management of Elephants in Burma*, published in Rangoon. The work contains such information as, "From the twelfth to the sixteenth month a pregnant female can do light work, but should on no account be made to *aung* in streams during rises as she may be struck by floating logs."

Despite the dearth of information, Belle's team attempted to project an air of competence, a feeling that they could handle any situation that might arise. Morgan Berry said that Belle was an especially sweet-tempered elephant. He had imported her from Thailand at the age of two months and hand-raised her for a year in the family's basement, treating her like one of the Berry children. Until she reached eight months and 400 pounds, she had particularly enjoyed motoring through downtown Seattle with the Berrys. Belle sat in the backseat of the family's open Cadillac convertible with her trunk wrapped lovingly around Morgan's neck as he drove. When she reached twelve months, and 660 pounds, Belle outgrew the basement and moved to a more permanent home at the zoo. Three years later, Berry imported baby Thonglaw, as a surprise gift for his children, and a few years after that, little Pet.

As soon as they were old enough, all three of Morgan Berry's elephants—Thonglaw, Belle, and Pet (whom Belle seemed to regard as her adopted daughter)—lived and worked at the Seattle zoo during the summer. In winter, Berry boarded them in the milder climate of the Portland zoo. Portland also owned two year-round female residents, Rosy, who was twelve, and eight-year-old Tuy Hoa. All in all, the Portland-Seattle arrangement was a cozy one, both for the animals and for the old codgers in charge. Although I could never prove it, I came to believe that Morgan and his pal Doc Maberry together had hatched the plot to import a male baby elephant and bide their time until it reach breeding age, whatever that might turn out to be.

Not only are captive elephants famously slow to mate; even in the wild, a longish courtship was believed to occur before the female would accept the bull's advances. But the high-spirited Thonglaw had turned out to be a formidable pachyderm Don Juan. By the time I met the elephants, Rosy was expecting her own calf in midsummer, Tuy Hoa in the fall, and though it was still a bit early to confirm the condition of little Pet, chances were that she would give birth the following winter.

Usually Thonglaw and his devoted harem shared the same spacious quarters. But every year or so since the age of ten the normally manageable bull had had to be hauled out and locked up alone in an isolation cell. Otherwise the animals' human attendants would not have had a chance to get anywhere near them. For about six weeks a year, the expectant father became a homicidal maniac who might charge any man who approached him, even Berry, with intent to kill.

Thonglaw's temporary insanity had no relation to his impending fatherhood. He was in heavy *musth,* Doc explained. *Musth* is a unique, periodic condition of mature male elephants caused or accompanied by a sharp rise in hormone levels. The condition is still not entirely understood, possibly because it renders the bulls unapproachable by human beings. Depending on age and general health, the animal experiences first *musth* at the age of ten to twelve. It lasts six to eight weeks, and recurs every twelve or fourteen months or so for the rest of his life. The cycle begins with the swelling of the temporal glands, a pair of unique organs that are set high on either side of the head, midway between eye and ear. The glands emit an evil-smelling, blackish, oily ooze that begins to drip down the elephant's cheeks. He may also dribble urine, and suffers other physical and behavioral changes triggered by a huge rise in his blood testosterone. He first becomes hyperaggressive, unpredictable, dangerous, restless, and perhaps more attractive to cows. But in later *musth* he turns moody, abstracted, and melancholy, and loses his appetite.

The word *musth* comes from the Urdu word *mast*, meaning drunk. In the wild, *musth* bulls fight. Part of the function of *musth* seems to be to establish a dominance hierarchy that determines which bull (or bulls) gets to mate with the "hot" cows. A wild bull in *musth* strides around jungle or savanna with his head held high, tusks forward, ears fanned out wide. He picks fights with other bulls and seemingly is searching for females that are coming into season. But although *musth* is related to sexual activity, the two do not always occur together. Many bulls in heavy *musth* appear stuporous and incapable of mating, and by the time *musth* subsides, the animal has lost weight and condition and is physically debilitated. Unlike deer, elk, and other herd animals that experience a simultaneous annual rut, each male elephant cycles individually, according to his own internal clock.

The phenomenon of *musth* fascinated early man; woolly mammoths with temporal glands adrip are depicted in prehistoric cave drawings. In ancient times the oily black secretion was variously thought to be a powerful aphrodisiac, an antidote to poison, and a substance guaranteed to dissolve pearls and to grow hair.

To deal with the "bulling problem," as *musth* is sometimes called in circus circles, castration has several times been attempted. One well-documented effort was made in the 1930s on mighty Pilate, a famed Hagenbeck & Wallace elephant who died almost immediately as a result. An elephant carries his testicles internally, leaving insufficient opportunity for post-op recovery. The huge creature cannot be kept tranquilized nearly long enough, and, as the fabled circus flack F. Beverly Kelley asserts in his memoirs, "the nervous disposition of the animal makes healing almost out of the question."

Musth subsides as mysteriously as it comes on, and the bull can then be rebroken, like a wild bronc. Using an electric cattle prod, Morgan Berry had successfully rebroken Thonglaw four times. But each time he had to wait until Thonglaw's galloping hormones settled back to normal.

Reflecting her gentle upbringing, Belle had continued throughout her developing pregnancy to be the very model of ladylike elephant deportment. Although she was certainly aware by mid-January of much unusual activity both inside her and out, she appeared not to notice. Sometimes her disposition seemed just a trifle edgy; this the zoo men could readily understand. It may be assumed that Belle had not the slightest idea what was happening to her. She had never known another elephant in her own ballooning condition. Neither, in fact, had any of the zoo men, and they were growing a trifle edgy themselves.

Each man on the team had his specific assignment. Dr. Maberry would supervise the expectant mother's general health, make examinations, keep records, and preside over the delivery. His equipment included surgical instruments, a resuscitator, a respirator, 110-volt electric prods to prevent the mother from trampling the newborn baby, floodlights, and a borrowed set of shipping-room scales. Maberry was prepared, but not prepared for, well, anything. In the event of difficulty, he might have to perform a cesarean, and he wondered how much anesthetic it would take to knock out an elephant, and how he would administer it. "Getting a mask on her might be a problem," he mused. He had an oxygen tent, but it wasn't big enough. He thought a pup tent would be about right, if he could make it airtight.

Someone asked him about transfusions. Even in an emergency, he said, whole blood would be out of the question; no information was available on elephant blood types. But he did have gallons of plasma substitute on hand. He also had a stethoscope with which he could pick up the fetal heartbeat loud and clear, and a homemade device for measuring Belle's temperature—a cattle thermometer he had lashed like a Neanderthal's spearhead to the end of a wooden yardstick.

Recently Portland had located the one man on earth known to have delivered an elephant in captivity, Dr. Eremanno Bronzini of the Rome zoo. The Portland phone company eagerly offered to put through as many gratis conference calls as might be necessary, and a high school Italian teacher was rushed to Doc Maberry's side to translate. Then it turned out that Dr. Bronzini had no telephone. Eventually the frantic callers roused Dr. Emmanuel Amoroso, an elderly professor emeritus at the Royal Veterinary College in London. In the 1930s, Dr. Amoroso had seen many African elephants born in the wilds of Ethiopia. The one reliable indication that birth was imminent, he told Doc, was a sudden dip in maternal temperature. The normal temperature of an adult elephant is 98°F, and a sudden drop of one to three degrees signaled that birth was twelve to twenty-four hours off.

Whether this symptom was equally valid for Indian elephants in captivity in Oregon no one knew. To be on the safe side, however, Portland's dedicated veterinarian had moved into the elephant house, placed his sleeping bag in the narrow lane between the concrete pipes and bulletproof glass, and had begun keeping detailed obstetrical notes as well as faithfully recording his patient's temperature twice a day.

We retreated to the haystack storage room. Suddenly a huge, shuddering thud shook the building. It felt as if Mount Hood had erupted, but Doc said it was only Thonglaw. Due to heavy *musth*, the big bull had begun angrily bashing his 8,000-pound body into the barred wall of his steel-reinforced concrete isolation chamber adjoining the room where we sat. Another isolation chamber, also equipped with massive hydraulic doors, was in readiness should Belle need to be alone.

The afternoon wore on. The public went home. The four females continued peacefully pacing their quarters. Before leaving the elephant house to get some dinner, Maberry stripped off his shirt and undershirt, Vaselined his right arm up to the armpit, and—with Keeper Tucker's help—induced Belle to back up to the bars. Seizing his homemade thermometer like a lance, and hooking his left arm around one of the bars for balance, he lunged for her rectum, and held his thermometer in place. Belle's temperature, he said when he withdrew it, had not changed.

Nothing else was happening, except that it was raining harder now. Somebody remarked that Belle's multicolored liver pills and antibiotic capsules would make excellent poker chips, and a few of the reporters started up a game.

Feeling itchy and smelly from my day in the straw, and depressed by a general sense of anticlimax, I returned to my hotel eager for a long, hot bath. In close quarters, the clinging, rotting-potato smell of elephant gets into one's hair and clothing and becomes overpowering. After a few hours in Belle's snugly warmed maternity ward, each heavy lungful of air seems to weigh on one's diaphragm like another rancid dumpling.

I stripped off my clothes and flipped on the TV news. The four females were eating the baby-bootie full of roses. After tearing the prickly bouquet apart, they carefully ripped off each crimson blossom with their trunks and cast it aside—as we might do with peanut shells—before dreamily munching on the long, thorny stem. One of them scooped up a fresh trunkful of roses from the floor, and stems and blossoms fanned out like a cat's whiskers on either side of her mouth, firmly clamped between upraised trunk and pendulous lower lip.

The following morning I returned to the zoo and found Maberry and the two doctors inside the elephant enclosure preparing to measure the baby's fetal heartbeat. The public was temporarily barred. The patient had been coaxed to lie down on her side, and the other three animals had been moved off to a far corner. I thought I could see Belle's great gray flanks twitch each time her unborn child administered a small, elephantine kick. But she lay there amiably enough while the doctors, aided by Keeper

Tucker, strapped on Metcalf's homemade equipment—a specially rigged contraption consisting of a length of canvas fire hose encircling Belle's midsection and attached to several feet of wire connected to an electrocardiograph. He also had brought gear for making blood tests. Later he announced the result of his calculations: Belle's blood volume would fill a fifty-five gallon oil drum. To supply her tremendous mass of tissue with energy, and rid it of waste products, her great heart needed to pump 320 pounds of blood a minute.

Time moved very slowly after that. The poker game resumed and went on all night. I survived on paper cups of black coffee, offering every third cup to Belle, who grasped it delicately with her trunk-tip and lowered the whole thing, cup and all, into her open mouth. Nothing was happening. I decided to go home to my husband and our six-month-old daughter. Doc apologized to the reporters for getting us up there too early, and promised to alert us in time, as soon as the situation changed.

In Los Angeles, I started reading up on elephants. Without some specialized knowledge of order Proboscidea, it was impossible for the general, peanut-throwing public to grasp the extent of the problems that shortly would confront Belle's six attendants. An elephant is the strongest animal on earth and is certainly not scared of mice. But it is easily startled by unexpected noises, bright lights, and strangers. Its sense of smell is so acute that it can be spooked even by a sudden whiff of Arpège. An elephant is a wild animal: it can be trained, but never tamed. Though it rarely uses its full strength, it is fully aware of its potential. It does sometimes kill, but never by accident. It is a vegetarian and does not eat people, ever. But because its digestion is only about 40 percent efficient, it must be eating something almost constantly.

A week later, Maberry called. The baby's kicking had become so much more violent and visible that he suspected her time was very near. I drove to the airport. At the zoo, I found Belle engaged in an intermittent weaving and rocking motion. Doc said she kept this up for hours on end, and he believed it might be an instinctive attempt to loosen the bones of her pelvic girdle, and perhaps also to move the fetus into position for birth. By now I knew that an elephant's cervix is located at about tail height, and at birth the infant slides down the five-foot birth canal as if in an amusement park chute-the-chute.

From January 25 onward, Maberry and one or more of his aides and a gaggle of reporters maintained a day-and-night vigil that became known as The Great Portland Elephant Watch. Headquarters was the back room of the elephant house, and we were forced to share the smelly space with two extraordinary wild animals. In a cage on the floor not far from where the unfortunate Thonglaw lurked, and occasionally lunged, squatted an Abyssinian ground hornbill, a turkey-sized, black, morose-looking bird with a beak like an iron banana. Periodically it shuffled around in the debris of its dinner and ran its beak along the bars of its cage, making a sound like a policeman's nightstick on an iron fence. Portland's hornbill was temporarily not on exhibition because the public found it too boringly revolting to look at.

At the start of our vigil, participants in The Great Portland Elephant Watch were a group of healthy, alert, eager animal experts and reporters, I the only female. We lounged in the hay pile swapping elephant tales; we read avidly through the scant elephant literature available; we catnapped occasionally, and rose often to poke, fondle, and feed the female herd. We munched our way through one hundred pounds of peanuts that a Portland nut merchant had sent to Belle, drank innumerable half-cups of coffee (the second half invariably saved for the expectant mother), and watched local TV on Keeper Tucker's grainy little black-and-white set. Life on The Great Portland Elephant Watch became mind-numbing, as well as olfactorily paralyzing. We elected ourselves members of a secret order called SPOPE, the Society for the Preservation and Observation of Pregnant Elephants, and devised and practiced a series of secret handshakes and grunts. Nothing helped.

The zoo switchboard was by now getting more than 500 Belle calls a day. Many callers were people in betting pools seeking hot tips on the likeliest day and hour of birth. Others were amateur obstetricians offering hot tips to the zoo men. Fill the enclosure with teak logs, suggested one, so Belle "would feel at home in the jungle." Another affirmed that all elephant babies are stillborn, but come to life if the other elephants are allowed to toss the infant back and forth with their trunks. A number of callers said it was well known that the gestation period of an elephant is three, or six, or nine years, so the Elephant Watch might as well go home. This particular suggestion soon came to have a strong attraction for the Watchers. We were all irritable, groggy, emotionally strung out, itchy from the hay, and sickest of all of the inescapable smell of elephant.

Although an adjacent twenty-by-twenty-foot maternity chamber was in readiness for Belle, if necessary, Maberry preferred to leave her for as long as possible with the other pregnant females. Elephants are herd animals, sociable by nature, and the doctor believed that the companionship of Belle's ladies-in-waiting would reassure her.

"Preservation of the young is the greatest instinct of all wild animals," he said. "But if you interfere, they'll often switch and try to destroy the young. The best procedure is to keep your mouth shut and your eyes open."

On the afternoon of Thursday, February 1, Belle had a sudden seizure. She moved away from Rosy, Pet, and Tuy Hoa to the opposite end of the enclosure. The seizure lasted two and a half minutes, then subsided.

That night Belle's temperature remained steady, but the temperature outside the elephant house dropped to 20°F, and an icy wind swirled snow along the deserted pathways of the zoo. Inside, Maberry, his aides, and the waiting press sipped black coffee and walked the floor. So did Belle. From time to time, Thonglaw charged the bars of his cage with a force that shook the building. Once he trumpeted so fiercely he roused the guard at the zoo gates, a quarter-mile away. At 5:10 A.M., Belle moved off alone again and squealed in the grip of a mighty spasm. This one lasted four minutes. Half an hour later, she had a third attack. An elephant in labor exerts about four times the force of a horse, and Belle's pains must have been gargantuan. Every time Belle squealed, the other females crowded close to her flanks and petted her with their trunks.

By morning all was quiet again. When there was absolutely no change in Belle's behavior throughout the rest of the long day, the six-man team decided again to consult the wonderfully named Dr. Amoroso in London. He said that, since this was Belle's first baby, her labor might last twelve hours. He added that the cord would break automatically, and told Maberry not to worry about tying the umbilical knot; Belle would do that job herself, with her trunk. He warned the Portland team to remain on the *qui vive* because, once Belle got into high gear, "it will be a rather precipitous birth."

Alas, it was about as precipitous as a glacier crossing the polar ice cap. On Friday, February 2, Maberry and Metcalfe ran another electrocardiogram. Belle's great, fifty-pound heart was thumping steadily at about thirty-eight beats per minute; the fetal heartbeat was eighty-five. On Monday, at 2:20 P.M., Belle trumpeted loudly twice. It seemed as though she had entered the acute stage of labor at last, but in retrospect Maberry feels that these early symptoms were false labor, perhaps stimulated by the unsettling presence of so many pop-eyed journalists.

For some reason, Belle always suffered most on Thursdays. After the first pains on Thursday, February 1, she slept little, ate little, drank little, and spent most of her time executing a curious, three-legged rocking motion. She kept her left rear leg half-cocked—whether to fend off meddlesome medics or just to relieve the well-known leg cramps of pregnancy no one but Belle knew for sure. Blood tests showed that Belle was becoming slightly anemic, so her diet was fortified twice daily with a pailful of diluted molasses. Belle took each dose with a single slurp of her trunk and downed it with the ecstatic expression of a child swallowing cough medicine on a TV commercial.

The next Thursday, February 8, Belle suffered several unusually severe contractions and for some hours stopped eating and drinking altogether. When Maberry and Metcalfe attempted to obtain a second blood sample, Belle bellowed and charged. The doctors ducked back outside the steel bars in the nick of time. "She snapped three steel chains just as if they were thread," Maberry said later.

The following Thursday, February 15, Belle had her worst night yet. She rocked and walked the floor until dawn. One of her elephant midwives always paced alongside and kept the miserable beast company, while the other two lay down and slept, snoring loudly through their trunks.

The next night, Maberry crawled into his bedroll just outside the bars, notebook in hand. When Belle's pains appeared to become especially severe, she "lay down flat and little Pet knelt beside her and gently massaged Belle's belly with her knee for fifteen or twenty minutes." During the massages, both elephants made odd snorting sounds. Pet even tried half-sitting on Belle's head. "Later Belle half-sat on Pet." Nothing seemed to help. When the pains were sharpest, all four elephants crowded close together and cried in unison. Sometimes the muscles between Belle's eyes knotted into a tremendous bulge, and tears rolled down her trunk. Although Maberry could see "very severe muscular contractions," the baby's kicking was no longer apparent. The doctor thought the baby probably couldn't kick because he was now holding in a vertical position, almost directly head down.

The assembled newsmen had also begun bellowing loudly. In a

rout of journalism by science, the reporters had been banished from the elephant house, and armed guards had been posted to assure Belle's privacy. Maberry was doing everything in his power to prevent having a premature elephant on his hands.

By then I had decided on a routine of my own: spend weekends in Portland, taking off every Friday evening after my husband came home, and leaving him to watch over our baby until Monday morning. Maybe I'd get lucky in my timing. My other problem was the perpetual, all-pervasive smell of elephant. One weekend at the staid old Benson Hotel, where I was by now a familiar figure, the grinning room clerks handed me the key to a single room that had two bathrooms.

On the evening of Friday, April 13, I called the zoo from the airport, as usual. All was quiet in the elephant house, so I went directly to the hotel and checked in. At midnight, I later learned, Dr. Maberry had made his regular check on bulging Belle and, noticing nothing at all unusual, had bedded down. Near 1:00 A.M., Doc was roused by an urgent telephone call: across town, a pet poodle was gravely ill. Leaving the regular night guard on duty at the elephant house, Maberry drove to the stricken dog's bedside. While he was attending to the poisoned poodle, the zoo guard telephoned and reported that Belle had suddenly begun thrashing around her quarters and throwing water over her head with her trunk, and that her three elephant midwives appeared greatly agitated. Maberry got back to his obstetrical patient about 2:00 A.M. The guard woke me at the hotel. "Better get on over here, ma'am."

I arrived by 3:00 A.M., by which time there was no question but that acute labor was under way at last. Belle was bellowing, her eyes were wide and bulging. She had been moved to her private room, and continually strained and pushed against the walls, throwing her head from side to side, alternately kneeling and standing. We watched through a small viewing window in her concrete wall. Doc had already telephoned Zoo Director Jack Marks and sent for two more keepers to help him control the three rambunctious midwives. Morgan Berry was in his pickup, driving down from Seattle.

By 5:30 A.M., the three excited females next door were still squealing shrilly, but Belle had quit bellowing and was busy rapidly crossing and uncrossing her hind legs. At 5:56 A.M., she suddenly began spinning rapidly and silently in circles, pivoting on her forefeet. After two minutes of this dervishing, abruptly at 5:58 A.M., Belle's 225-pound infant quietly dropped to a heap on the floor—hind feet first, and backside front—and gazed about him with bright red but wide-open eyes. As he lay huddled under Belle's great belly, his mother swiftly knotted or clamped the umbilical stump with her trunk. Then she gave her newborn son a couple of swift kicks in his fuzzy flanks. Slowly but firmly he rose up on his stout legs. He was hairy all over, and the color of boiled veal. His pink-tipped trunk was so small he looked as much like a fatigued anteater as a baby elephant, and he seemed to have no idea what to do with the strange appendage dangling before him, and no control of its movement.

We heard a high, thin squeal, like a leaky balloon. Gently shoving the baby with her trunk and forelegs, Belle was nudging his head around to her breast. At 6:30, the baby managed to get his trunk out of the way and took his first swallow of elephant milk, a thin but very rich liquid that is said to taste like diluted coconut milk. He seemed to enjoy his first breakfast, though much of it was lost dribbling down the fringes of his hairy chops. Occasionally his tiny, flabby, pink-tipped trunk seemed to quiver with gourmet appreciation, and he emitted more high squeals of delight.

At 7:00 A.M., Zoo Director Marks was manning the telephone, describing the blessed event to the press, when he got so excited that he collapsed to the floor in a dead faint. He was rushed to the hospital, put to bed for a couple of hours, and sent home to rest.

Soon a brilliant spring sun was shining over Portland. A blue elephant flag fluttered from a shopping center flagpole, and the city's children were trooping to the zoo grounds to view the newborn elephant, and also to take part in the annual Easter egg–rolling contest on the zoo lawn. Inside the elephant house, the newcomer was alternately nursing and stumping sturdily back and forth through his mother's legs. The mayor announced that, by a vote of the city's schoolchildren, the little fellow's name was Packy. His proud owner, Morgan Berry, finally dashed in from Seattle, clutching a tape measure, and soon revealed that the baby stood thirty-five inches high, measured forty-six inches at the chest, fifty-three inches at the abdomen, and eight inches at the trunk. Later he announced that Belle and Packy could be purchased for $30,000, and the schoolchildren of Portland immediately started a fund-raising drive to meet the price.

At 10:00 A.M., Keeper Tucker forked Belle her morning meal of hay, bread, apples, and lettuce, and she devoured the mess with gusto. After twenty-one months of pregnancy, she appeared within four hours to have returned completely to her old, sweet-tempered, high-spirited, gentle-hearted self. So indeed had Dr. Maberry. The lines of fatigue and tension from attending a 6,000-pound female through three months of on-and-off labor had vanished from his face. As Maberry, Belle, and Packy lounged amid the hay wisps, regarding one another with an air of total contentment and pride in a job well done, the director of the egg-rolling contest poked his head through the doorway. He suggested that Belle, as Portland's first lady, should have the honor of stepping out onto the lawn and rolling out the day's first Easter egg.

"I don't think so," said Maberry. "Belle has already rolled her egg for today."

CHAPTER 2

ALPHA ELEPHANT

I HAD GROWN fond of Morgan Berry over the long months of waiting for Packy's birth, and later paid several visits to his unusual home, an eighty-acre spread of virgin forest between Portland and Seattle, near the hamlet of Woodland, Washington. He called his place Elephant Mountain, and scattered about the mountaintop were various wild animals that Morgan currently was offering for sale—some caged, others roaming freely among the evergreens and wildflower meadows. But no matter what other fauna might be in residence, the mountain's ever-changing population of big cats, bears, tropical birds, zebras, and other ruminants always included a few elephants.

By profession a wild-animal importer and part-time Seattle zoo keeper, Morgan Berry was quite likely the most knowledgeable self-taught elephant man alive. He and his sons had built the big farmhouse themselves, and the sprawling living room was dominated by an immense Hammond organ on a raised platform. Morgan liked to entertain guests with popular songs of the 1930s and '40s, played in a bright, peppy style, while his wife and daughters prepared lunch, and an occasional monkey or giraffe peeked in through an open window. Morgan's wife, Louise Berry, was a devout Seventh Day Adventist, and eventually she and a daughter moved permanently to Colombia to do missionary work among the Indians.

Morgan had started out in life as the music-minded son of a midwestern politician. While attending the Juilliard School of Music, he had collected musical instruments of every variety, and could more or less play, or at least coax a sound from, all of them. In the 1930s he worked as a jazz band drummer and trombonist, often aboard trans-Pacific cruise ships. During World War II he saw military service in Southeast Asia, and later returned to the region, first as an importer of tropical fish, then birds, and finally as a supplier of all manner of wild animals for zoos and circuses. Morgan's love for animals equaled his love of music, and he struck me as a kind of modern Orpheus, improbably returned from the underworld wearing spectacles and khaki coveralls and fated to push an eternal elephant broom back and forth between Seattle and Portland.

H. Morgan Berry was as mild a man as his name, sandy and middling in every visible aspect save for the company he kept: increasingly, and for the last fifteen months of his life exclusively, elephants. He seemed to be in as perfect harmony with these most beguiling, mysterious, and—to me—sad of God's creatures as it is possible for man and wild beast to be. Some say that Morgan was possessed by elephants, as Ahab by whales. But Morgan was not a huntsman. His special relationship to elephants was more akin to that of Saint Jerome and his lion.

I moved back east in 1969, but Morgan and I remained pen pals, and I saved his occasional, brusque letters to enrich the book on elephants that I planned one day to write.

April 17, 1975

Dear Shana,

I have been single since 1970 and live alone here on the farm. I do have a partner who trains animals for fairs and the circus. Have an act of 5 male Indian elephants and one of the three African elephants. My partner has an act of 6 bear, 3 lions, 2 tigers and a leopard in Puerto Rico.

Thought you might be interested in knowing that the elephants at the Portland zoo are not doing too well. Thonglaw the male after fathering 15 babies died just before Christmas. Everyone at the zoo from top to bottom are new. There was not the interest in the breeding that there used to be. From standing in his own droppings, Thonglaws feet almost rotted off and his feed was cut from 2 bales of hay to 1/4 bale a day and before he died he looked like a skeleton.

Would like to see you next time you are out this way.

Your friend,
Morgan

My last letter from Morgan is undated, but probably was written in the autumn of 1978:

Dear Shana,

Life has sure changed for me up at the farm. On May 5 my partner was killed up in Canada by Teak, son of Thonglaw and Pet. The circus phoned that if I did not get up there right away, they would kill all the elephants as well as the cats and bear. . . .

The following spring, a stranger called me at home in New York. "We feel sure Morgan would have wanted you to know," he said, and identified himself as Dr. Warren Iliff, the present director of Portland's Washington Park Zoo. A few days earlier, Morgan had died suddenly, under rather mysterious circumstances.

I was shocked. "What happened?"

"Of course you heard about Eloise . . ." Dr. Iliff said, and explained that Morgan's partner for a decade had been Eloise Berchtold, daughter of a middle-class Cincinnati family whose passion for wild animals had driven her to run away from home at age fifteen to join the Ringling Brothers, Barnum & Bailey Circus. She first became the sideshow snake charmer, the only job then available, but rapidly worked her way up to training and showing bears, big cats, and elephants all over North and South America. By the time she hooked up with Morgan, Eloise was internationally known and billed as "The World's Greatest Female Animal Trainer."

Eventually I learned a bit more: Eloise had come to live at the farm with Morgan and help care for his animals, and in return, she sometimes took his animals on the road. All three of the elephants Eloise was putting through their paces at the time of her death were males in *musth.* But I wasn't surprised that Morgan found these matters too delicate to mention in his letter about losing his partner. Everyone I have ever met who has anything to do with wild animals professionally—be he circus roustabout or distinguished professor of mammalian behavior—invariably takes the side of the animal. Disaster is never the animal's fault.

At the time of Morgan's death, a year after Eloise's, he was still living on Elephant Mountain, entirely alone now except for nine elephants, plus a few lesser beasts. The elephants were experienced circus animals, trained to waltz, stand on one leg, or two, and throw batons with their trunks. Some could even stand on their heads. But for more than a year the only creature on Elephant Mountain who had done any work was sixty-eight-year-old Morgan Berry, and he had done it all.

The next person to telephone me after Iliff was Randall Moore, a young biologist who said he was looking desperately for a way to keep Morgan's herd together. Otherwise the beasts would probably have to be sold off, individually. To keep them would require one and a half tons of food a day, plus the necessary hands to feed and water the animals, and clean up afterward. Temporarily in charge of the herd was one of Morgan's sons, Kenneth Berry, a sometime Seattle zoo attendant.

A few years earlier, back when he was an itinerant semi-hippie, Moore had taken a temporary job as an elephant hand, and later became the road man for a traveling circus act, five Asian bulls billed as "The Five Tuskers of Thailand." The animals were owned and trained by Morgan and Eloise, and the experience changed Randy's life. "They were like grandparents to me," he said.

Moore decided to earn an advanced degree in animal studies, and devote his life to the preservation of wild species. Now twenty-eight, he had been camped on a remote beach in Mexico rescuing Atlantic Ridley sea turtles from extinction when word reached him of Morgan's death. He had barely made it back in time for the funeral, and was calling me now to ask if I would be willing to return to Portland to write the final chapter of Morgan's story. He thought this might help save the farm. Perhaps the place could be made into an elephant reproduction and research center. After all, elephants by now were approaching extinction in both Africa and India.

In prehistoric times, huge herds of mammoths and mastodons had ranged over the entire planet. By the time human civilization had got under way, let us say 10,000 years ago, order Proboscidea had dwindled down to just two species, African and Asian, but both were abundant in the wild and freely roamed the earth from Carthage to Cathay. By 1980, only 27,000 to 40,000 Asian elephants remained in the wild, and their numbers dwindled daily. The African species was vanishing even faster, due to the depredations of ivory poachers and loss of rangeland to inroads of civilization. Despite the magnitude and urgency of the problem, however, the only proven source of elephant replenishment in the entire world remained the breeding herd at the Portland zoo.

Moore sent me some clippings on the case from the Oregon

newspapers. "It is thought Berry suffered a heart attack as he struggled with a chained elephant," said one. But another writer had dug up the coroner's report, and it mentioned "traumatic injuries caused by a six-ton elephant." Yet another account said that postmortem tests for a possible heart attack had been "inconclusive." In truth, no one knew for sure what had happened to Morgan.

On the airplane I reviewed the cast of characters, human and animal. In addition to Dr. Iliff and Randy Moore, there was Joe Wodeage, the neighboring farmer who, along with Morgan's son Ken, had discovered the body. Two more veterinarians had arrived at Elephant Mountain, separately, later on the fatal morning. One was Dr. Michael Schmidt, who in 1973 had come to Portland almost straight out of veterinary school and had run the show at the zoo, scientifically speaking, ever since. The other vet was my old friend Dr. Matthew Maberry, Schmidt's predecessor, the man who, at least as much as Morgan and Thonglaw, was responsible for putting Portland into the elephant business back in 1962. The zoo administration had changed several times since then, and at some point all the old crowd had been forced out, including Doc Maberry. Through the wars he and Morgan had remained staunch buddies, and I particularly looked forward to seeing Doc again. Like Morgan, he was a plainspoken man of great charm. Besides, I wanted someone I could trust. I sensed that I was about to walk into a still tense political tangle, a group of troubled, grieving, mutually suspicious people delicately bound together by their common love of Morgan, and elephants, and each holding a slightly different theory about what had really happened, and why. The situation reminded me once again of the Indian fable of the six blind men who "saw" six different elephants—except, of course, that Morgan's friends were not blind (although each, understandably, was a bit blindsided)—and the sixth blind man was me.

How on earth, I wondered, was the Berry family going to dispose of nine elephants? Circuses and zoos are always eager to acquire a baby elephant, or a cow, but seven of Morgan's herd were feisty bulls of thirteen to fifteen years and already experiencing periodic *musth.* On the other hand, since it had proved to be extremely difficult to breed elephants in captivity, with the notable exception of Portland, tractable male elephants would be of enormous value if a reliable artificial insemination technique could be developed.

Randall Moore met my plane. He was tall and slender, and his flashy, gypsy-like good looks contrasted oddly with his somewhat drifty demeanor. "Hope you don't mind riding in a pickup truck," he said.

The drive north to Morgan's farm took us an hour, and on the way I asked him to run down the elephant cast of characters for me. To most people, all elephants look more or less alike. But elephant professionals see each animal as a distinct, quirky individual with a unique personality that is stable—except for the violent vagaries of *musth*—and instantly recognizable.

Buddha, Tunga, and Thai were three young Asian bulls that had been imported by the Berrys, father and son, about a decade before, Randy said. Buddha was still chained in the same spot where Morgan's body had been found. "That elephant was bad from the word go," Randy said. "Been trying to kill people ever since I've known him. But Morgan used him as his work elephant. Had him up there in harness, logging Douglas fir after he started losing his view out his picture window. Buddha's worked for Morgan ever since he was two years old. But he was so bad they couldn't keep any help—even me." Buddha had probably stomped Morgan to death, Randy believed, and then possibly slept on him. "But I think he was Morgan's favorite," he added.

Tunga was a behemoth who would almost certainly become the largest elephant in the United States when he reached his full growth. He was the zoo's choice to share stud duties with Packy. As for that, there was a possibility that he, along with two Asian females, might be sent to a circus breeding farm. Randy termed him an "escape artist," because he was always slipping his chains, and told me he was the elephant that had been loose on the fatal night.

In that case, couldn't he have been the killer, I inquired.

"Not a chance. That elephant never hit anybody."

Teak still came next in order in Randy's mind, just as he had in the family act, even though he was dead, destroyed after he went berserk and killed Eloise. "Teak was the most lovable, personable animal! Fat, jolly, and very playful. But you *can't* play with elephants." On the day Eloise died, Randy said, "Tunga, Teak, and Thai were all in heavy *musth*, and Eloise was worried." Just before going into the ring, she had telephoned Morgan from Toronto and asked him what to do. The crowd expected to see a three-animal act, she told him, and she didn't want to disappoint them. Morgan advised her to just work one.

"Well, the roly-poly fat boy seemed safer than great big Tunga, so she made the wrong decision. One hour later Teak put both tusks right through her in front of thousands of people.

"The place went crazy." Teak had begun taking down the big top when he was shot by the Royal Canadian Mounties. "People started freaking out, and Thai took off right through the sidewall of the tent."

I did not learn the full details of the story until many years later. Randy, true animal man that he was, had toned down his account of the tragedy for my benefit. In fact, two of the bulls—Teak and Tunga—had been fighting seriously for several days, and on the phone Morgan had pleaded with his partner to cancel the performance entirely. But she refused.

Midway through the act, Eloise had tripped on a ragged piece of canvas flooring and fell headlong in front of Teak. In a flash, the "roly-poly fat boy" dropped to his knees and stabbed both tusks through her body. He then lifted the disemboweled woman still impaled on his tusks and flung her ten meters across the ring.

Next he walked over to the mangled corpse, tusked her through once more, and stood over her remains, daring anyone to approach.

The remainder of Morgan's nine-elephant herd were three Africans, a bull and two cows, one of which had become pregnant in 1977. Morgan imagined himself the first person in history to breed both species in captivity, "But one of the Asians beat her up and she dropped her calf." The premature delivery of the unborn African had begun the series of tragedies.

• • •

Turning off highway I-5 at Woodland was like stepping back into the 1930s. Woodland is logging and cattle country, with worn red barns, lots of wildflowers and dense stands of fir. We circled the three miles up Elephant Mountain. Randy unlocked the enormous gate that barred the last turn, and we drove out onto the broad mountaintop of bare rock. Off to our left in the middle distance stood Buddha, almost white in the sun's glare, lashing his trunk in nonstop, snakelike coilings. His agitation was eerie, scary even at 300 yards, although the creature was now chained front and back, stretched almost like a hammock between two large trees. Kenneth Berry, thirty-eight, a big, smiling man in coveralls, strolled up to us, stuck out a hand, and introduced himself. We followed him over toward the tallest barn. "Tunga's still in *musth*," Randy noted.

"Tunga is wrecking the barn," Kenny said. The behemoth was outgrowing his quarters and had begun systematically destroying the rafters twenty feet up.

Both elephant men urged me to come closer and inspect the blackish, oily ooze running down the side of Tunga's head. But for the first time in my life, I felt terrified of elephants, any elephants, and quite unable to approach. Purple thistles, white cabbage butterflies, and the distant mountains were all I wanted to look at.

The three gentle Africans, seemingly untethered, walked up out of a field of goldenrod and stared at us from ten yards off. Kenny's helper drove a pickup truck full of carrots around to each elephant and dumped off a load. I watched Buddha, his trunk still writhing, bathe in dust and eat carrots. He had an unusual lower lip, pointed, pendulous, and cruel, like certain portraits of depraved French noblemen.

"All this motion, this agitation, is new," said Randy.

"It's a huge job taking care of elephants," Kenny said. "My father killed himself with work." He spoke of happier times, when a hundred species of animals lived together at the farm in seeming harmony, and Morgan rode around bareback on a hippopotamus, inspecting his Noah-like domain.

Kenny produced a stack of photographs: Morgan in a white tuxedo as a trombonist in the thirties; Buddha clumsily balanced on his right foreleg atop a drum. "You know, Buddha was the best in the act," Kenny said. "He could do the one-foot stand before he was three years old."

The posture was so unnatural, so unelephantlike, with trunk tightly curled and three limbs awry, that I could scarcely imagine seeing it in a Babar book, let alone performed by a living elephant. "Oh, but he was clever! And very easy to train. It only took old Buddha a couple of weeks to learn this. He could do the headstand too. You could teach him anything.

"You know," Kenny mused, "if I can get rid of the others, it would be nice to maybe take three nice elephants out on the road again. It's very hard to get out of the elephant business. I can't *imagine* being out of it."

An elephant reunion and cookout was scheduled at the Iliffs' house that evening, and Randy picked me up at the hotel in his truck. Doc Maberry's hair had turned white, but his quizzical face had scarcely aged. Our hostess, Ghislaine Iliff, a Belgian, had grown up as the daughter of an elephant-park superintendent in the Belgian Congo, she told us, and after that the talk turned immediately to the recent tragedies. Eloise had been killed during a pirouette routine, someone explained.

"Morgan said it was because elephants haven't got good eyesight," Dr. Iliff said. "They can't see straight down."

"Then why do they put their eye to the crack, instead of their trunk?" asked Doc quietly. He was referring to the massive sliding steel door used in the breeding experiments now taking place at the zoo's elephant house. "With Eloise gone, the first time Morgan went in to work 'em alone, he put on Eloise's overalls, just to be safe."

"Tried any of our Zoo Doo on your garden, Doc?" Dr. Iliff inquired. Since elephants are nonstop eating machines, the zoo had begun selling elephant dung, at seven dollars a pickup load.

"I'll tell you," said Doc, "with elephants you gotta shovel a lot of food in one end, then shovel a lot of stuff out the other. That's known as job security to a zoo man."

Jack Marks, the zoo's original director, now long retired, smiled. "I'll tell *you,* monkeying with wild animals is a form of insanity. And there's no cure for it."

The next morning Doc stopped by my hotel. "The week before he died, Morgan was so weak he couldn't walk ten feet. I don't know how he managed to carry food and water. But one thing he did do, he did take care of those elephants. I'm pretty sure he had a heart attack. 'Course the only two who know for sure is him and Buddha, and Buddha ain't talking.

"Morgan had no use for young Dr. Schmidt," Maberry added, referring to his successor. "He started to experiment with the animals. Knockin' 'em down with drugs. Doing artificial insemination, which to me is immoral and illegal. These are public, not private, animals. His job is to keep them in exhibitable condition, not to use the place like a private research institute. The zoo sure isn't like it used to be! Morgan didn't want any of his elephants to go there. He told Eloise's mother, 'If anything happens to me, shoot all the elephants.'

"You know, after Eloise died Morgan was never the same. It really broke him up when they killed Teak. That was his favorite elephant."

"Doc," I interrupted, "that was no heart attack. I think Buddha really did it."

"Yes. But if we say Buddha did it, somebody's sure to start shooting. . . . Maybe Morgan got caught between the loose elephant and Buddha. Being males, they could have been fighting."

I told Doc that Randy Moore believed Buddha had stomped Morgan to death. Doc looked skeptical. "Elephants don't usually trample anything. They can tear it up, or lean on it. They'll hit you with their trunk. Even do a headstand on you. But they're very careful where they place their feet. Of course, you gotta remember that an elephant just leaning on you in love leaves nothing but a grease spot. A man is a very fragile creature."

• • •

It was time for me to revisit the zoo. In the eighteen years since I'd been there last the pink-painted elephant house had faded to gray. Warren Iliff was waving cheerily, eager to show me the recent $300,000 remodeling job, especially the new hydraulic "crush," a squeeze-cage that in theory will enable Schmidt and his staff to get close to the big bulls without danger of getting hurt. We stepped into the fetid gloom of the back room where Morgan and I had first met. "Little" Packy, now six tons and close to ten feet high at the shoulder, entirely filled the huge concrete chamber.

A fresh-faced young man appeared, dressed in a white medical jacket and carrying a clipboard. This was Mike Schmidt, D.V. M., who for more than five years had been running systematic "sniff tests" to determine his elephants' estrous cycles, information essential to collect before an artificial insemination program could become feasible. Schmidt stationed himself outside Packy's four-inch-thick steel bars and invited me to watch through a small window in the concrete wall. A keeper took his position at the hydraulic controls, the machinery whined, and the outer door of the chamber slowly opened. A keeper escorted a cow indoors from the patio and maneuvered the huge beast until her hindquarters faced the moveable steel wall behind which Packy waited. A louder whining and the wall slid open just wide enough to admit Packy's trunk and mouth. One of his eyes was visible. He felt between the female's legs with his trunk, tasted the urine, and backed off, disappearing back into the gloom of his concrete chamber.

"That's it!" yelled Schmidt. The wall closed, the first cow was moved out, and the next one backed in. Again the wall slid open. One rolling eye and Packy's trunk again appeared, sniffed, tasted, and a tremendous shudder shook the entire building. This cow *was* in estrus, and Packy had lunged.

"That's it!" Schmidt yelled, and noted the bull's erection on his charts. Another earthshaking lunge, another cry of "That's it!" and the third female was replaced by a fourth. Again the Everest of gray longing and pink frustration loomed in the concrete crack, sniffed and withdrew, and we watched the droopy, wobbly loins of the female as she trudged slowly out through the patio door back to daylight, and perhaps disillusion.

"God, you'd think it was the end of the world every time!" her keeper complained. At this, her big head swung around and the saddest eye imaginable came balefully, briefly into view.

The head keeper gestured with his elephant hook toward the big enclosure that housed the zoo's eight cows, several of them gravid, and one still unweaned calf. "Teak, the one that got Eloise, was born right in here," he said.

"You know all their routines," I said. "Was Buddha trained to stand on his head?"

"Buddha and Thai could *both* do headstands," he replied. "But what's the difference? Dead is dead. With any luck, he died almost as fast as Eloise. . . . Well—gotta run and clean up after my girls!" Springing to his wheelbarrow and broom, the keeper rushed off.

The following day Randy and I drove up to Joe and Mary Wodeage's place at the base of Elephant Mountain. While Mary fixed supper, Joe, a retired Cowlitz County road inspector, drew on his pipe and talked. "We don't know what'll happen now. When Morgan was up there, he had complete control of those elephants at all times. He'd often have four running loose at once, for exercise, and he'd say, 'Buddha, go to the barn! Thai, hang on to his tail! Teak hang on to Thai!' They'd all do exactly what he said. He'd say, 'Buddha, leg up!' Never even have to bend down to chain him.

"But Morgan was working awful hard. After he was alone, he always slept in a chair, this kinda vibrating rocker he had. Never even lay down. And I don't think he was eating well. Morgan didn't smoke or drink. He was a very fine gentleman. Never a mean man, never spoke evil of anyone. But you talk about work! You gotta feed 'em when you get up, feed about noon, feed again about four, then about ten at night you give 'em an extra load of hay. That's nine loads of hay every four hours. Then there's the other end—you gotta shovel! Then you gotta water. 'Course, Morgan had made that big muddy wallow under a tree. He'd keep it full of water, and in the afternoons he'd sit out there in his reclining rocker with the loose elephants and enjoy watching 'em play in the mud wallow. When they was loose like that, he'd never leave 'em alone. You couldn't. They have to be chained, because they destroy everything. I've seen 'em tear up thousands of feet of water hose, the pump, the barn. Wreck everything. One time we left a wheelbarrow nearby and they ate the wood handles off it."

After Eloise's death, Morgan agreed to call the Wodeages every night before bedtime. One night the call didn't come, and Joe told Mary, "We'd better go check."

They got some flashlights and drove up the mountain and

found only eight elephants, four staked out and four in the barns, but no Morgan. "All the elephants were standing, including Buddha. We hunted in all the buildings, and hollered. It was pretty close to midnight when we phoned Kenny in Seattle, and he said he'd start driving down, but to call the sheriff." With an unknown elephant on the loose, however, the sheriff elected to wait for daylight.

"Next morning Kenny come by our place around six or seven o'clock, and when we all got up to the farm, I noticed Buddha was lying down. We checked the barns first, didn't find nothin', and when we come out Buddha was up on his feet, kinda workin' toward us, occasionally lunging, and his trunk sorta lashing and coiling up on itself like a python. I'd never seen anything like it. Then we seen this object that we hadn't noticed before lying on the ground. It looked like an old rag—no, maybe more like a deer hide. Kenny got a pitchfork and raked this hide out and started to unfold it. With the fork. He unfolded the first flap and two strings come out and they was legs. Then two more strings come out and they was arms. Unfolded it a third time and we saw this face. It was Morgan's profile. A perfect image but absolutely flat, no eyeball even, and that's the first time we even knew what the thing was. Kenny said, 'That's my father.' Then he said, 'Buddha, how could you *do* this!' Then we spotted his coat laying there, and one shoe, so I raked them out, and Kenny went to call the coroner."

• • •

When I went to visit Dr. Schmidt in his laboratory, I asked him to tell me what he knew about *musth*, and this led him to the best explanation I'd heard yet of Morgan's fate. "Nobody knows exactly what it is yet. If an elephant is healthy he goes into *musth* regularly every year, or if he's very healthy, like Packy, twice a year. It's very much an individual variation. The glands do swell, and it might create a severe headache. Usually an Asian bull in *musth* is looking for a fight. In the wild, he will challenge the dominant bull. *Musth* is something you've got to think of in terms of evolution."

Elephants are herd animals, he explained, and *musth,* like rut in deer, is probably nature's design to encourage young bulls to challenge the herd bull. The extra hormones give the smaller animals the courage to attack the largest one, and the result is that the strongest, bravest, quickest bull will sire the next generation of calves.

But in captivity, when there is no other bull to challenge, said Schmidt, "I think they go for the dominant human being. I got the idea one day when I was watching our cows, and something happened that I couldn't figure out. Rosy is our dominant cow, but if a keeper's in there, she defers to him. One day we let in Metu's calf. Now you gotta remember that elephants are ferocious mothers. Then we let in Tamba, who's a teenager, so she could learn *how* to be a mother, and Tamba started to knock that little calf around, but the others did nothing about it. I was astounded. How could the aunts and mothers allow this? Then a light bulb went off in my head: Rosy is boss, so they all keep their eye on Rosy. But when a human is in with them, *he* becomes alpha elephant, and Rosy abdicates her leadership. So it would make sense that, up at the farm, Morgan was recognized as alpha elephant.

"I see what happened that night as this: Buddha's in *musth.* Morgan's got him and is taking him to tie to the tree. Morgan's getting older. His hearing and vision are not as good as they were. He was probably very tired. His back was hurting him. If Morgan was sharp, Buddha wouldn't have tried anything. But remember, Buddha wants to challenge. And he says to himself: *It's now or never.* Or possibly Buddha was going after Morgan, Morgan began to fight back, *then* he started to get a heart attack, and Buddha saw his chance."

• • •

After Iliff, Moore, Maberry, and Wodeage, Mike Schmidt was the fifth blind man, and I thought his version probably made the most logical sense. But by then a logical explanation could not entirely satisfy me. I was the sixth blind man, and I had my own vision. It grew out of a poem by Walker Gibson that I had carried around in my wallet for many years without entirely knowing why. It was written in the late forties, and it describes the fate of a circus ship that was lost in the Caribbean in 1948, all the circus acts tumbling down through blue water, the high-wire artists, the lion tamer, and . . .

> Then while the brass band played a languid waltz
> The elephant, in pearls and amethysts,
> Toppled and turned his ponderous somersaults,
> Dismaying some remote geologists.

The poem came back to me that night as I slept fitfully, and then I began to imagine Morgan's own last night, sitting and dreaming in his vibrating chair, grieving for the departed Eloise and Teak, and then perhaps imagining, or perhaps *really seeing* Thai—who was loose, after all—and Buddha out in the moonlight toppling and turning through their ghostly routine of headstands and footstands and waltzes under the maples and aspens and firs, and then Morgan himself somehow becoming caught up in, and a part of, that final, fatal performance.

CHAPTER 3

A UNIQUE CREATURE

THE ELEPHANT IN both anatomy and temperament is the strangest of all mammals on earth and sea, with the possible exception of ourselves. It is also unique among living creatures: no other land animal is anywhere near as big, none enjoys the miracle of a trunk, none endures the mysteries of *musth*. Indeed, no other animal is even remotely like it. Its physiology is truly extraordinary, far stranger even than the blind men in the fable could possibly have imagined. Strange, too, are the byways of evolution. Let us take a moment to wander down one of them.

Insofar as the elephant is concerned, evolutionary branching is believed to have begun at the start of the Eocene epoch, about fifty-eight million years ago, and today the nearest relatives to order Proboscidea—indeed the elephant's *only* living relatives, mammoths and mastodons being long extinct—are a couple of unlikely animals commonly called the sea cow and hyrax. Sea cows, also known as dugongs, are shy, water-dwelling mammals native to the tropical coastal waters of the Indian Ocean, the Red

Sea, and the southern Pacific. They feed on underwater vegetation and bask on rocks in warm seas and streams. At the approach of a boat, they submerge promptly. A sister species to the dugong is the manatee, found in the warm coastal waters of Florida, northern South America, West Africa, and the Caribbean.

Dugongs and manatees are classified as sirenians, for reasons that will shortly become apparent, and both are about the size of large dolphins. The face of the manatee is almost hairless, whereas the dugong is decidedly hirsute.

The hyrax is a furry, wide-bottomed desert creature weighing no more than seven or eight pounds, and to me it looks less like an elephant than almost any other animal I can imagine. Except a sea cow. I saw my first one at the break of dawn one morning in the Serengeti, in East Africa, the most spectacular wildlife habitat in the world. In the chill dark, having been teased awake by the far-off roaring of lions, I heard high-pitched, cheeping noises just outside my window. "Cheep, cheep! Skre-e-e-k! Cheep." I raised the blind, and saw the rock pile outside the window alive with bright-eyed creatures larger than guinea pigs madly chattering and scampering over the stones. They had short legs, no tails, and strange, round feet with—I later learned—five toes on the forefeet (only three of them functional) and three toes on the rear ones. The toes of elephants are encased in a "mitten" of skin, though with the nails on the outside. Hyrax feet have suction cups on the bottom that enable them to "scramble or even gallop about on sheer rock faces," says the renowned naturalist Ivan T. Sanderson. "The heads are rodent-like but the teeth quite different. . . . At the extremity of the upper jaw [is] a pair of small tusks. . . . Their back teeth look like those of tiny rhinoceroses."

Hyraxes are the "conies" referred to in the Bible (Psalms 104:18)—"the rocks are a refuge for the conies." Judaic dietary laws condemned the animals as *trayf* (nonkosher, unclean) because they are a creature that "chews the cud but does not part the hoof," and at one time their noisy, slap-happy colonies could be found all around the shores of the Mediterranean. Today hyraxes dwell only in the Middle East, East Africa, a few other sections of Africa, and in South Africa, where they are universally known as dassies (Afrikaans for "little badgers").

Sirenia, the hyrax, and the elephant share certain characteristics not found in other mammals. All three have similar, rather primitive hearts with a double apex. The males carry their testicles tucked up inside their abdomens. Unlike most mammals, the females have two mammary glands on their chests, instead of four or six nipples near their hind legs. Strange are the ways of modern taxonomy. The aardvark, a burrowing African mammal with immense front claws that enable it to feed exclusively on giant termite mounds, is sometimes lumped in with this group of odd creatures.

Sanderson states flat out that hyraxes have given scientists "more trouble than almost any living mammal . . . their anatomy [is] 'all wrong.' " Accordingly, modern zoologists have assigned hyraxes an order of their own, Hyracoidea. They are tiny monsters, all the scarier for not resembling anything else in the animal kingdom. I grant you the hyrax may not be much of a monster by classical standards—chimeras, fire-breathing dragons, and such—but times are lean. Science long ago contrived to sabotage fable, and today's garden of possible monsters is a sadly empty zoo containing only a few Himalayan yetis, Scottish sea serpents, and an occasional undependable blob up from the ocean floor. So, whatever hyraxes may be, I'm glad to have them around.

As for Sirenia, far-fetched as it seems (and in the case of dugongs, a luxuriant crop of whiskers notwithstanding), early naturalists thought that distant glimpses of these animals reclining on far-off rocks must have inspired the widespread belief in mermaids, sirens, and the Lorelei. To me this seems highly unlikely. In aquariums—the only place I've seen them—sea cows look like jowly seals with swollen tails, puffy forelimbs, and no rear limbs nor fins at all. But when the females rear up out of the waves, they do indeed have breasts on their chests . . . so who is to say? Does anyone really know for sure what a sailor may see on a dark night?

• • •

But enough mooning over lost monsters; back to order Proboscidea. At one time more than 160 species and subspecies of proboscideans roamed the planet. The two that remain—Asian and African elephants—evolved from different stocks. Generally speaking, the differences between them are these: a mature male Asian elephant, *Elephas maximus*, weighs from 6,615 to 11,020 pounds, and stands seven to twelve feet tall. A male of the still larger African species, *Loxodonta africana*, weighs 8,820 to 15,430 pounds, and may be ten to thirteen feet tall. Its heart alone may weigh fifty or sixty pounds, sufficient to circulate the fifty-gallon blood supply. The large and small intestines are about fourteen and forty feet long, respectively, and the rectum is positively enormous.

In contour, the African elephant is a bit more lanky-looking, the Asian more compact. The African has a slightly concave back, and enormous, fanlike, multiveined ears, the largest of any animal in the world. Flapping them helps it cool its huge volume of blood, reducing the blood temperature ten to fifteen degrees Fahrenheit in the time between entering and leaving the ears. Throwing foliage or mud up onto its back and head with its trunk serves the same purpose, as do frequent baths.

The Asian elephant's ears are proportionately smaller, but it keeps cool in the same fashion. The Asian species is also distinguished by smoother skin, a more humped or rounded back, and a more compressed head, with large dorsal bulges and a dished forehead. Until recently, Asian elephants were considered more intelligent and tractable than African elephants. But that assumption more and more appears to rest on the historical fact that in Asia men and elephants have lived and worked together since the dawn of civilization, while the African animals have remained entirely wild.

Today many experts believe that Africans are at least as manageable as Asians, possibly more so. Around the turn of the century, King Leopold of Belgium set up an ambitious elephant training program in the Congo, and imported a cadre of mahouts to do the training, but little came of it.

A century ago the world elephant population was about 1.4 million, and reasonably stable. The numbers began to drop at around the time of World War I, and the decline accelerated steadily until, in the terrible 1980s, the combined effects of ivory poaching, the spread of automatic weapons, and human population growth wiped out well over half of the remaining Africans.

Accurate elephant-counting has always been notoriously difficult, for political as well as topographical reasons. Reflecting this difficulty, the World Wildlife Fund, in January 1999, was only able to estimate the remaining number of Africans at "somewhere between 280,000 and 600,000 in the 37 African range countries. No one can be sure."

The WWF put the number of surviving Asian elephants as "between 45,000 and 50,000 in the 13 Asian range countries. But this figure too is somewhat speculative." One-fourth to one-third of these animals are probably captive, and classified as "working, domesticated" beasts.

Although Africans are far more numerous than their Asian cousins, the two species are considered equally imperilled, Africans mostly by the threat of poaching, Asians primarily by loss of habitat.

Among ecologists, the elephant is known as a *keystone species*, that is, an animal capable of shaping or modifying its habitat, to the benefit of many other species. For example, vast caves have been dug in the side of Mount Elgon in Kenya by elephants searching for salt. These extensive excavations also serve salt-hungry monkeys, hyraxes, and a variety of ungulates (hoofed animals), as well as bats and birds, and also provide shelter. Remove the keystone, and the entire arch crumbles.

Elephant habitats in both species vary greatly. We find them living in open grasslands and savannas, in swamps and marshes and riparian areas, in near deserts, and in dense forest and jungle. They thrive equally well at sea level and in mountain uplands. But wherever they live, the extraordinary demands of elephant metabolism mean that "a proboscidean's life must virtually be an everlasting meal or it dies of starvation." For eighteen hours out of every twenty-four, elephants are on the move, feeding and foraging for food and water.

Let us begin our anatomy lesson with the six-and-a-half-foot trunk. In structure a radical elongation of nose-plus-upper-lip, it is surely one of the most eccentric organs in the animal kingdom, and almost certainly the most versatile. Strong enough to swat a man to the ground, uproot small trees, or lift 450 pounds, an elephant's trunk is also so sensitive it can stealthily untie a child's shoelaces, or pick up a single grain of rice with its moist, finger-like tip. The African elephant's trunk has two tips, opposed, like our thumb and forefinger; Asians make do with one, on the dorsal side. Modern anatomists like Cairo-born Dr. Jeheskel Shoshani, now of Wayne State University and founder and president of the Elephant Research Foundation (formerly Elephant Interest Group), have estimated the number of individual muscle fascicles (small bundles) in an elephant's trunk to "at least 150,000, and counting."

Being prehensile, the trunk is adapted for seizing, grasping, or holding, especially by wrapping around an object: think of a monkey's prehensile tail. A primary trunk function is to harvest and gather up the nonstop supply of forage that must be fed into the mouth. Its myriad, intricate muscles make it capable of extending somewhat in the manner of a telescope to reach fruit as high as twenty feet off the ground. The trunk can also serve as a shower, of dust or water, as the occasion demands. When the animal is swimming, the trunk becomes a breathing tube. On land, it gives the elephant a far keener sense of smell than a dog's, and it can function as an "olfactory periscope," telling the male whether a female miles away has come into estrus and hence may be receptive to his advances. Conversely, it tells a "hot" cow where the bulls are. Elephants that must perform heavy labor, on the road with the circus or in logging camps, never use their valuable trunks for the job; they push with their massive heads and nudge with their forefeet. The trunk is employed only to balance a heavy load carried on the tusks. An angry elephant about to charge will first curl its trunk tightly toward its body to protect it from harm.

One of the first things a newborn elephant must learn is how to use this odd organ. At birth, it has no idea; the trunk appears to be just a rubbery, eight-inch, dangling object that interferes with nursing, and the infant flops it back onto its forehead in order to suckle. It takes six or eight months to learn to control it. The problem is similar to that of a human baby learning to use his hands, and nothing is funnier to watch than a baby elephant trying to feed itself the same way its mother does. One of the grimmest consequences of elephant poaching is that it leaves very young elephants with no knowledge of how to feed themselves, and starvation is sometimes a consequence.

Tusks, which are found mostly in Asian males, and in African elephants of both sexes, are actually hugely elongated upper incisors. No animal that has come along since the dinosaurs is more impressive than a mighty African bull flourishing grandly curving ivory incisors that can be up to eleven and a half feet long and weigh 220 pounds each. Most Asian males have tusks, but some—like my old friend Packy at the Portland zoo—have only what are sometimes known as tushes. These are overgrown incisors far shorter than tusks, and composed of softer ivory. Tuskless males occasionally occur in both species.

An elephant's tusks grow at a rate of about three inches per year, but failure to grow them does not put an elephant at a disadvantage, according to the self-styled "Elephant Bill"—Lt. Col. J. H. Williams, O.B.E.—who spent thirty-odd years bossing logging elephants and their *oozies* (riders) in the teak forests of Burma. "From the age of three all that the animal is saved by not having to grow tusks goes into additional body strength, particularly in girth and height of the trunk. As a result the trunk becomes so strong that it will smash off its opponent's solid ivory tusk as though it were the dry branch of a tree."

No other animal has teeth like an elephant. Its huge metabolism requires it to be a ceaseless eating machine, and nature has given it teeth that are unique in size, in shape, and in the way they grow. Its only front teeth are the tusks. The work is done by two pairs of molars, an upper and a lower on each side, which work like millstones, grinding the intake of forage necessary to sustain the creature over its sixty- or seventy-year lifetime. All elephants, of both species, have a total of twenty-six teeth: two upper incisors (tusks), twelve deciduous premolars, and twelve molars. The grinding surfaces of these teeth are composed of sharp ridges of enamel, dentine, and cement, and cross-serrated like a kitchen meat tenderizer. As someone said, you could grate carrots on them. The four molars working at any one time may weigh up to eleven pounds apiece and measure twelve inches in length. Since the ridges on the tooth's surface run across its width, not the long way, elephants chew with a forward and backward motion of the lower jaw. Other animals chew from side to side, like a cow chewing its cud.

As the elephant's first set of molars grinds along, a second set of four slightly larger molars is growing in behind the first, and gradually moving forward in the jaw. Before the first four have been ground down and are ready to crumble and fall out, the second four have moved into position to take up the mighty task. As Dr. Shoshani describes it:

> Elephants do not replace teeth in a vertical manner (a new tooth replacing the old one from above or below) as most mammals do, but rather in a horizontal progression. A newborn elephant has 2 or 3 small cheek teeth in a jaw quadrant, and as it ages, new, bigger teeth develop from behind and slowly move forward to replace the lower ones, as if on a conveyor belt. This occurs 5 times during its lifetime, over a period of about 50 to 70 years. Worn teeth move forward, fragment, and fall out of the mouth or are swallowed.

The sixth set of teeth is in place by age forty or fifty, and all or part of it remains in place until the elephant dies. Gradually these last teeth grind away their ridges and become perfectly smooth, eventually forcing the animal to leave the herd to seek out the softer vegetation that grows along the edges of rivers and swamps. Old elephants tend to die alone, at the water's edge, and their remains either sink into the marshes or are picked clean by predators. When the rains come, the bones are swept away. The fact that elephant skeletons are so rarely found is probably responsible for the erroneous belief that somewhere in the jungle is a secret graveyard where old elephants go to die.

The only other animal in which teeth migrate through the jaws is our timid friend the manatee, which spends most of its time feeding off the bottoms of lakes and rivers, although it must occasionally come up for air.*

Wild elephants are migratory animals, and herd leaders choose their routes in accordance with their remembered knowledge of the terrain, of the change of seasons, of the places where succulent forage may be found after the rains, and of the locations of

*Since manatees eat coarse grass that quickly erodes the teeth, sets of replacement teeth are lined up, ready to move into position horizontally, from behind. Still, the first set of teeth comes into the jaws vertically, as in other mammals.

the best water holes along the way. Most herbivores pull up grass to eat, or pull the leaves off bushes. But elephants grind up leaves, twigs, even small branches with those massive molars. This can have a beneficent effect on wild plants similar to what pruning does for a garden shrub: the remaining plant growth thickens and fills in. But if a herd of elephants is really hungry, if the rains are late in coming, or if other factors intervene, they may destroy everything in their path, yanking out young trees and second-growth shrubbery by the roots.

The pachyderm's digestive system, though overworked, is not especially efficient; an elephant digests about 44 percent of its hay intake, compared with 50 to 70 percent in a milk cow. Large chunks of food, or other items such as pieces of tires, plastic bags, beverage containers, and old boots, pass unbroken through its digestive tract. A lot of weeds and seeds pass through untouched, which means that elephants are very valuable in propagating the plants they enjoy most, thereby expanding their own range. In Africa, at least thirty species of trees rely entirely on elephants for seed dispersal.

Unlike cattle, elephants cannot digest cellulose. Nor do they have multiple stomachs, or chew their cud. Rather, they have a simple stomach about five feet long, and a large, baglike organ between the small and large intestines, called the cecum, which is filled with zillions of amoebas and protozoa that aid digestion by breaking down the food. A wild elephant digests fifty tons of forage annually. The infant elephant eats its mother's dung to acquire its own microbe supply. A byproduct of all this microbial activity is a prodigious daily amount of methane gas—sufficient, someone has calculated, to power a car for twenty miles.

It takes from twenty-one to fifty-five hours for food to negotiate the elephant's entire digestive system, depending on what it has eaten. The animals are always described as strict vegetarians. But I've read of a circus elephant that liked to steal the cut-up fish prepared for the seals. And George "Slim" Lewis, America's premier elephant handler, tells a macabre story about a young bull named Chang in the Zurich zoo who came there as an infant, and soon became the spoiled darling of the staff. One night an especially devoted office worker named Bertha appears to have sneaked into his cage with a loaf of bread. The next morning nothing unusual was seen but a bit of blood on the straw. Nothing, that is, until Bertha's undigested clothing, hat, and handbag made their somewhat beat-up reappearance. Later, Chang turned on and killed his beloved keeper, and was shot.

Many experts agree with Ivan T. Sanderson that elephants "have some *other* sense as yet unexplained which tells them unerringly what is poisonous and what is not, and what is good to eat and when. . . . Doping [an elephant] is quite easy, but killing them with poison is virtually impossible."

Elephants in the wild require about sixty gallons of water per day. Drinking is accomplished with the trunk, which sucks up about 1.5 gallons at a time, after which the animal puts the trunk deep into its mouth, tilts back its head, and squirts the water down its throat. The renowned British expert Richard Carrington likens the procedure to filling a cistern with a bucket, and says that the sound is like "a gurgling drain."

The nineteenth-century writer G. P. Sanderson describes a peculiar noise made with the trunk that seems to express dislike or apprehension. He likens the sound to a large sheet of tin being rapidly doubled. "It is produced by rapping the end of the trunk smartly on the ground, a current of air, hitherto retained, being sharply emitted through the trunk, as from a valve, at the moment of impact." Ivan T. Sanderson amplifies this: "All of them can produce an astonishing noise by rapping on hard ground with the tips of their trunks. This has best been likened to the noise made by waggling a large piece of thin sheet-metal or by a saw improperly played with a bow. It is the most extraordinary noise made by any animal."

Dr. Shoshani recently discovered the existence of a canteen-like bag located halfway down the elephant's throat that holds an emergency supply of water that can be sucked up again and drunk, or squirted onto the head for cooling purposes. Heretofore, writers had conjectured that the elephant was able to put its trunk down into its stomach and suck the water back up, a theory that betrays an ignorance of elephant anatomy.

Carrington reports that "They break wind with unrepressed abandon, and excrete the waste products of their enormous intake by frequent defecations. The elephant body is, in fact, like a gigantic and rather wasteful factory, using far more fuel than is necessary to ensure its own efficient operation, and squandering at least 50% of its potential in the form of imperfectly digested boluses."

The very act of walking has a laxative effect on the huge beasts, hence the necessity of the man with the broom who follows the elephant in the circus parade and in the ring. On average, an elephant defecates fifteen to seventeen times a day, leaving behind about 250 pounds of manure as well as fifteen gallons of urine. But, like other wild animals, elephants on the march learn to hold their water so as to avoid wetting their legs.

Elephants are more powerful swimmers than any other land mammal. They use their trunks as snorkels, and the many air-filled sinuses in their spongiform skulls may lend added buoyancy. In the 1880s, the sailing ship *Agra* had left India laden with a cargo of wild animals, snakes, and birds destined for sale to zoos and circuses in the United States, when it ran into heavy fog and struck an underwater reef. The fearful sounds of tearing wood mingled with the screams of the trapped beasts, and the vessel sank almost instantly. Panthers, tigers, cheetahs, leopards, hyenas, apes, orangutans, and rare birds all went down with the ship. But when the mists cleared, a herd of elephants was seen swimming easily back to Ceylon.

The reliable Carrington has seen a herd swim for six hours without touching bottom, rest briefly on a sandbank, and swim another three hours, without a single animal being lost. One elephant went for an island-hopping swim all around the Bay of Bengal, taking twelve years to complete the circuit, "and some of the hops from island to island were across at least a mile of open ocean."

In Africa, no running water is terribly deep, but herds have often been seen fording broad rivers by walking on the bottom, with only the tips of their trunks above water. Indeed, in times of great hunger, this sight provides tribesmen with an ingenious means to a surefire dinner: from a canoe, they skewer a trunk with a weighted spear, causing the animal to drown. Intestinal gasses soon make the carcass rise again, so that it can be recovered, butchered, and eaten.

An elephant's legs, also unique among land animals, are stout columns engineered so that the femur sits directly above the tibia to support the enormous weight. Ancient superstition held to the mistaken belief that elephants cannot bend their knees. In *Troilus and Cressida,* Shakespeare has Ulysses comment that, "The elephant hath joints, but none for courtesy. / His legs are legs for necessity, not for flexure."

In fact, an elephant's rear legs bend at the knee, like our own, and its front "knees" are really wrists, with a bone structure like that of no other creature, excepting, once again, the hyrax and the manatee. Okay, let's get this over with: most mammalian wrists, including our own, are composed of rows of carpal (wrist) bones in a staggered arrangement, like bricks laid in a wall, whereas the unique carpals of the elephant, hyrax, and manatee are stacked one on top of the other like bricks in a pile. Zoologists therefore assign these three animals to a class all their own, the Uranotheria.

Elephants rely on their front feet, analogous to "hands," to deliver deadly kicks, both forward and backward, and also to play football. A glance at their skeletal foot shows that they walk on the very tips of their toes. An X-ray of an elephant's foot and the foot of a ballerina *en pointe* are similar in this regard. The bulk of the elephant's "foot," or "sole," is a huge, spongy pad similar in shape to the cork sole of a woman's "wedgie." It spreads when the creature takes a step, and contracts when the foot is lifted—another weight-bearing accommodation. When walking in swampy territory, the pad splays out like a snowshoe and prevents the animal from sinking too deeply into the mud. Elephants that do very little walking grow a thick pad at the bottom of the foot, which becomes hard and must be trimmed down frequently, lest the animal wear down one side more than the other and make the foot crooked.

The massive leg structure means that neither species of elephant is able to run, jump, or leap, but only to walk or amble, keeping at least one foot always on the ground. However, a mature African bull can achieve speeds of thirty miles per hour and outrun an Olympic sprinter. The normal speed of Asians, says Ivan T. Sanderson, is about three miles an hour, "but they can make four or even five miles per hour and keep it up for ten miles. During a stampede, [Asian] elephants can increase their speed to 15 miles per hour for short distances."

My own observation is that the rear view of an elephant attempting to run looks alarmingly like the man in baggy pants in the Imodium A-D commercial trying to make it to the men's room in time; when running, it keeps its back legs very close together.

If the maximum stride of a large male is six and a half feet, he will find a seven-foot-wide, sheer-sided trench impassable, a limitation that makes it possible to exhibit zoo elephants behind moats rather than behind bars.

Tracking a herd of wild elephants on the move in Burma, Elephant Bill saw the lead animals pause atop the eight-foot-high banks of a river, then plunge their forefeet into the edge of the bank, "breaking it away and, sitting on their haunches, [making] a toboggan slide for the herd following them."

Another writer says that to descend a steep bank, the elephant will kneel at the brink until its chest touches the ground, then extend one forefoot over the edge. If it then fails to find a chink or standing place, it will kick a foothold into the bank, and then kick a second, lower foothold for the other forefoot. This cautious kicking or pressing-in of the earth continues, inching downward until the hind legs come over the edge, using the same footholds made by the forefeet. Clumsy as this may sound, the elephant can by this method descend a mountainside or riverbank at an angle steeper than forty-five degrees. The animal is unusually surefooted, even when climbing the steepest inclines, making it an invaluable beast of burden to mountain peoples.

In truth, elephants are never clumsy. They never trample man or beast by mistake, and a herd can slip noiselessly and near-invisibly through the thickest jungle. In certain respects elephants are exceptionally strong. The famous American circus elephant Tusko "with one leg pulled two loaded trucks with their wheels locked. . . . They can do the work of 200 laborers, or two bulldozers, or four tractors of medium size," says Ivan Sanderson. They are "used to shunt railroad cars, and a bull elephant jerked to a start 21 such cars on a level track and then rolled them five miles."

Great as they are at pushing, pulling, and dragging, elephants cannot carry a great deal of weight proportionate to their size; their backs are too weak, and their legs are already supporting close to the maximum. Pound for pound, an ox or donkey is a far better load-bearing bet. But an elephant, better than any piece of machinery, can maneuver in mountainous, inaccessible terrain, traversing water and forests, with minimal environmental impact.

Another elephant anomaly is the unusually thick skin on some parts of its body, as much as an inch thick across the back and parts of the head—hence the term *pachyderm* ("thick-skinned")—yet paper-thin around the mouth and eyes, inside the ears, and at the anus. Although it enjoys a hearty slap on flank or trunk, a fly or tickle on other parts of its skin drives the animal crazy. Elephants love wallowing in mud because it cools down their tough-looking but delicate hide and, after it dries, protects it from insects. Being relatively hairless, it is subject to severe sunburn, which it soothes by constant bathing in water or dust.

Their scant body fat affords elephants very poor insulation and makes it difficult to maintain a constant body temperature of 99° to 100°F, so that elephants often suffer fevers and chills, in addition to such common problems as breathing difficulties, broken tusks, sore foot pads, and splintered toenails. Their deeply wrinkled skin aids somewhat in promoting heat loss, since it has a much greater surface area than smooth skin would have. Its crevasses also retard the process of evaporation after a bath. All this is important because of the elephant's great problem in keeping cool.

Pachyderms lose moisture through their skin, though they do not seem to have sweat glands. They do have salivary glands, but not two of them like most mammals; they have four, like rodents. So how is it that circus elephants don't seem to mind having their sparse, wiry hair burnt off by blowtorch? Hard to say. Yet it is undeniable that the few widely spaced, stiff hairs on its body feel like cactus prickles to a bare-legged rider. Similar hairs grow on the underside of the trunk.

The thick skin of the flanks weighs about six pounds per square foot, according to an autopsy report issued by the San Diego Zoo on a 7,500-pound Indian male of fifty-five or sixty years. The brain weighed 9.5 pounds, the heart 28.5 pounds, the lungs 53 pounds, the three-lobed liver 69 pounds, the spleen 39 pounds, the kidneys 7 pounds each, the testicles 5.5 pounds apiece.

The reproductive organs, habits, and idiosyncracies of elephants are utterly wild and, again, unique. Not even the hyrax can compare. First, the weight problem: the gross thrusting pelvic movements employed by males of other four-legged species would be too precarious for a ten-thousand-pound animal balanced only on its rear toes above a female only half or one-third its size. Second, there are anatomical eccentricities: unlike horses, dogs, and other four-legged mammals, the female elephant's vulval opening is not beneath her tail but just forward of her hind legs, making it considerably more difficult for the male to find and enter.

The male's erect penis, nearly four feet long and as big around as a man's thigh, is somewhat S-shaped, to better conform to the contours of the female. It is equipped with its own tendons and voluntary muscles, which wave the last foot or two from side to side and up and down, like a python, while delicately maneuvering into place. Although copulation takes less than a minute, and may occur six or more times a day, it is an utterly astonishing sight each time, and one has no difficulty understanding why the elephant is a phallic god of mythic power and potency.

Douglas Chadwick, author of the 1993 prize-winning book *The Fate of the Elephant,* loses his cool somewhat at this point in his narrative:

> The Masai call the elephant *ol tome* or *olenkaina,* meaning he with the hand. They often snicker when they say this, for it may also be taken to mean he with the long, active penis. . . .
>
> I had never seen anything remotely like a sixty-plus-pound articulated penis in action up close. My whole impression of this beast shifted onto a mythic plane. He became one of the ancient earth gods, the generative phallic force incarnate, fashioned from mud and mucus and overpowering crotch perfumes: Mighty Bull Elephant, lord of creation, bent upon sowing his seed across the land and filling it with his indomitable life force. For the moment, he was my totem.

The advent of heavy *musth* in the African male, and perhaps the Asian as well, brings on a partial erection and a perpetual dribble of urine down a rear leg. Leg and penis soon turn greenish-black, and the condition has been labeled by Drs. Joyce Poole and Cynthia Moss, its preeminent researchers, "green penis syndrome."

Elephant mothers have but two nipples, on a pair of rather human-like breasts between their forelegs (like the aforementioned hyrax, dugong, and manatee; about the aardvark, I remain ignorant). Since elephant gestation takes nearly two years, and females do not come into estrus again until their young have completed nursing, and elephants very rarely have twins, this works out to one calf per adult female every four or five years, or an average of six calves per lifetime.

In theory, African and Asian elephants should not be able to interbreed, as they are classified as two distinct genera. Nonetheless, in 1978, at the Chester Zoo, England, a freak exception occurred: Jumbolino, a male African, mated with Sheba, a female Asian, and their offspring, Motty, became the only known instance of an African-Indian crossbreed. Motty showed characteristics of both his parents—his large ear with pointed lobes were African, and his single-fingered trunk was Asian—but unfortunately, he lived for only ten days.

There are many ways of measuring human intelligence, all of them imperfect, including the once-revered Stanford-Binet IQ tests, so one is not surprised that attempts to measure or compare animal intelligence have been far from satisfactory. One yardstick has been brain size. Most mammals are born with their brains 90 percent developed, leaving very little room for growth, and therefore improvement—or so the theory goes. The brain of a human infant, however, is only 27 percent of its adult weight, and that of a newborn elephant 35 percent, which would seem to leave comparable room for growth—i.e., learning—in both species. Another measure of brain development is the degree of convolution in the cerebral cortex, and here again the elephant brain, like that of dolphins and great apes, is a highly convoluted organ.

Most experts rank elephant intelligence as somewhere between that of dogs and apes. However, the temporal lobes, those parts of the brain involved in memory, are even more convoluted in elephants than in humans, suggesting that the elephant's capacity for memory storage may surpass our own. Helped by its keen olfactory system, an elephant has no difficulty in recognizing at least 200 different individuals, and possibly many more. Certainly elephants detect many smells that we cannot. Moreover, they hear many sounds we cannot hear (see below, chapter 12).

Chadwick describes elephants that learned how to unscrew the bolts holding their cages together. The famed animal trainer Gunther Gebel-Williams of Ringling Brothers, Barnum & Bailey, who worked extensively with many wild animals—all the big cats, including lions and tigers, and horses and dogs, as well as elephants, and was without question the premier wild animal trainer of all time—credited elephants with being "by far the most intelligent of circus creatures."

Ivan Sanderson in his chapter on training performing elephants states: "They are very intelligent, far more so than any dog, horse, bat, or even ape or pig." In 1884 a famous elephant trainer, George Conklin, taught an elephant to "read"—that is, he stationed a fifteen-year-old bull, Rajah, in front of a blackboard. Rajah already knew simple commands, such as "March." Now Conklin slowly printed MARCH on the blackboard while Rajah watched, then shouted "March!" Soon Rajah would start marching as soon as he recognized the forming letters as M-A-R-C-H. Conklin was able to teach him to recognize S-T-O-P and obey the command, in the same way. Probably he recognized the "M" and the "S" as symbols indicating he should perform a certain action. While it was not precisely "reading," the experiment did indicate a high degree of intelligence in a wild animal.

We also read (especially on dull news days on the AP wire) of elephants who can paint. One such was the late Ruby, in the Phoenix, Arizona, zoo. Ruby was also said to refute the assumption that elephants are color-blind, and appeared to enjoy color-matching. If she saw a red truck parked nearby, she selected her red brush. If a woman in a bright orange dress came by, Ruby shifted to orange. Indeed, her handler claimed that Ruby was so deft—and, hence, such a big attraction—and received so many sweets and buns from the public in tribute to her abilities, that a pair of African elephants caged alongside her began scratching patterns on the walls of their compound with sticks held in their trunks. I don't much care if this is true or not; I like the story.

Given their eons-long history, and enduring mystery, the number of fables and misconceptions about elephants is not surprising, three of them being that elephants never forget, that they are afraid of mice, and that they go to a secret elephant graveyard to die. None of these are true.

The fact is that elephants do indeed have remarkable memories, and can readily recall and obey more than fifty commands, yet, like people, they forget things all the time.

I don't know how the myth got started about the elephant's fear of mice; relative size may have had something to do with it. But elephants in the wild fear nothing and have no natural enemies, no predators, except man. Indeed, captive elephants have been known to keep mice as pets, and rats as well, saving up and feeding them choice tidbits. The myth, widely believed by the ancients, that elephants demonstrate their superior wisdom and intelligence by copulating face-to-face need not, I think, these days, be dealt with.

The elephant's enormous brain is protected by a massive skull filled with tens of thousands of air sinuses. The substance is sometimes referred to as "pneumatized bone." Its spongelike construction lightens what would otherwise be a head too heavy to carry. The immense skull is needed to support the weight of the tusks, and to provide sufficient surface to attach the huge muscles that move the head.

One reason big-game hunters have had such a difficult, often messy, time of it with elephants is that the brain "rests upon a plate of bone exactly above the roots of the upper grinders; it is thus wonderfully protected from a front shot, as it lies so low that the ball passes above it when the elephant raises its head" to charge, which it always does, says Ivan T. Sanderson. Consequently, the hunter's best hope is to have others turn the beast, in mid-charge, and try for a temple shot behind the ear. This is usually fatal if fired from not more than ten or twelve yards. But it is hard to get closer than fifty yards without risking a charge.

Who taught the first elephant to stand on its head? Surely it happened in India, where the history of performing elephants extends back more than five thousand years. Indians traditionally divide captive elephants into six categories—warfare, hunting, transport, work, parading, and performing—and the training for each is different. But essential to all elephant training is the one-on-one relationship between performer and teacher that must be maintained throughout the animal's lifetime. Indeed, the trainer becomes a slave to his elephant, as much as the other way around. And let there be no mistake about traditional elephant training, in every country. For thousands of years, the animal learned to do what was asked because it had been taught to expect certain pain if it failed to obey the trainer's commands. The term for this method is "negative reinforcement." Today we know that "positive reinforcement"—praise, affection, and immediate rewards for compliance—can be equally effective. Modern zoos and menageries increasingly have been switching to the new system. One zoo-bred calf I know of was recently trained to follow, lie down on either side, present each foot for inspection, and accept a leg restraint solely with the use of physical affection and Oreo cookies.

Perhaps this is the place to mention the astonishing number of similarities between elephants and our own species, starting with the fact that, as Dr. Shoshani writes, "Ever since . . . elephant numbers and distribution have been recorded, it has been observed that elephants favor the same habitat as humans," a coincidence that, as we shall see, will have a profound effect on the survival of Proboscidea. Our two species have the same long life span of seventy or so years, and maintain the same lifelong family ties. Newborns go through the same lengthy maturational process, and are not considered fully adult until they reach their late teens. Like us, elephants are by nature inquisitive and exploratory, and the elders hand down from generation to generation the knowledge acquired from experience. Tool-making and the ability to communicate through language were once considered the essential qualities that distinguish men from beasts. But elephants make and use tools, and we now know that they are in constant communication with one another through elaborate, highly developed sound signals inaudible to the human ear (see below, chapter 12). Like us, elephants modify their habitat, both by varying their grazing patterns and by digging for water and minerals.

Both our species are highly socialized. Elephants of every age like to fondle and caress one another. Newborns nurse until about age two, and, until then, stroking and cuddling between mother and child is nonstop.

Not only is the structure of our limbs similar, both species having "wrists" and "ankles"; we also fold our legs the same way when lying down. No other four-legged beast does this. Like us, elephants have a relatively naked epidermis and are vulnerable to sunstroke and sunburn. They catch colds and look after each other's children. Elephants suffer and die from many of the same diseases that afflict mankind, in particular cardiovascular disease, pneumonia, and arthritis. Sometimes they feign sickness or injury. They appear to grieve and mourn their dead, and may refuse to leave a dead comrade. Often they cover a carcass with earth and branches. Mothers may carry a dead calf on their tusks for several days. A number of observers report having seen elephants weep.

Sanderson relates the following anecdote:

> Once upon a time . . . eight elephants and two men [were] in a large building in a place called Lancaster, Missouri. The youngest of the elephants, a female named Sadie, apparently just could not understand what was required of her during a course of training for forthcoming circus performances. The two men were professionals of long experience in this exacting business. They were good men but hard-boiled; their work was difficult, and they knew, or thought they knew, its every aspect. But, as one of them told his biographer, they still had something to learn about these marvellous creatures. What happened was this.
>
> Sadie finally gave up and tried to run out of the training ring. The men ordered her back and began to "punish" her . . . for her supposed stupidity and for trying to run away. At this, Sadie sank to her knees and then lay down on her side, and the two men, as the chronicler records, "stood dumbfounded for a few moments," for Sadie was crying like a human being. "She lay there on her side, the tears streaming down her face and sobs racking her huge body."

Sanderson totally believed this story, and found himself profoundly moved, as do I.

Tales of elephants weeping, and mourning their dead, are legion. Dr. Cynthia Moss in *Portraits in the Wild* retells a story she'd heard from a park warden:

> Elephants appear to make allowances for other members of their herd. One African herd always travelled slowly because one of its members had never fully recovered from a broken leg suffered as a calf. A park warden reported coming across a herd with a female carrying a calf several days dead, which she placed on the ground whenever she ate or drank; she travelled very slowly and the rest of the elephants waited for her. This suggests that animals, like people, act on feelings as

> such, rather than solely for purposes of survival. It suggests that the evolutionary approach is no more adequate to explain animal feelings than human ones. A single example such as this one, no matter how well documented, may not challenge the entire evolutionary paradigm for feelings, but it raises questions that biologists have yet to face. There appears to be so little survival value in the behavior of this herd, that perhaps one has to believe that they behaved this way because they *loved* their grieving friend who loved her dead baby, and wanted to support her.

If animals can cry, can they also feel the opposite emotion—can they laugh? Sanderson believes that apes, elephants, and perhaps other animals have a "sense of humor," but that they lack a "sense of the ridiculous," which is found only in man (a distinction I fail to understand).

Douglas Chadwick agrees: "They have an immense capacity for amusement, and, I think, joy, not surprising in a life-form supreme in its realm."

One day I asked Dr. Mike Schmidt, the very knowledgeable Portland vet, "Do you believe animals have 'feelings,' as we understand them, that they experience grief, laughter, compassion, and so on?"

Yes, they do experience grief, he said, adding that elephants are one of the few species, like whales and dolphins, that understand and naturally accept humans as their masters. "Elephants sort of identify with humans." This was not as surprising to hear from a white-coated scientist as it once would have been. It was becoming clear to me that people of all eras and locales have identified with elephants, so why not vice-versa?

Mike carried the thought further. "There is a pecking order among elephants. They fit people into it . . . and that's where zoo keepers get killed."

As further evidence that elephants have "feelings," he told me that when young Hanako's calf was born, she showed no interest in nursing it. Observing this shirking of maternal responsibility, two of the older females literally "picked Hanako up and bounced her against the wall. Those two wise old cows realized she wasn't doing her job as a mother. They did it two or three times—until Hanako allowed the calf to nurse.

"They didn't just adopt a hungry baby and take care of it; they forced the mother to do it! Elephants are watching and thinking and figuring about the world all the time. Some elephants would make great baby-sitters for humans. They'd be very gentle, they'd watch the toddler all the time, and gently pull it back if it started to stray. No other animal would do this. You certainly wouldn't want to give your infant to a chimp!"

Finally, Sanderson says it flat out:

> Let me be bold, therefore, and forthrightly say that I believe elephants are exceedingly intelligent; that they have a form of intelligence which manifests itself in many ways that are very like our own; and that, in these respects, they stand as far apart as we do from all other living things—the great apes not excluded.

Summing up the elephant character, he writes:

> Despite their majestic and for some strange reason docile and kindly appearance, elephants are really very dangerous creatures. . . . They know their strength, but they don't use it aggressively and they abhor fighting or physical violence of any kind. Most of them show noticeable signs of revulsion to bloodshed or death in any form and display distress in face of these things.

In conclusion, Sanderson makes the important observation that "although they work at it, *they don't like performing*," a reference to the same quality—the powerful "sadness"—I myself saw, or sensed, when I watched the Stravinsky-Balanchine *Elephant Polka* at the age of eight.

The admirable aspects of elephant temperament have long been remarked on. In the 1920s, an American science magazine declared:

> The normal elephant has a sanguine and serene temperament, his nerves are not jumpy, his perceptive faculties are keen and precise, and his patience is infinite. . . . Without any exceptions, *every* wild Indian elephant quickly learns that mind is superior to brute force, that it is wisest to accept the inevitable, and to become a cheerful and dependable civilized worker. This is not true of any other adult wild animal with which we are acquainted.

All elephants, wild and tame, seem to have a passion for alcohol, which tends to make them boisterous and unsteady, yet another characteristic they share with man. Several traveling circus elephants in Colonial America were readily trained to pull the cork from a bottle, drink the contents in one gulp, and pass the empty back to the trainer.

W. H. Drummond, in *The Large Game and Natural History of South and South-East Africa,* reported that elephants migrate to a certain spot each year at the time of the ripening of the fruit of the *umganu*-tree, "of which they are passionately fond, and doubtless come in search of. This fruit is capable of fermenting into a strong intoxicating drink, and the elephants after eating it become quite tipsy, staggering about, playing huge antics, screaming so as to be heard miles off, and not seldom having tremendous fights." How one would enjoy spying this bacchanal one moonlit African night!

Elephants need very little sleep, and until recently it was believed that they slept standing up. But Dr. Joyce Poole and others have shown that elephants spend between one and three hours a night lying down, sometimes snoring through their trunks, and often catnap on their feet for a few moments during the daytime. Oddly, the elephant's heart rate speeds up when it lies down, a suspicion confirmed by careful experiments with a cardiotachometer. The standing pulse rate is about thirty-four; asleep, it is about forty.

The elephant has so many organs and attributes found in no other animals (except hyrax and sea cow) that it is time to mention some things the elephant does *not* have. Their bones have no marrow. Their skeleton has no collarbone. Their guts have no gall bladder.

I think we will skip the elephant's paleontological background or heritage, well-traced and oft-described though it has certainly been. The most remote ancestor of both Asians and Africans on the evolutionary tree is a repulsive-looking, smaller, hairless, trunkless, short-legged, piglike creature named Moeritherium that once inhabited the wilds of Egypt. Forty million years on, mighty mastodons and, somewhat later, mammoths covered the planet (with the exception of Australia and Antarctica), and were hunted by primitive man. A climatological change wiped them both out, leaving only Asian and African elephants. The newest theory of elephant evolution posits that they were originally land mammals that for some reason moved back into the seas, became aquatic, developed trunks for breathing, and then for some other unknown reason switched back to terrestrial life.

For the penultimate word on elephant physiology, let us return to the redoubtable Richard Carrington. An elephant's tongue, he reports, "is very pink and fleshy, and as soft to the touch as velvet." Furthermore, its tip is turned inward.

The last word on elephant physiology should probably be awarded to the ancient, still-venerated Arab zoologist Ibn

Quatayba, who, in a section on *Fîl* (Arabic for "elephant"), after discussing the unique form of the elephant's tongue, pauses to remind his readers of the belief firmly held throughout India and all of Asia that "if the [elephant's] tongue were *not* inverted, it would be able to speak."

PART II

SEEING THE ELEPHANT: LOOKING BACK

CHAPTER 4

IN RELIGION AND IN MYTH

WHEREVER ON EARTH the elephant has lived it has entered the culture and belief system of the people to a degree matched by no other animal. Evidence of the extraordinary intimacy between our two species is strewn across North Africa, Egypt, Babylon, India, China, Siberia, and Southeast Asia. The earliest representations of elephants and mammoths—painted, carved, and etched in ivory—date back about 30,000 years. Paleolithic paintings and carvings of elephants have been found in several parts of the Sahara. Elephants also appear in Egyptian art, and elephants found on a wall tomb in Thebes date from about 1500 B.C. Curiously, they look more like Asians than Africans, and stand about half the height of a man. Could they have been the ancestors of the pygmy forest elephants some say are still found in Africa today?

Representations of fighting or rampaging elephants may be found throughout history, but they are more often depicted as benign, or as a defender embattled with an evil being—dragon, lion, or serpent.

Roman coinage over many centuries is replete with elephants. "In view of the belief that elephants were worshipers and proteges of Helios (the sun), their role as symbols of light and life and of victory over darkness and death can be readily explained," says J. M. C. Toynbee in his book *Animals in Roman Life and Art*. Their symbolic purity, however, did nothing to protect elephants from the Romans' lust for luxury. Ivory was carved into jewelry, into combs, hairpins, handles, and countless other small artifacts. The earliest "memo pad" was the diptych, two notepad-size slabs of ivory linked by cord hinges into a kind of sandwich. Their inner surfaces were faintly hollowed out and filled with a thin layer of wax on which one could write with a stylus. Close the sandwich and the writing was safely preserved. The diptych was often used by the Bishop of Rome and other high clerics. Eventually came the triptych, as well as crucifixes, crooks, pastoral staves, reliquaries, and every other possible sacred object made of ivory. "Even the *flabellum* devised in the East to waft flies off the sacrament was traditionally made of ivory in the West," says Ivan T. Sanderson. "In fact, we have a more continuous record of ivories than we have of any other European art form, with the possible exception of manuscripts, and despite its friability, more of it has come down to us than of any gem or metal."

Ivory was used in fine Roman furniture, both as a veneer and as inlay. The much admired, massive, ornate ivory-and-gold figures called chryselephantine were developed by Egyptian and Greek artisans. The great fifth-century B.C. sculptor Phidias constructed colossal statues sheathed in ivory and gold, including a forty-foot-tall Minerva for the Parthenon, a seated colossus of Jupiter fifty-eight feet high at Olympia, and a gigantic Zeus, one of the Seven Wonders of the World. All exposed skin was covered in ivory painted in skin tones; beards and moustaches of human hair were attached as necessary. Fingernails were fashioned of highly polished cow horn. Robes were gold sheet or leaf, gem-studded. The Greeks had learned the art form from still earlier peoples—perhaps the Jews, who had thrones, beds, and other pieces of furniture paneled in ivory, or perhaps from the Phoenicians, whose rowers sat on ivory-covered benches. The trick was a now-lost method of softening the ivory with chemicals before molding it, then hardening it again with other chemicals. It could also thus be flattened into four-foot-wide "planks." The Roman emperor Caligula reportedly built an ivory stable for his horse.

The passion for chryselephantine, which reached its zenith during the Roman Empire, required the slaughter of tens of thousands of animals. "In all likelihood," says Richard Chadwick, the Roman market for ivory "played a key part in eliminating Asian elephants from the eastern parts of their original range. . . . North Africa's last elephants vanished around the second century A.D., primarily because of the Roman Empire's insatiable demands for ivory tusks."

A word or two more about those tusks: the ivory trade got started around the time of Christ, when hundreds of thousands of mammoth tusks excavated in Siberia began to find their way to China. By the year A.D. 1000, Arab traders dominated the enterprise. In the 1600s, the British started buying up the mammoth ivory. But its source was unknown in the West until the early nineteenth century, when an entire frozen mammoth was dug up in Siberia. Its hair alone weighed thirty-seven pounds, and ten men were needed to lift its hide. Before that time, the tusks were believed to be the teeth of an extinct species of giant burrowing rodents killed off by the sun's rays when they inadvertently emerged from underground.

When Marco Polo returned to Venice in 1295 and described the goods and glories of the East, chief among them ivory, every seafaring nation in Europe began to search for sea routes to India and the Far East. The Portuguese expeditions were partially financed through ivory sales; all along the coasts of Africa and

India, from Mozambique to Goa, they set up small "stepping stone" colonies to harvest the local ivory before moving on.

A history of ivory poaching would have to go back to the Portuguese navigators. In modern times, some experts maintain that poaching was inevitable because of economic realities: "In most parts of Africa, a man can make more money by killing an elephant and selling its tusks than he can by working at his job for a whole year," writes Suzanne Jurmain. Between 70,000 and 100,000 elephants died each year during the 1980s to supply the demands of the world ivory trade, and nearly all were killed by poachers. Prices continued to rise and, by the end of that disastrous decade, a pair of tusks was worth more than its weight in silver.

The most important event in the long history of the ivory trade occurred on January 18, 1990, when the African elephant was placed on the international Endangered Species List. No species on the list, nor its parts and products, could be imported or exported for commercial purposes. The Asian elephant had been on the list since 1973.

Six months later Daniel arap Moi, president of Kenya, dramatized his country's commitment to the cause by setting fire on international television to a mountain of more than 1,200 illegal elephant tusks. The conflagration entailed a loss of more than $3 million in sales.

But even then, the ordinary ivory customer was no more concerned with the plunder and near-destruction of an entire species than the ancient Romans had been when they sat on ivory benches telling their beads, combing their beards, and nodding their agreement with the great historian and naturalist Pliny the Elder that the main natural enemies of elephants were well known to be dragons.

• • •

By the Middle Ages, moral attitudes had changed and people considered themselves to be far more pious and less barbaric than the bloodthirsty mobs that once gathered at the Circus Maximus and the Colosseum. It was now believed throughout Christendom that elephants were "special creatures of grace," because they possessed "innate knowledge of the difference between good and evil." In fact, these convictions were but the latest flowering of ancient ideas that had been part of both Aryan and Asian beliefs. Indeed, traces of the same ideas can be found in every major religion. Always, the elephant symbolizes a morally ordered universe. Always, man sees the elephant as the embodiment of the good. Always, elephants are recognized as benign—kind and gentle—beings.

The ancient belief systems of Asia tend to twist and bend back upon one another, to intertwine and imbricate, and disentangling them is difficult. I am thinking primarily of the many varieties of Hinduism and Buddhism. In both religions, man and the elephant make their first appearance in the cosmos together and, in both, elephants are associated with water and rainfall, the primordial giver of life to dust.

Joseph Campbell offers a useful distinction between the two major religions of Asia when he writes, in *The Mythic Image,* that

> Hinduism, like Judaism, is basically a racial religion: one is born a Jew, born a Hindu. Buddhism, on the other hand, is, like Christianity, a religion founded on belief: a credal religion, hence a world religion, open to all equally, no matter of what mother born. And that, finally, is the meaning of the symbol of the virgin birth. It is neither of race nor of caste, but absolutely of the spirit, from aloft—as in the strange scene below.

The "strange scene" is a charming medallion in bas-relief from Bharhut, India, now in the Calcutta Museum. It depicts the dreaming queen Maya surrounded by her handmaidens, while above her recumbent body floats an enchanting little elephant wearing a jeweled cap. One can imagine Campbell smiling as inscrutably as any bronze or granite Buddha as he pens his caption:

> The subject here—one of the earliest monuments of Buddhist art, ca. 100 B.C.—is the dream of the Buddha's mother, Queen Maya, the night she conceived the Savior. She thought she saw descending through her sleep from the heaven of the highest gods (where the reincarnating monad of the one now to become the Buddha had been dwelling between incarnations) the form of a glorious white elephant, radiant, with four brilliant tusks, which on reaching the earth walked thrice around her bed in the auspicious sunwise direction, struck her right side with its trunk, and entered the womb.

The dream was interpreted to mean that the unborn child had received the spirit of a holy white elephant. The infant princeling was given the name Gautama. When he grew to manhood, he renounced his riches and worldly possessions and became a wandering monk. Thereafter he traveled the world preaching that the way to enlightenment was to forget worldly things, learn to love the truth, and care for others. Soon Gautama became known as *Buddha* ("the enlightened one") and regarded as founder and godhead of one of the world's most enduring, powerful, and elegant religions.

In Hindu religion, the elephant guards the tree of life, rules the sky, and venerates the moon and stars. It is able to cause lightning, and congregating elephants induce rain. Long, long ago, elephants had wings. Disney's Dumbo is only the most recent in a long line of flying elephants stretching back forty centuries, and the ancient image retains great power. The Viennese singer Lotte Lenya, hardly a sentimentalist, wrote to her husband Kurt Weill in 1942 after seeing *Dumbo,* "I cried my eyes out. When that mother elephant takes Dumbo in her arms that's like a Botticelli madonna. Just beyond words."

At one time, elephants could not only fly but change their shape, like their close cousins, the clouds. One day, in the foothills of the Himalayas, an ascetic who was devoting his life to meditation in the shade of his beautiful banyan tree happened to glance up and see a great flock of elephants flying straight at him. When they alighted on an overhead branch it broke and fell, killing a number of his students seated below. The elephants simply winged off to another bough, but the yogi, righteously enraged, put a curse on the entire species, removing their ability to fly, or to change shape. From that day forward, elephants have been clouds condemned to walk the earth, ridden by men and servants of men. They are revered as blessings, bringers of fertility and life, because when their relatives the clouds arrive to visit them, the boon of rain descends.

In Sanskrit, the classical literary language of India, orthodox Hinduism is called *Vedanta,* or Brahma. The oldest Hindu sacred texts are the four Vedas (the Sanskrit word for "knowledge"). Brahma, the creator-god, is conceived chiefly as a member of a triad that includes both Vishnu, protector and preserver of worlds, and Shiva (also: Siva), destroyer and restorer of worlds.

Chief among the early Vedic deities was Indra, associated with both rain and thunder, and variously referred to as "Lord of Heaven," "God of Thunder," and "Knight of the Clouds." As all-powerful lord of the atmosphere, Indra brought rain and hurled thunderbolts. He was at once the god of war, the symbol of fertility, and scourge of all the malevolent forces of nature. When depicted with four arms (sometimes he has only two), one holds a bow, another an arrow-like thunderbolt, and the third and fourth hold elephant goads.

Indra lives on Mount Meru, the Asiatic Olympus, somewhere amid the swirling clouds to the north of the Himalayas. He rides a mighty, white, four-tusked elephant, Airavata, who is venerated as the ancestor of all elephants. Together they rush through the air, bringing storms. Some people say that Airavata's trunk is actually a giant waterspout for pouring water on the thirsty earth. Indra and his queen, Indrani, are attended by voluptuous celestial dancers, the Apsaras, and their Gandharvas, the dissolute musicians who partner them.

In Laos and Thailand, people venerate the three-headed elephant figure Erawan, who represents the three supreme Hindu gods—Brahma, Vishnu, and Siva—and appears on the Laotian flag.

Although Buddhism is the newer religion, and was founded by a man—a royal prince, not a god—the Buddhist explanation of how earthly affairs began is very like the much older Hindu belief. The most recent incarnation of Buddha *before he became a man* was as a white elephant, which is why Buddhists consider white elephants sacred in themselves. Buddhists also believe that the elephant is the Father of God.

Of all the Hindu deities, the best loved is Ganesha (also: Ganesa, and Ganesh), a god with the body of a man but the head of an elephant. He is a great and good spirit, the god of wisdom, learning, and the arts. Hindu poets begin their books with a prayer to Ganesha. In Bengal, a particularly bright schoolboy is sometimes honored with the nickname *Gonesh,* yet another way of pronouncing the god's name.

Ganesha lost his original human head while attempting to prevent the Lord Shiva from visiting his mother, the goddess Parvati. In retaliation, Shiva struck Ganesha's head from his shoulders, though afterward he relented. But instead of restoring Ganesha's original head, he ordained that he should be awarded the head of the first animal to appear. This, providentially, was an elephant.

A variation of the legend says that Ganesha was born a normal child. In due course his mother, Parvati, invited the other gods and goddesses to come see her handsome new son. The god

Shani, who could kill with a single glance, stayed away, fearing he might injure the infant. When Parvati insisted, Shani came, took one look, and the baby's head instantly became a smoldering heap of ashes. The assembled gods and goddesses demanded that Shani go find a new head. After searching the world over, Shani came upon a sleeping elephant, the wisest of all creatures, and in a flash cut the head off, brought it back to Parvati, and placed it on the shoulders of Ganesha.

Small, stocky, cheerful, and potbellied, Ganesha has four arms and carries in his hands an elephant goad, a rosary, and a begging bowl. His fat belly is the sign of his insatiable gluttony. One day, after gorging himself with offerings, he decides to take a ride to ease his digestion. Mounted on his rat—his customary steed for riding around the heavens—he is ambling along in the moonlight when a huge serpent bars his way. The frightened rat leaps to one side and Ganesha falls off, bouncing so hard his fat stomach bursts open. He then picks up the serpent and uses him to bandage his damaged belly.

He is preparing to continue on his way when suddenly he hears great shouts of laughter ringing across the sky. It is the moon, mocking and jeering at him. In a rage, Ganesha breaks off one of his tusks and throws it in the mocker's face with a terrible curse. Ever after, the moon has been periodically deprived of its light.

Another version of the story says that Ganesha tore out his tusk to use it to write down the *Mahabharata*, the immense epic poem of ancient India. The poem has been difficult even for holy men to remember, being about eight times as long as the *Iliad* and the *Odyssey* combined.

That Ganesha is the patron of literature is only fitting, as he combines the natures of the two most intelligent beings, man and the elephant. He has a gentle disposition and is a mountain of common sense, amiability, and friendliness. Gentle, calm, and propitious, Ganesha loves men and is loved by them. He bestows riches, and assures the success of every undertaking. Nothing should be begun, not even the worship of another god, without first doing honor to Ganesha.

One group of Hindus believes that the weight of the world is carried on the back of an elephant. In the beginning, Brahma sang seven holy melodies over the two halves of an eggshell, which he held, one half in each hand. From the shell in his right hand Airavata emerged, followed by seven more male elephants; from the shell in his left hand eight females emerged. "These were . . . the ancestors of all the elephants," writes Carrington. "They also became the caryatids of the universe, four of them supporting the world at the four cardinal points of the compass, the remainder at the intermediate points."

Good fortune, knowledge, and wealth await the man who speaks the twelve names of Ganesha at dawn, noon, and sunset. At school examination time, children bring cake and cookies to Ganesha's shrines. Like all elephants, he loves sweets, and the children hope that in return for their offerings the god will assure them high marks. Travelers pray to Ganesha before beginning a journey, and businessmen pray to him before closing a deal. Indeed, Ganesha is the most frequently invoked of Hindu deities, far more so than his father, the omnipotent Shiva.

The elephant in India is also a symbol of royalty. The supreme Hindu god Indra rides on Airavata, and white elephants are sacred to the Sun, just as white horses were for ancient Greeks and white oxen for British druids. To Buddhists, the jolly, elephant-headed god is known as Nakhanet and is the god's last incarnation before assuming human form. Among devout Buddhists, the white elephant plays a curiously similar role to the white dove of Christianity.

In sum, a huge chunk of the planet—not just Asia, but wherever elephants were known—seems to have been haunted, and protected, for millennia by saintly guardian elephants.

• • •

Ancient Greeks and Romans believed that elephants were the only animals capable of worshiping the gods. According to Jurmain,

> When the new moon appeared, they thought that elephants plucked leafy branches and waved them toward the sky in honor of the moon goddess. And when the shining sun rose in the east at dawn, they believed that the elephants respectfully lifted their trunks in prayer.

Some of this veneration survives today in Sri Lanka, the former Ceylon. For fifty-eight years, in Kandy, the beloved bull elephant Raja led the annual summer parade of more than fifty lavishly bejeweled elephants honoring Buddha and was celebrated as the nation's "most venerated moving monument." In a golden casket on his back, he carried the golden tooth relic of Buddha. Raja was declared a "national treasure" in 1985 and, when he died three years later, at the age of sixty-five, Buddhist monks paid tribute, and thousands of mourners passed by his bier. Now mounted and stuffed, Raja stands in a museum in Kandy beside the Temple of the Tooth Relic.

Many elephant legends and tales deal with the intimate relationship between elephants and death. The notion of a secret elephant graveyard is pure myth. Nonetheless, it plays a major part in Arab fantasy and folklore. The Seventh Voyage of Sinbad the Sailor, for example, tells of Sinbad's being kidnaped by pirates, sold as a slave, and bought by a rich merchant. The captive is ordered to sit in a tree with a bow and arrow and shoot any elephants that pass, because the merchant wants the ivory. Sinbad is a fine shot and kills many animals, until one day the elephants turn around and charge his tree, pulling it up by its roots and dragging off the startled marksman. He is thus brought by the elephants to a vast hillside blanketed with the tusks and bones of dead elephants. In this manner the merchant gets his ivory, the sailor wins his freedom, and the elephants thereafter live in peace.

In the real world, many travelers have reported seeing elephants carrying the bodies of dead calves for days, or carrying the bones and tusks of a dead elephant. They describe elephants "burying" their fallen comrades under branches, earth, and leaves. "If a herd comes across a long-dead elephant," says Ian Redmond, "the members will feel and sniff the remains, pick up and scatter bones, draw the tusks from the skull, and sometimes smash them. Even when no sign is left, they may pause where a relative died, as if recalling the lost family member."

In the early 1920s, archaeologists in Pakistan discovered a mysterious mound of earth at Mohenjo-daro. It was a buried, forgotten city, 4,000 years old, and included all the amenities of the great cities of antiquity. Everywhere, the excavators found not only shops, bathhouses, granaries, forts, and temples. They found thousands of seals picturing elephants wearing saddles—clearly they were domesticated creatures even then.

Bringing matters down to the near present, in 1839, depictions of elephants along with their riders and assorted elephant paraphernalia were found amid Mayan carvings in the jungles of Guatemala. According to Ivan T. Sanderson, American ethnologists date the stelae (carved monuments) to between the first and fourth centuries A.D.; the British put them between the sixth and ninth; the Germans think perhaps a bit later. That is to say, the stelae were carved at about the beginning of the Dark Ages in Europe. How could such a thing have come about? Most likely, thinks Sanderson, it was the work of the Phoenicians, who were phenomenal sailors. Indeed, the Mayan turbans do look exactly like the ones the Phoenicians wore (and the Assyrians, too, for that matter).

Among the Mayan pyramids and other grotesque stelae, notes Sanderson,

> The two top and dominant figures on each edge of one stele are most perfectly and naturalistically represented heads of elephants—not loxodonts, mammoths, or mastodons, but obvious *elephants* richly caparisoned in the manner well known in India and Cambodia. One of these figures carries on its neck a mahout, wearing a typical Oriental turban on his head and holding in his hand a traditional square elephant hook!

Elephants are also found in the indigenous, pre-Hindu animistic religious art of Java and Bali; indeed, Sanderson thinks these elephants have a "strangely Ganesha-like form." He finds more of them in southern China, and among the great carved figures lining the avenues to the fifteenth century Ming tombs at Peking and Nanking. He points to still more elephants on the altars of Buddhist monasteries in Tibet. In Mongolia, in Japan, "and in the temples of inner China there were great silver statues of elephantines having as many as six tusks."

Elephants turn up from time to time in Christian belief as well. Historian John of Ephesus in the sixth century A.D. reported on a herd of elephants in Constantinople that had become so devoutly Christian that every time they passed a church they stopped to kneel in prayer and make the sign of the cross with their trunks.

In Europe during the so-called Dark Ages, civilization was kept alive by the phenomenal sweep of Islam throughout Spain, Asia, India, Mongolia, and Indonesia. After the death of the Prophet in 632, it was the writings of Arab scholars that kept the lamps of knowledge burning and preserved the intellectual wealth of the ancient world. And Arab writings are loaded with elephants. The first written recognition that the African and Indian elephants were separate though related species is found in an Islamic text. There is even a "Chapter of the Elephant" in the Koran (number 105), which includes a prohibition against the eating of elephant flesh, because of the mistaken belief that elephants are carnivores.

An important Muslim legend relates that the year Muhammad was born in Mecca, 570, Abraha, king of Yemen, set out to conquer the city. He led his armies toward Mecca, mounted on an enormous elephant, followed by a company of war elephants. But as they neared the city's walls, Abraha's mount suddenly stopped in the dust and knelt. The other elephants did the same, and their riders could not budge them. Abraha tried to trick his mount by ordering it to go away from Mecca. When the beast readily obliged, Abraha attempted to turn him back toward the walled city, but he refused to obey. Just then a great flock of birds crossed the sky, each one carrying a rock in its claws with which to bombard Abraha's army. The entire company was slaughtered save for Abraha, who lived to tell the tale "of how God had commanded the elephants to save Mecca and the life of the Prophet Muhammad."

A final thought: although the elephant has been semisacred to man since the dawn of time, and benevolent elephants appear in the religion and mythology of all peoples who have known elephants, every real elephant remains a wild animal. As zoo men say, "It can be trained, never tamed." And even trained ones are difficult to manage. Given the choice, the first pair of animals Noah would have pushed overboard would surely have been his elephants. They eat too much, excrete too much, destroy too much, take up too much space, and, being both migratory and gigantic, have always been virtually impossible for man to manage.

CHAPTER 5

IN WAR AND IN HISTORY

MILITARY HISTORIANS LIKE to describe the war elephant as "the ancient equivalent of the tank." And certain it is that history's great generals, from Alexander to Hannibal to the sixteenth-century Mogul, Akbar, employed elephants in their armies. But in truth the elephant's chief importance in warfare has always been as an inciter of terror, in men and in horses—a value that diminishes, of course, with each successive encounter.

Elephants are indeed useful as scouts and lookouts, and for transport of matériel across difficult terrain. As recently as World War II, the British in Burma used them to carry field artillery pieces, to drag disabled planes across airstrips, and to help build the famed bridge over the river Kwai. In Vietnam, the Viet Cong used them to transport rocket launchers. During the latter part of that war, reports surfaced that American fighter-bombers had been ordered to "interdict" elephants along the Ho Chi Minh Trail because "they were suspected of being used to transport military supplies."

Early in 1968, the U.S. Special Forces had actually tried to parachute live elephants into the high jungles of Vietnam. They ordered them chained and staked to wood pallets, fitted with outsize parachutes, shot with tranquilizers, then pushed out of low-flying transports, all in a misguided effort to aid our friends the Montagnards, who relied on elephants to carry rice and other necessities up and down steep mountain trails. The poor beasts all died hideously. An elephant's body, like a human's, is composed mostly of water; its leg has the structural strength of a stalk of celery.

Returning to the classical world as quickly as possible, elephants were first employed in the West as instruments of war in 331 B.C., when Alexander the Great, having already conquered Greece, Macedonia, Egypt, and Persia, attempted to extend his empire to India. Marching eastward, he often received gift elephants from local potentates whose lands he traversed. By the time he got to India, he had about a hundred animals under his command, but used the beasts only for transport. When he reached the river Hydaspes (the Indus), however, which marked India's western boundary, Alexander saw a mighty army drawn up on the opposite bank. One witness reports 50,000 foot soldiers, 3,000 horsemen, 300 war chariots, and 200 war elephants. The leader, King Porus, was seven feet tall and mounted on an enormous elephant.

Alexander at first was stopped cold. But eventually he got across, fought a desperate battle, routed the Indian army, pursued and captured the gigantic rajah, and then converted him into an ally. "At last!" sighed Alexander, not yet thirty years old. "At last I have met a danger worthy of the greatness of my soul."

Or so the story is usually told. Recently I heard a variation from Dr. Bets Rasmussen, an eminent elephant authority who is a biochemist and molecular biologist with the Oregon Graduate Institute. Porus's mount was the leader of his herd, its matriarch. At the height of the battle, however, she heard her hungry calf back in camp begin bawling for its dinner. At once she turned and ran back to feed her baby, causing the mighty king's entire army to disintegrate. How one hopes this version is the correct one!

Elephants had been used in India as beasts of burden for two thousand years before Alexander arrived. For about a thousand years, the Greek word *elephas* had been translated as "ivory," but traders from the West did not know whether the true nature of the substance was animal or mineral. The answer had to wait until the Macedonian general marched east, saw his first elephants, and decided to bring a few of the astonishing creatures back home with him as gifts for his old teacher, Aristotle, then at work on his *Historia Animalium*. More than three hundred years before Christ, he wrote:

> Of all wild animals the most easily tamed and the gentlest is the elephant. It can be taught a number of tricks, the drift and meaning of which it understands. . . . It is very sensitive, and possessed of an intelligence superior to that of other animals. . . .
>
> The elephant of either sex is fitted for breeding before the age of 20. The female carries her young, according to some accounts, for two-and-a-half years; according to others, for three years; and the discrepancy in the assigned periods is due to the fact that there are never human eyewitnesses to the commerce between the sexes.

After Alexander's death, in 323 B.C., his empire and his elephants were divided among his generals, and the armies of the Seleucids of Syria became famed for their corps of trained war elephants. Seleucus had been one of Alexander's generals in the great battle with King Porus, and the experience haunted his life. He later made Indian elephants the emblem of his dynastic house and established a private pachyderm army, animals he acquired by surrendering all of the provinces that Alexander had annexed en route to the Indus in exchange for large numbers of war elephants. Seleucus's decisive victory at the battle of Ipsus, in Phrygia, in 301 B.C., was won by pitting these animals against the forces of his rival in Asia Minor, Antigonus, who had only seventy-five elephants.

The Seleucids of Syria obtained their Asian elephants overland from India. Their rivals, the Ptolemies of Egypt, relied on African elephants captured in Ethiopia and shipped up to Alexandria from trading posts on the Red Sea.

It should be mentioned, incidentally, that all war elephants had to be trained to kill, and backsliding to their natural condition of docility was frequent. Often they were fed prebattle wines and drugs in hopes of rendering them more bellicose.

There is some disagreement as to when Romans first encountered elephants in war. Some historians say that when Pyrrhus, king of Epirus and a second cousin of Alexander the Great, landed in Italy in 280 B.C. he had an army of 25,000 men and twenty war elephants. J.M.C. Toynbee believes that—despite the poet Juvenal's description of "an African beast"—these were in fact Indian elephants brought from Carthage after traveling there by way of Arabia and Egypt. Thereafter, most elephants encountered by the Romans were African, as this species was more readily available, though the Romans remained quite familiar with the Asiatic species.

Pyrrhus was at first successful in his deployment of these animals. By stationing them on the wings of his forces, he terrified and overwhelmed the Roman cavalry. But when he rode to the Roman embassy atop an enormous pachyderm and demanded return of his prisoners, the grand gesture failed to provoke the hoped-for peace offering.

The following year, in the battle near Venusia, Pyrrhus's tactic was again to place elephants on his wings. But on the second day of battle he switched and attempted to use them to open breaches in the Roman lines; once more his victory was indecisive. The year after that, he brought his elephants to Sicily. But when he tried a fourth time, in 275 B.C., he lost many animals. "Another victory like this and I shall be ruined!" he famously exclaimed.

Later that year, the Romans captured four of the Pyrrhic elephants and brought them back to the capital in triumph. This was the first occasion on which Rome had actually seen an elephant, and as they had originally been sighted in Lucania, the Romans referred to the strange creatures somewhat derisively as "Lucanian cows."

All the elephants portrayed in early Roman art and coinage were almost certainly based on these four. A beguiling elephant selection can be found on carved or painted objects displayed in Rome's tawny-colored, majestically serene Villa Giulia museum, and it is pleasing to think of them there, forever at rest amid the gardens of umbrella pines.

Carthage, on the coast of North Africa more or less opposite the toe of the Italian boot, was the other great Mediterranean power of the ancient world. In Carthage, elephants were used for hauling as well as warfare. Before being sent into battle, they were partially armored, and were trained to use their trunks to swing stout clubs tipped with heavy bronze knobs, or long, double-edged knives. When not actively engaged in campaigns, they were kept in a public park, where they were much admired by the citizenry.

Many writers, including George Blond, dean of French military historians, date the first encounter between Roman legions and elephants to 255 B.C., at the Battle of Tunis, one of the great set pieces of ancient warfare. At the start, the Roman and Carthaginian armies faced each other on a great plain, less than one mile apart. The Romans, led by Atilius Regulus, included 15,000 infantrymen and 500 horsemen. Opposite were 16,000 Carthaginian mercenaries—12,000 foot soldiers and 4,000 horses—under the command of the Macedonian general Xanthippus. The general also had a "secret weapon"—a corps of mighty war elephants.

The Carthaginians advanced first. Having little faith in their leader's secret weapon, they had pledged to fight to the last man. The Romans, too, moved forward, and suddenly saw a swirl of dust out of which a glittering army of brightly painted elephants hurled themselves forward like tanks, crushing in their frenzy some of the Carthaginian soldiers.

Although the Roman general ordered his troops to advance, their horses, maddened by the elephants' size and smell, reared and threw their riders. Only 500 Romans survived the battle, after which Xanthippus's men herded them all the way back to Carthage, the humiliated Regulus chained in their midst.

Roman emperors often appeared before the populace in, or had themselves portrayed in, elephant-drawn chariots—as, for example, on the medal of Augustus. Ptolemys II and III valued elephants as curiosities, as well as for use in war, and both kings were active in the ivory trade. "However, at the battle of Raphia in Palestine in 217 [B.C.]," says Toynbee, "Ptolemy IV's 73 African elephants proved . . . greatly inferior to the 102 Indian beasts of Antiochus III."

Ever quick to adapt, the Romans soon had war elephants in their own armies, and only four or five years later, at Palermo, the Roman general Metellus marched a group of them against Hannibal's brother, Hasdrubal. A few decades later, however, mindful of the great difficulty Hannibal had in getting his elephants over the Alps in 218 B.C., the Romans elected to concentrate on perfecting their anti-elephant defenses, rather than training the huge beasts to attack.

Foot soldiers wielding axes were taught to go first for the trunks. Hacking these not only caused great pain, but "broke the animals' enthusiasm for battle." Some soldiers wore spike-studded armor to prevent the elephants from grabbing them with their trunks. Others were equipped with long lances and drove light chariots swiftly past the plodding pachyderms. They were taught to jab the lance at the elephant's vital parts and to target the mahout. Other soldiers had long poles with heavy stones attached by a line to their tips. Still others were taught to harass elephants with javelins and arrows. While not fatal, these weapons upset the animals sufficiently to minimize their effectiveness. Then the Romans moved in to attack at closer quarters with hamstringers, who carried sharp-edged axes, and cataphracts, who wore armor studded with points and cutting edges. Some men allowed themselves to be picked up by the elephants' trunks, enabling them to hack at their vulnerable bellies and the backs of their forelegs. Catapults flung stones and, most effective of all, flaming torches and arrows rained down on the beasts. Projectiles coated with burning tar and resin or sulfur stuck to the elephants' skin and so maddened them that they attacked their own keepers, who then had no alternative but to kill them. Livy reports that the most common method of execution called for the rider to hammer a chisel into the neck of the crazed elephant, just behind the ears. The cut is similar to the matador's *descabello;* the medulla is severed, and the animal drops dead.

The Carthaginian defeat in Sicily, which ended the first Punic War (264–241 B.C.), left Rome in command of the sea. ("Punic" refers to the Phoenician dialect spoken in Carthage.) Many of the Carthaginian troops were mercenaries who had not been paid; after the defeat, they mutinied. At home, a peace party took power. Appeasement became the prevailing political climate. But the fierce and warmongering Carthaginian generals, all of them related by blood and led by the mighty Hamilcar Barca, "The Thunderer," already were plotting gory revenge on Rome. A surprise attack from the north, they concurred, would have the best chance of success, even though it would mean marching overland some 1,500 miles, carrying all their own supplies, since no support could be expected from the home front.

When Hamilcar died in 228, he was succeeded by his son-in-law, Hasdrubal. After his murder, seven years later, Hamilcar's four sons—Hannibal, Hasdrubal, Hanno, and Mago, known collectively as "the lion's brood," successively took command. The greatest of these, Hannibal, had been only a boy of nine when Hamilcar induced him to swear that Rome would be his enemy for life.

The Second Punic War occurred in 218 B.C. Since the Romans were expecting a seaborne attack from Carthage, Hannibal employed a novel strategy—a surprise invasion by way of Spain and France, and then across the Alps and down into northern Italy. Armored with swords, spears, sling stones, and elephants, he would destroy the Roman armies in France and northern Italy before attacking Rome.

Two years earlier, he had besieged, and in eight months conquered, the Roman stronghold of Segentum on the sunny Spanish coast. He rested and restocked for a year and, the following spring, set out with 38,000 foot soldiers, 8,000 horses, and 37 elephants, leading them across the Pyrenees and northeast through southern France to a point on the steep banks of the rushing, roaring Rhône river. He had decided to make the difficult crossing not far upriver from Arles, where the waters were about 300 yards wide.

To get his men and animals across, Hannibal constructed a "bridge" by first building a flotilla of boats. Then he started work on a series of fifty-foot-wide, loosely connected wooden pontoons. If necessary, they could swiftly be cut adrift. When his remarkable contraption extended about 200 feet out over the water, Hannibal fastened a pair of enormous floats to its far end, each one large enough to carry one of the herd's two lead matriarchs. Several boatloads of oarsmen, guyed to the bridge by lines, rowed continuously upstream to steady and stabilize it.

The entire route was then covered with earth and branches so as to resemble an elephant's forest path, and the two big females went first, to show the rest of the animals that all was safe. The plan went well until the two lead elephants stepped onto the big floats, whereupon these inadvertently separated from the rest. When other boats endeavored to tow them toward the opposite bank, the remaining thirty-five elephants rocked "from side to side in great fury and disorder," and seemed about to panic. Some were sufficiently "disordered by their fears" to throw themselves into the rushing stream, drowning their mahouts. But the animals quieted and became more cooperative once they realized that they were completely surrounded by water and, by day's end, all had made it to the opposite shore.

Next came the fearful task of getting men, horses, and elephants across the trackless glacial barrier of the Alps. Many men and beasts died of exposure, and others disappeared into bottomless crevasses. Those elephants that came through were in miserable shape. Nonetheless, Roman historians such as Livy and Appian acknowledged that these elephants were a decisive factor in Hannibal's first engagement with Roman troops, at Trebia. The Roman horses were terrified by the sight and smell of the huge animals, and the allied Gallic tribesmen who fought alongside the Romans were equally spooked. But the Apennines still lay ahead, and during this ruinous crossing many more men and animals perished. By the time Hannibal's exhausted men reached the Arno, they had only one elephant left, which the general rode at the head of his men.

Since Hannibal crossed the Alps in November, and early snow had only just fallen on the Italian side, there must have been fairly plentiful elephant fodder for the greater part of the time, and they did not have to rely entirely upon a grain ration. The crossing was calamitous nonetheless, and more than two weeks of bloodshed ensued, a nonstop battle against wild mountain tribesmen, hunger, blizzards, and rebellious troops.

"It is not clear what [Hannibal's] object was in bringing the elephants with him," says Jurmain. In India, the chief importance of war elephants was to knock down fortified walls and, in particular, gates, during the final assault on beleaguered cities. The animal instinctively uses its massive skull as a battering ram, and Indian city gates frequently were studded with iron spikes three to five feet long, specifically to prevent elephants from pounding them with their heads. But why bring elephants all the way from Carthage to attack the then ungated Rome? While it is possible Hannibal wanted to use them for siege purposes, it seems more likely that they were brought along primarily as a form of psychological warfare.

Jurmain's account continues:

> The Carthaginian general kept marching toward Rome, but it was a bitterly cold winter and the army was sick and hungry. A violent infection left Hannibal blind in one eye. Men and animals died. Soon there was only one elephant left: Surus, the bravest. . . . When Hannibal became too sick even to ride his horse, his physicians wrapped him in blankets and mounted him on Surus's back. All through that long cold winter, the one-eyed general and his elephant led the tired, freezing army through Italy.

Hannibal never actually reached Rome. At the news that the Romans, led by Scipio Africanus, were threatening to invade Carthage, the great general hastened home to organize the defense. He ordered a fresh elephant hunt to take place in the then forested mountain ranges of North Africa, and by the time he and Scipio met at Zama, in 202 B.C., the Carthaginians had the support of eighty new war elephants.

But the Roman general had for once made a careful study of the innate weaknesses of elephant warfare and, in consequence, it was at Zama that Hannibal and his army were finally thrashed. Scipio stationed his foot soldiers widely apart, so they would not be trampled by charging elephants, and ordered his cavalrymen to dismount and face the onrushing elephants on foot, to avoid panicking their horses. Then he ordered his buglers to blow a fearful charge. It was the elephants that panicked, and the rest, as they say, is history.

Jurmain adds the final note: the defeated Carthaginians were forced to give up their elephants forever, and to forswear training any new ones. But they never forgot them. Years later, at the end of the Third Punic War, in 146 B.C., "when the Roman armies were at the gates of Carthage and the desolate city was about to be destroyed, the Carthaginians wandered helplessly through the streets. Some wept; some prayed. Others shouted the names of their elephants—perhaps hoping for a miracle that would bring the mighty animals back to save them."

The penultimate appearance of elephants on a Roman battlefield was during Julius Caesar's crushing defeat of his rival, Pompey, at Thapsus, southeast of Carthage, in 46 B.C. Caesar had imported war elephants from a state-owned herd in Italy, but reserved them to train his cavalry for the coming battle. In the battle itself, Pompey positioned his elephants on the wings, but to no avail. "Terrified by the blows inflicted on them by Caesar's slingers and archers, by the whir of the slings and the impact of the stones and lead, they trampled on the men of their own side and crashed their way back to . . . camp," says Carrington.

During the reign of Caesar Augustus (27 B.C.–A.D. 14), war elephants were pitted against horse and foot soldiers at a ratio of twenty elephants per 500 men. Later, the proportions were elaborated: each elephant carried a tower holding at least a half-dozen armed men. But for the emperor's preferred commando technique—rapid marches and surprise sorties against an unsuspecting foe—the animals could prove more a hindrance than a help, and often he consigned them to the rear.

Yet, on certain occasions, "Even a solitary war elephant could be highly effective." In Julius Caesar's invasion of Britain in 54 B.C., as Sir Gavin de Beer describes, Caesar wanted

> to cross the Thames, which Cassivelaunus, King of the Britons, fought to prevent with many horsemen and chariots. But in his army Caesar had something which the Britons had never seen before: a huge elephant, protected with iron armor and bearing on its back a tower in which were archers and slingsmen, who were ordered to advance across the river. The Britons were terrified at the sight of such an outsize animal, against which horses were unavailing. For as in the case of the Greeks, horses bolted at the bare sight of an elephant. Nor could the Britons stand up to this armored fighting animal possessed of firepower and shooting arrows and sling-stones at them. With their horses and their chariots they turned and fled, and the Romans were able to cross the Thames without danger because their enemies took fright at one animal.

The last representation of draft elephants in classical times is a fourth-century A.D. ivory panel now in the British Museum that depicts a four-elephant car with four mounted mahouts bearing an effigy of the emperor's soul. The emperor's hairstyle and beard most closely resemble those of Julian the Apostate (331–63), and Toynbee speculates that the piece dates from the fourth-century pagan revival that Julian initiated.

To give Toynbee the last word on Rome, let us contemplate

> a fascinating terracotta statuette of an Indian war-elephant of the Roman period, now in the National Museum at Naples . . . found at Pompeii. The elephant, which has small ears, wears a heavy saddle-cloth sweeping to the ground, and on it, fastened by chains to the beast's body, is a tall,

crenelated tower. In front of the tower sits a mahout, inserting a loaf or cake into the elephant's uplifted trunk.

Of all the mighty elephant warriors of history, my own favorite is the half-legendary Assyrian queen Semiramis, daughter of a great general and a goddess, who warred against the Medes and Chaldeans in about 800 B.C. Most of what we know about her comes from the frequently flawed and incomplete writings of Diodorus Siculus. But he describes her as an exquisitely beautiful woman with boundless ambitions. Like Alexander and Tamerlane after her, the one thing she most wanted was to conquer India . . . and the one thing she did not have, and sorely needed, was elephants. Since Assyria in her day had no elephants, Semiramis decided to make her own. She assembled a battalion of artisans, and in due time they created a mighty army of elephant puppets—in fact, creatures made of ox-hide stuffed with straw and mounted on the backs of camels, each one carrying two soldiers. The ruse might have worked had not a few Assyrian soldiers tipped off the Indian forces. The Indian horses were terrified by the strange monsters, but eventually the real elephants of the enemy trampled the puppet army of Semiramis to bits.

In Europe's Dark Ages, the elephant all but disappeared from the Continent. In A.D. 797, the emperor Charlemagne received the gift of an elephant from the Caliph of Baghdad, Haroun al Rachid (of *The Thousand and One Nights* fame). The beast, named Abbul Abuz, came to Italy by sea, and then was marched over the Alps and into Germany. The emperor so adored his elephant that he took it along on his travels. After it expired, during a campaign in Saxony, he had a drinking cup made from its greater tusk, and had the remainder of its ivory carved into a set of chessmen, some of which still survive.

The indefatigable British researcher Richard Carrington can find but one other elephant in Europe over the next millennium, an animal "obtained in the Holy Land by St. Louis (Louis IX of France)" in 1254. The French king presented the creature to England's Henry III, who stabled him or her in the Tower of London.

Marco Polo's late-thirteenth-century accounts of his travels in India and China are replete with references to elephants. They describe a religious procession in what is now Peking that included a parade of 5,000 elephants caparisoned in gold-embroidered silk robes. He relates how Kublai Khan, emperor of China, was carried into battle in a wooden "castle" mounted on the backs of four elephants. Of course, Marco Polo also describes a huge eagle-like bird capable of picking up an elephant and flying off with it.

A century after Marco Polo's travels, the peoples of the Near East and Central Asia spoke in whispers of "the great gray wolf" who was eating the earth. This was the dreaded Tamerlane (also: Timur, and Tamburlaine), who had reassembled, and extended, the enormous empire of Genghis Khan, which once constituted half the known world, but had fragmented after his death, in 1227. By 1398, the gray wolf had swallowed up most of present-day Iran, Iraq, Turkey, Syria, and Afghanistan, and his empire stretched from Central Asia to Turkey to southern Russia to India's northern border. At age sixty-two, the cruel Mongol emperor determined to take on India.

He divided his forces in three and marched one section on Lahore and another toward the Punjab. He himself led the third force over the most punishing route—across the high mountains of the Hindu Kush. Everywhere they murdered and looted without mercy, slaughtering children, enslaving adults, and dragging with them huge baggage trains of ivory, gold, gems, cattle, and slaves. Reaching the great walled city of Delhi, for centuries the political and cultural center of India's rich civilization, the Mongol hordes reportedly strangled 100,000 Indian slaves in less than one hour, before prostrating themselves to beg the aid of Allah in the coming battle.

By trickery, Tamerlane managed to lure the Indians to attack. The huge gates opened, and out poured 40,000 foot soldiers, accompanied by 10,000 horsemen, and 3,000 trained and armored war elephants led by Prince Mahmoud. The animals had poisoned daggers lashed to their tusks, and bore huge wooden towers on their backs, each holding archers armed not just with bows and arrows, but also rockets and vats of boiling tar. "The great brass drums thundered, the cymbals crashed, the trumpets screamed, and the great Indian army poured out through the city's gates," says Jurmain, and were met by 90,000 Mongol horsemen "disciplined to act as one." The path of the elephants had been mined with barbed stakes, and catapults hurled pots of burning pitch at the terrified animals, who quickly stampeded, injuring and killing many Indians.

When it was over, Tamerlane had killed or captured every living thing, and all the elephants appeared to kneel and bow their heads in homage. Elephant Bill tells us that "all of them had snuff put into their eyes so as to make them appear to weep tears of grief at the outcome of the battle." Before leaving, the Mongols piled a tower of human heads at each of the city's four corners. Tamerlane's top commanders returned to Samarkand with at least a hundred slaves each—none of his followers had fewer than twenty—and Delhi was not rebuilt for another 150 years.

One hundred years after Tamerlane, the European Age of Exploration began. Portuguese accounts of work elephants written at the time of Columbus heap praise on the numerous animals employed in India, Bengal, indeed all over Southeast Asia, and as far north as the Himalayas. Most of all, the travelers were impressed by the elephant's sagacity, which, they reported, surpassed that of any other animal. "On occasion," says Ivan T. Sanderson, "elephants were used on a massive scale. During the siege of Columbo in 1587 . . . the Sinhalese were said to have deployed a force of 2,200 war elephants against the Portuguese."

In 1513, the election of the Medici pope Leo X, an aesthete, epicure, and scholar of renown, ushered in the Florentine Golden Age. "God has given us the Papacy," he proclaimed. "Let us enjoy it!" Artists, poets, and men of letters descended on Rome by papal invitation, and soon made the Eternal City the cultural capital of the Western world. But despite Leo's joie de vivre, he suffered bouts of such profound melancholy that sometimes he was unable to leave his bed unassisted. Painful piles and severe obesity intensified his gloom, and he was quick to lavish gifts upon anyone who could relieve him of his "black dog." In the first year of his reign, Manuel I of Portugal earned the Holy Father's lifelong gratitude by presenting him with Hanno, an elephant captured in Cochin by the explorer Tristan da Cunha. An impromptu baptism of sorts took place in a Vatican courtyard when Hanno sucked up a trunkful of water and squirted it all over His Holiness. The little elephant became at once the pet of the papal court and accompanied Leo everywhere, contributing, in time, to the vehemence of Martin Luther's denunciation of ecclesiastical excess.

The only complete suit of elephant armor was made in India in about 1600. It has 8,439 overlapping metal plates linked with chain mail and sewn onto cloth, and weighs 350 pounds. The behemoth who wore it was also equipped with swords attached to his tusks. The monstrosity was acquired by the wife of the governor of Madras, Lady Clive, who brought it back to England in 1601.

Carrington has dug up obscure records relating to three or four other elephants in Europe. Louis XIV kept one at his Versailles menagerie, where it became celebrated for its appetite for French cooking, insisting upon at least twelve pints of wine a day and swallowing huge pailfuls of Gallic soups, into which it dunked its French bread before downing both.

A word must be said here about the longtime employment of elephants as work animals. Although African elephants were widely used throughout the ancient world, the last such on record were a pair of bulls that pulled a chariot at Axum, in Abyssinia, in about A.D. 500. The employment records of Indian elephants of course span the entire history of Asia. Britannia would never have been able to rule the waves had it not been for the eighteenth-century discovery and conquest of Burmese teak forests. Elephant Bill tells us that the English ships that defeated Napoleon at Trafalgar were built of Burmese teak. "Heretofore," he reminds us,

> the British navy had been build of stout native oak. And there was never quite enough. An oak must be 80–120 years old before its lumber is of sufficient size for ship-building, and a single warship can require 700 trees. Then Britain discovered Burma's teak forests, source of one of the toughest, longest-lasting, most rot-resistant of woods. Elephant labor was the only way to get the precious teak out of Burma's dense forests. The terrain is as steep and serrated as the tooth of a giant elephant, and teak trees appear only intermittently amid the choking growth.

In our time, the outstanding elephant war story is told in a much-beloved children's book that to me seems utterly bizarre. It is read aloud on Japanese radio and television every August to mark the anniversary of Japan's 1945 surrender to the Allies that ended World War II. First published in 1951, *Faithful Elephants* has since gone into more than seventy printings and has been widely translated all over Southeast Asia. In it, an elderly Tokyo zookeeper relates a tale of "a long time ago when . . . bombs were dropped on Tokyo day and night, like falling rain." People began to worry about what might happen if bombs hit the city zoo, allowing dangerous animals to escape and run wild through the city. "It would be terrible!"

The army therefore orders that all dangerous animals be poisoned. After all the lions, tigers, leopards, bears, and big snakes have been killed off, it is time for the zoo's three elephants to die. Big John loves potatoes, so the soldiers mix a few poisoned potatoes into his dinner. "John, however, was a very clever elephant. He ate the good potatoes, but each time he brought a poisoned potato to his mouth with his trunk, he threw it on the ground, *kerplunk!*"

So they decide to inject the poison, but no needles will pierce John's thick hide. They decide instead to starve him to death, and seventeen days later poor John dies. Now it is beloved, gentle Tonky and Wanly's turn to die. Their keepers stop feeding them, and they grow weak. But every time someone walks by their enclosure, they totter to their feet and pitifully beg for food and water. Weak as they are, one day Tonky and Wanly managed to stand on their hind legs, raise their trunks high in the air, and "do their banzai trick." Their trainer cannot bear it. Sobbing, he rushes to bring them food and water. The other trainers pretend not to see him, because "everyone is praying that if the elephants could survive only one more day, the war might be over and the elephants would be saved." But the bombs keep falling, the elephants sink to their knees, and finally die leaning against the bars of their cage, trunks extended, still trying to do their banzai trick.

Raising their fists, all the keepers cry, "Stop the war! Stop the war! Stop all wars!"

The final page recounts how "not even one drop of water" could be found in the dead elephants' stomachs. The accompanying illustration, prettily bordered with cherry blossoms, shows the now white-haired old keeper, still weeping, patting the elephants' tombstone "tenderly as the cherry blossoms fell on the grave, like snowflakes."

CHAPTER 6

IN ZOOS AND IN CIRCUSES

PEOPLE HAVE ALWAYS loved watching elephants; and the animals need not perform; their very existence compels. The first zoological gardens we know of were constructed in the ninth century B.C. in Assyria, by Assurnasirpal II, and at about the same time, exotic animals were exhibited at a Phoenician zoo in Kalhu. In both places, the most popular attractions were the elephants.

The first performing elephants appeared in India in the early Vedic era (before 1000 B.C.), when Indian princes staged elaborate entertainments in their palace courtyards, and elephants trained in acrobatics invariably took part. From India, the custom spread to Mesopotamia and Abyssinia. But the most skilled animal trainers among the ancient peoples were the Egyptians. They worshiped many species as gods—Apis the bull, Anubis the jackal, Horus the falcon, and the crocodile-headed Sobek, for example—and encouraged wild animals to roam at will through their temples and gardens. Egyptian hunting cats were taught, like canine retrievers today, to recover waterfowl the huntsman had shot with an arrow. Armies of sacred baboons were taught to weed gardens, stack firewood, sweep out temples, serve at table, and perform obeisance to the setting sun. Holy elephants bathed themselves and each other in the Nile. They wandered untended through pavilions of white limestone and freely browsed the sacred groves of sugarcane and dates and bananas.

Romans valued wild beasts equally as household pets and as participants in spectator sports of unbelievable cruelty and excess. Over the 700- or 800-year existence of the Roman games, the entertainments grew increasingly bloody. Girls were torn apart by teams of oxen and lashed between poles as bait for hungry crocodiles. Dwarfs and morons gouged each other to death, and wild animals were slaughtered by the tens of thousands.

The immense, horseshoe-shaped Circus Maximus was the largest structure in ancient Rome, one-third of a mile long and capable of accommodating 250,000 spectators, one sixth of the city's population. By way of comparison, the New Orleans Superdome seats 95,000. The Roman Colosseum, still standing today, seated 50,000. Completed in A.D. 80, the Colosseum was inaugurated with one hundred days of games, during which 5,000 wild beasts, 4,000 tame animals, and uncounted numbers of slaves and captives were slaughtered. Its arena could be flooded, for reenacting naval battles, and even had a collapsible ship, so that spectators could enjoy watching the slow sinking of an ark loaded with screaming wild animals.

Some of the elephants stabled in the city were there for training in the gladiatorial arts, and others were kept for breeding purposes. Since fighting does not come naturally to elephants, handlers employed every sort of mechanical goad, torture, and drug to incite war elephants into more furious combat. The breeding elephants, on the other hand, were treated with immense tenderness, and responded with exemplary behavior.

Elephants had appeared in the Roman circus as early as 655 B.C. At first they were matched against one another; later they fought bulls, and, finally, men. A favorite spectacle was the trampling to death of convicted criminals and army deserters by a herd of deliberately maddened elephants. Wholesale slaughter reached a climax under the emperor Trajan (A.D. 98–117) with the butchery of 11,000 animals to celebrate his Dacian triumph. "But for refinement of cruelty to animals, Commodus took the palm," writes Toynbee. "He kept animals at home in order to kill them: in public he despatched with his own hands 100 bears, six hippopotamuses, three elephants, several rhinoceroses, a tiger and a giraffe." According to Herodian, who also mentions lions and leopards among the emperor's victims, he "shot ostriches with crescent-shaped arrowheads devised to decapitate the birds, whose headless bodies went on running."

Roman training schools turned out performing elephants that could dance, throw darts with their trunks, and execute all manner of difficult, dazzling tricks. On one occasion, four elephants entered the arena bearing a litter on which lay a fifth pachyderm thrashing as if in the pains of childbirth. Both Pliny and Seneca were present when a full-grown elephant walked a tightrope down from the top level of the arena to the stage. They also describe a troupe of elephant clowns, and a pantomime in which twelve elephants costumed as patricians in gilded wreaths and gorgeous togas assembled onstage for a classic Roman banquet. They assumed various lounging positions on immense divans and nibbled their victuals with utmost delicacy and hauteur—until one elephant filled its trunk with water and drenched the most elegant member of the company. A water fight at once broke out, and continued until all the Romans were soaking wet and howling with laughter.

Romans were quick to notice their elephants' particular sensitivity to music. When captured in the wild, they were at first spooked by the sounds of clashing cymbals, but could be readily taught to "listen enraptured to the sound of flutes and tap out the rhythm with their feet." On occasion, a troop of tame, music-loving elephants was brought to a theater to march in precision, turn circles, and toss flowers to the audience—a corps of ponderous pachyderm Rockettes.

With the collapse of the Roman Empire in A.D. 476, all the spectacles, chariot races, circuses, and attendant pomp and ceremony disappeared, and the circus was not seen again in Western Europe for almost 1,400 years. One or two elephants were seen in England in Elizabethan times, and Shakespeare certainly knew of them, but they were thought of more as rare and exotic creatures, to be exhibited in menageries, than as performers.

• • •

Save for a few scruffy little touring menageries and the occasional hanging, organized entertainment in Colonial America was virtually nonexistent. This dearth was due only in part to the lack of roads; more important was the strict piety and Puritan heritage of many settlers. Women of the day considered theatrical entertainments ungodly, and many men agreed. Card-playing and billiards were against the law. Concerts, musicales, and even formal dinner parties were unknown. Apart from a few big centers—Boston, New York, Philadelphia—major American cities in the early 1800s lacked the money to support museums and other temples of culture. As Mrs. Trollope noted when she reached Cincinnati, in 1832, "I never saw any people who appeared to live so much without amusement."

In America, the traveling menagerie—often no more than a wagon containing perhaps a monkey, a burro, a parrot, a snake—preceded the circus. Gradually acrobats, clowns, jugglers, bareback riders, and other acts were added. Then one day in early April 1796, the trading ship *America,* on its return voyage from the Far East to its home port of Salem, Massachusetts, put in to New York Harbor to unload cargo. The meticulous keeper of the ship's log, Seaman Hawthorne (father of the writer Nathaniel), noted that part of the cargo in question was a young elephant.

Captain Jacob Crowninshield had bought her for $450 in Bengal and, ten days after arriving in New York, sold her for $10,000 to a canny Scot, John Owen of Charleston, South Carolina. Owen placed advertisements in newspapers up and down the Eastern Seaboard, "Come to see The Elephant! 25 cents!" and immediately set off, traveling by night to prevent the impecunious from getting a free look. People came, in droves.

Mankind has always needed monsters—their existance helps affirm our own humanity—and in the rigorous and pious world of Colonial America, fabulous beasts were rare, and the provincialism of the populace difficult to overstate. We were a nation of rubes. In 1761, a New York newspaper solemnly described the arrival in Manhattan of a monster captured in Canada, which it identified as a "gormagunt . . . larger than an elephant [with] three heads, eight legs . . ."

Around 1800, a ship carrying an Indian elephant from England to be exhibited in Philadelphia foundered in a storm. Fishermen at the entrance of Delaware Bay the next morning were astonished to see a "huge, strange, five-legged creature" wandering along the beach.

Meanwhile, walking from town to town under cover of night, Owen's Elephant—the only name she was ever given—plodded up and down the nation for a decade. Only a single onlooker is reported to have been unimpressed, a newly arrived slave in North Carolina who took one look and scoffed, "Hie, Massa! He *calf*!"

It was probably this animal who gave rise to the common nineteenth-century American expression, "He has seen the elephant." To see the elephant could mean, "to get around," "to survive difficulty and hardship," or "to become more worldly, less provincial." As Mark Twain wrote in *Following the Equator,* "I've seen the elephant, and I've heard the owl, and I've been to the other side of the mountain."

America's preeminent circus historian, Stuart Thayer, has established that by 1804 at least two elephants were touring the

United States. Owen's Elephant was followed by Old Bet, a four-year-old African who landed at Boston Harbor after being purchased in London for about twenty dollars. She lived twelve years before being murdered one Sunday in Maine by a crazed, god-fearing farmer outraged by the wicked violation of the blue laws, which forbade working on the sabbath. Shouting that Old Bet was the dreaded behemoth of the Old Testament, he ran up and plunged a heavy-gauge shotgun into her ear, then fired both barrels into her brain. "The poor Elephant was destroyed," a clergyman pointed out, ". . . because he took money from those who could not afford to spend it." The thrifty owner, Hackaliah Bailey (no relation to P. T. Barnum's future partner James A. Bailey), saved her bones and hide and, after the taxidermists had done their job, the animal worked the road for four more years, stuffed, before being sold and put on permanent display at the American Museum in New York City.

Bailey also owned the first American performing elephant, Little Bet, no relation to Old Bet. She arrived in the United States in April 1817, and could kneel, stand on one foot, present her trunk for mounting, as well as sit, lie, or stand on command. She could also draw the cork from a bottle, drink the contents, return the container to her keeper, bow, and whistle.

Hack Bailey took to boasting that Little Bet's hide was so thick it was impervious to bullets, and one day, just outside the hamlet of Chepachet, Rhode Island, five small boys, determined to see for themselves, set up an ambush behind a roadside elm tree next to a wooden footbridge. The instant Little Bet stepped onto it, the boys sprang out and fired. A rifle bullet entered her eye, and she fell dead. She had survived twenty-two years in America, and died instantly—a somewhat kinder fate than befell most of the elephants who followed her to these shores.

The first circus tent on record appeared in Wilmington, Delaware, in 1825. That same year the Erie Canal was opened to link the Hudson River at Albany to the Great Lakes, and the boom in westward travel began. By 1849, a full-fledged circus was already playing to Gold Rush audiences in San Francisco, though admittedly it had arrived there by way of a sea voyage around Cape Horn. By 1834, twenty-one field shows—seven circuses and fourteen menageries—were touring the Northeast. Elephant rides for children were widely available and, to advertise the fact, a circus parade marched down the main street of Albany, New York, in 1837 with a pair of furiously ruffling drummer boys, each one mounted on elephant-back, bringing up the rear.

Twenty years earlier, in Danbury, Connecticut, Phineas Taylor Barnum, the greatest showman of them all, had been born into a Yankee farm family. He started out in life as a rustic mathematics prodigy employed in his father's general store in Bridgeport. By age four he had collected sufficient pennies to trade for his first dollar, and it was said that thereafter the budding capitalist never let up. When he was twelve, his teacher bragged that he could calculate the number of feet of wood in a wagonload within five minutes. Bets were made, young Barnum was awakened from a deep sleep, gave the correct answer in less than two minutes, and fell back into bed.

He married at nineteen, bought a printing press, went into business as a newspaper publisher, and before long was jailed for libel. Upon word of the young wizard's imminent release, the admiring townspeople of Bridgeport organized a forty-horse parade, followed by a marching band blasting out "Home, Sweet Home!" and sixty carriages loaded with jubilant citizens.

Barnum's talents made him an ideal ticket-seller and a natural showman. Soon he had organized a circus of his own, and was ballyhooing a bright, twenty-five-inch-tall English midget, dressed in a tiny Civil War uniform, whom he called "General Tom Thumb." Preceded by prodigious advertising, Barnum eventually brought the general to London to sing "Yankee Doodle" to Queen Victoria, and to impersonate Napoleon for the Duke of Wellington. (When he died, in 1883, 10,000 people attended his funeral and, as Barnum's biographer Irving Wallace points out, "The showman would never forget that of the 82 million tickets sold by his variety attractions, 20 million had been sold by Tom Thumb alone.")

The winsome general was but one of many attractions Barnum offered in a lifelong panorama of museums, exhibitions, and road shows displaying freaks, fossils, giants, midgets, flea circuses, and humbug of every variety, including the memorable signpost, "This Way to the Egress." The course of Barnum's life was an eighty-one-year roller coaster of triumph and catastrophe. The first big crisis occurred when the burgeoning showman was in his late thirties and alcohol appeared likely to destroy not merely his career but his life and marriage. Then one thrashing, sleepless night, after attending a temperance lecture, Barnum summoned up unsuspected depths of willpower, descended to his voluminous wine cellars, knocked the heads off sixty or seventy bottles of champagne, and ended up signing a temperance pledge, which he honored for the rest of his life. He had barely escaped, he felt, and later wrote, "I had gone so far in the miserable and ruinous habit of . . . 'liquoring up,' that this unnatural appetite would soon have become stronger than resolution and I should have succumbed."

Instead, Barnum became an outspoken temperance lecturer. But he never let his new faith interfere with his inborn Yankee wit. When years later someone offered a bottle of whiskey to Barnum's latest acquisition, Jumbo, the largest animal in the world, the showman turned purple and spluttered, "Now look what you've done—stunted his growth!"

By 1841, booming, filthy, frenetic New York City had become the third-largest city in the world. Broadway, its main drag, ran for three miles from its root at the Battery straight out into the countryside, and in part was more congested than any thoroughfare in Paris or London. At the omphalic address of Broadway and Battery stood P. T. Barnum's huge, marble-walled Great American Museum, his "ladder to fortune."

In 1850, Barnum sent agents to the Far East to collect elephants and other wild animals for his projected "great travelling museum and menagerie." This, he correctly perceived, would be the best way to out-gross even his biggest popular successes to date, Tom Thumb and Jenny Lind, "the Swedish Nightingale," his top road-show attraction. By the time of her death in 1887, the singer had grossed more than $700,000 for the showman.

In the years before the Civil War, Barnum introduced Americans to George Washington's nurse (fake); to their first bearded lady (real); their first mermaid (fake); and their first "Siamese" twins, Chang and Eng (real—they were joined at the stomach—but not Siamese. Their entire family was Chinese). Barnum's agents returned from Ceylon with eight elephants. Barnum added two more, harnessed all ten to a chariot, and paraded them up Broadway. A four-year road tour followed, billed as "Barnum's Great Asiatic Caravan, Museum & Menagerie." At its conclusion, Barnum in 1855 decided to sell off the entire show—animals, cages, tents, the works—and keep only a single elephant, and its keeper, "for agricultural purposes." In fact, this was a scheme to advertise his American Museum. Barnum had the animal hitched to a plow, dressed up its keeper in vaguely oriental garb, and stationed them on a six-acre plot of Connecticut farmland he owned that bordered the tracks of the New York & New Haven Railroad. He gave the man a railroad timetable, and ordered him to start plowing every time a passenger train was expected. He could skip the freights. When the story hit the papers, as it did worldwide, it amounted to a free announcement that Barnum was using elephants as draft animals. Furthermore, he let it be known that this single elephant also helped him to build fences and stone walls, to harvest fruit in his orchards, plant corn, water the lawn, and assist in milking the cows. Hordes of people flocked to see the spectacle, and, as Barnum wrote in his autobiography, "The six acres were plowed over at least 60 times before I thought the advertisement sufficiently circulated, and I then sold the elephant."

The showman's entire life was punctuated by a series of disastrous fires. In 1857, Iranistan, his palatial seaside castle in Connecticut, burnt to the ground. In midsummer 1865, his American Museum was reduced to ashes. Three years after that, the museum he had rebuilt on the very same spot was totally destroyed by fire. He replaced that one with his Hippotheatron, a structure that would burn down five years later, wiping out his new circus and menagerie, and incurring a $300,000 loss in property and livestock.

Barnum was broke again, but he could not be kept down for long. The public loved him, and when he decided to go into politics, they readily elected him a Republican member of the Connecticut State Legislature, where he served two terms. But circus was his natural forte, and the rapid expansion of the railroads after the Civil War had made possible a boom in the traveling circus business.

Nothing spurred the development of the American circus more than the advent of railroads. The first passenger service opened for business in 1830, running thirteen miles, between Baltimore and Ellicott's Mills (now Ellicott City). By the start of the Civil War, the nation had 30,000 route miles of track, crossing the Mississippi River and opening up Texas, Arizona, California, Oregon, Washington, Idaho, Montana, and of course Canada to the circus trains. The war put a temporary hold on railroad expansion, but transcontinental tracks finally were completed in 1869.

Railroad travel was far superior to wagon travel for America's touring circuses. As an early rail advertisement put it in 1856:

> No more skeleton team horses! Rickety wagons! Tarnished trappings! Worn out ring horses! Tired performers as with the old fogy wagon shows, traveling all night over rough roads, but Fast Men! Fast Women! Fast children! and performers well rested! Ring horses of spirit! and Trapping lustrous!

In the spring of 1869, forty-two traveling shows took off. By autumn, a terrible summer of unprecedented, near-ceaseless rainfall had driven twenty-two of them out of business. But Barnum's enthusiasm was unquenchable. Upon learning that the first railborn circus had taken in one million dollars cash in less than six months, the sixty-one-year-old Barnum had leaped joyously back into showbiz.

By 1872, eight circuses were touring by rail, although only Barnum's carried a whole show for the full season: circus, menagerie, parade equipment, and personnel. In the stock cars, the elephants were packed tightly together, standing at right angles to the tracks, to prevent injury from falls or sudden stops. By 1880, the largest circus conglomerate in existence was the London-based Cooper, Bailey & Hutchinson, incorporating Sanger's British Menagerie and Howe's London Circus. International in scope, the huge show carried an incredible 168,000 yards of canvas, toured as far as Australia and Java, Brazil and Peru, and maintained a thriving winter headquarters in Philadelphia, Pennsylvania. In that city, on March 10, 1880, a twenty-three-year-old 7,000-pound Asian elephant named Hebe gave birth to Little Columbia, long believed to be the first baby elephant born in America, although the mother was almost certainly pregnant before arriving in the United States.* The newborn weighed 214 pounds, had a six-inch trunk, and was about the height and length of a Great Dane. Barnum immediately wired the owners an offer of $100,000. When the gleeful reply came, "Will not sell at any price!" Barnum, always a realist, recognized in Bailey a man he could not beat; eventually they would have to join forces.

Meanwhile, other circus entrepreneurs had begun to take advantage of the new market in wagon-borne and rail-borne enter-

*The inimitable Stuart Thayer has recently documented the birth of another infant elephant, in St. Joseph, Missouri, in 1875. The baby, however, did not survive.

tainment. In 1884, five of the seven strapping and musically talented Rungeling brothers, sons of a harness-maker in Baraboo, Wisconsin, went on the road with a 600-seat tent and a modest show that could be loaded into nine borrowed homemade farm wagons. By the time they added their first elephant, in 1888, "Rungeling" had become "Ringling," their show had grown to include sixty horses, a menagerie of numerous other animals, and a host of new acts housed in fancy, tarted-up wagons and chariots, and billed as the "Ringling Brothers United Monster Shows, Great Double Circus, Royal European Menagerie, Museum, Caravan and Congress of Trained Animals."

The four Sells brothers had been proprietors of an Ohio livery stable until they saw the light and took to the star-spangled road. By the early eighties, they boasted that their circus had eight elephants. In 1902, the colorful Henry Tammen and Fred Bonfils, co-owners of the *Denver Post,* launched a small dog-and-pony show, chiefly for their own amusement, and named it after their sports editor, Otto Floto. In time, after another merger, the Sells Floto Circus became one of the best shows in the land.

By 1889, the Ringling show carried 110 horses. The following year they used two rings and a stage, and began traveling in two railroad cars. The next year they owned twenty-two cars, and the year after that, thirty-two. Barnum and Bailey had finally merged at the close of the 1887 season, and their union became a synonym for razzle-dazzle showmanship that is still in use today. Merger papers had been drawn up by Barnum's lawyers, the notorious Brooklyn legal team of Howe & Hummel, who also represented Lillie Langtry, Lillian Russell, John L. Sullivan, Stanford White, and John Barrymore, and more than one thousand alleged murderers. Like their clients, the lawyers were famed as masters of fraud, hoax, and humbug, qualities that, as we shall see in the next chapter, also characterize the history of the elephant in North America. The pair endeared themselves to Barnum by including a clause in all his new contracts forbidding "all consumption of alcohol by freaks" while in his employ.

When the showman heard of the existence in Siam of "sacred white elephants," he was determined to obtain a specimen and again sent agents to Asia. While they were gone—on February 2, 1882—Queen, one of Barnum's twenty-two elephants, gave birth in winter quarters at Bridgeport, Connecticut, to a 145-pound calf. Barnum arranged to have this event witnessed by "60 scientists, medical men and reporters," and the resultant press—"more than 50 columns of details of the birth" in the American papers alone—insured that the circus that year, opening five weeks later at Madison Square Garden, would be a smash.

Barnum's sacred white elephant dragnet paid off on March 28, 1884, after a three-year search and alleged expenses of $250,000. Before the animal arrived, Barnum disclosed that Toung Taloung came not from Siam, as anticipated, but from the despotic, and broke, Burmese king Theebaw, next door. Earlier, Barnum had offered a $10,000 bribe to the U.S. minister to Siam, with the promise of more to come. But various delays ensued. Being sacred to Buddha apparently rendered an elephant untouchable by Christians. One of Barnum's agents who approached the king directly on the matter was forced to flee the country for his "blasphemous presumption."

King Theebaw finally offered to make a deal for $6,000, explaining that he would need to have his sacred white elephant painted red and blue to get it past the eyes of watchful priests and safely out of his country. Barnum had been advertising his prize as "pure white," and was dismayed upon washing off the red and blue to find the animal's natural color to be a dirty gray with a few pink spots, and pink eyes. "Well, he's whiter than I expected," he told reporters lamely, but later confessed, "I have had my share of disappointments in my long career, but I doubt whether I was ever more disgusted in all my life."

Barnum's disgust became the opportunity of his nemesis and archrival, the wonderfully named Adam Forepaugh, a former Philadelphia butcher and dealer in used horses who changed careers the day he delivered a meat order to a traveling circus and realized that there was more money in showbiz. For years thereafter, Forepaugh had dogged Barnum's heels, once shouldering him out of Madison Square Garden by booking the space far in advance. He also hired away the wildly popular acrobat-minstrel-clown-strongman Dan Rice, a longtime star attraction at Barnum's Museum, for $1,000 a week.

To launch his 1884 season, Barnum with great fanfare had his "white" elephant, Toung Taloung, led into the ring by a retinue of saffron-robed Buddhist priests. On learning of this, Forepaugh sent to London for a large elephant, had it whitewashed, and imported it to New York as "The Light of Asia." Crowds flocked to see the beast. Barnum retaliated by whitewashing one of his own elephants, and ordering his advance men to put up posters: BARNUM IMITATES 4-PAW . . . A WHITE ELEPHANT JUST LIKE FOREPAUGH'S WHITE-WASHED ONE. WAIT FOR BARNUM.

Forepaugh thereupon invited the press to preview "The Light of Asia" at his headquarters in Philadelphia, where an alert journalist crawled up to the beast with a wet sponge and demonstrated that it had in fact been whitewashed. But then, with Yankee ingenuity equal to Barnum's own, the man suppressed his own scoop, selling it to Barnum instead. In the end, people didn't care. Forepaugh's beast was whiter, and crowds preferred it.

At season's end, Forepaugh put out word that his elephant had conveniently "died" before Barnum's experts could examine it closely. "It was dyed already!" Barnum exulted.

In showmanship, timing is everything. As the decade of the 1880s begun, America prospered as never before. Great fortunes were being amassed in mining, banking, railroads. Technology had brought the skyscraper, the telephone, the transcontinental railroad, the phonograph, steamships, electric light, electric trains. For diversion, rich and poor alike flocked to see P. T. Barnum's great traveling circus. Barnum urgently needed a super attraction to underline his merger with Bailey, bigger than Jenny Lind, more outlandish than the Wild Men of Borneo, more rare than his fabled midgets Tom Thumb, Tom's thirty-two-inch-tall bride, Lavinia Bump, and their twenty-nine-inch sidekick, Commodore George Washington Nutt.

The world's greatest showman had had his eye for years on the world's greatest animal, Jumbo, an enormous yet gentle African elephant famous for giving rides to children in London's Zoological Gardens. Of all the elephants who ever lived, mighty Jumbo remains the most famous even today, and his name has become part of our language. The origin of the word is not from the Swahili word "Jambo!" meaning "Hello, there!"—as has been claimed. Others say his full name was Mumbo Jumbo—the name of a type of West African priest who protected villagers from evil spirits. Most likely the name comes from the West African word *onjamba,* which simply means elephant. At any rate, Phineas means "mouth of brass" in Hebrew, and certainly P.T. was aptly named. The man *invented* ballyhoo. His Jumbo posters depicted a beast thirty-six feet high, not twelve.

Jumbo was the first African elephant Britons had ever seen. He had been captured in what is now Zimbabwe, walked to Cape Horn, and thence taken by ship to Paris's Jardin des Plantes. Another version of his history has him captured by Hamran Arabs in Ethiopia and spending some time in Cairo before being sent on to Paris by the Viceroy of Egypt. By 1865, the London Zoo wanted to add a sixth elephant to its herd, and the Paris Zoo found itself in need of an Indian rhinoceros. When London suggested a swap, Paris was so pleased by the deal that it threw in a couple of spiny anteaters.

But when Jumbo's shipping crate was pried open in England, it revealed a sick and half-starved creature seemingly near death.

An assistant keeper, Matthew Scott, was assigned to nurse the four-year-old elephant back to health, and over the many months of convalescence, a bond of total trust formed between man and beast. Jumbo then stood sixty-five inches high, and measured nine and a half feet in girth. His gentle nature never varied, and he was put to work giving rides to children, a task at which he was adept, quiet, and well-behaved. They loved to feed him biscuits and sweets, which he accepted gently, with a delicate movement of his trunk-tip.

For fifteen years Jumbo could be seen daily plodding the gravel pathways of Regent's Park, a howdah full of happy children on his back. Under the constant care of the devoted Scott, Jumbo grew steadily, and ultimately may have reached eleven feet or more in height. (It is notoriously difficult to measure the height of an adult elephant. The unique, weight-bearing structure of the shoulder allows the leg to sink into the joint when the animal stands, and the spongy foot also compresses markedly when weight is put upon it.) After importing Jumbo, Barnum put out a story that he'd had him scientifically measured by a pole vaulter in flight. This whiz had determined that the elephant stood exactly ten feet and nine inches at the shoulder.

The British people and press adored Jumbo. By the early 1880s, the total number of children to whom he had given rides was reckoned in the hundreds of thousands, his fame was international, and Barnum's periodic attempts to purchase him for exhibition in the States were routinely rebuffed. Unbeknownst to Barnum, however, Jumbo's behavior had begun to change. As he approached his twentieth year, he occasionally turned obstreperous and, in the course of these fits, did considerable damage to his quarters. Quite likely, the animal was coming into *musth*. However, the cause may also have been dental; autopsy reports indicated that his fifth set of molars never came in properly, and may have afflicted him with chronic toothache.

Soon his attacks on his quarters became so violent that he

broke off both tusks near the gum line. As the splintered ends began to grow back in, they caused abscesses that had to be lanced. Scott took up a position with his bag of tools under Jumbo's colossal jaw, and the elephant permitted his keeper to cut around the circumference of each tusk with a razor-sharp hook so it could grow out again in a normal fashion.

Whatever the cause—raging hormonal impulses or a mighty toothache—Jumbo was now subject to sudden rampages, especially at night, when his beloved Matthew Scott was not nearby. If he ever got loose, his potential for murderous mayhem was so appalling to contemplate that the zoo's superintendent had quietly petitioned Parliament for permission and the means to destroy the monster, should this become necessary for public safety.

Although Barnum believed he had no chance of getting Jumbo, his need was great, and in 1881 his agents made a no-hope bet, a feint: they offered 2,000 pounds sterling, or $10,000. A scant two days later, the deal was made, contracts signed. The zoo's ready agreement was greeted with horror by the British press and public. The only worse crime, said one writer, would have been a decision to sell the Americans Queen Victoria. Judging from the hue and cry, the elephant might have been a Gainsborough. Schoolchildren were mobilized. Thousands of them wrote to Barnum begging him not to deprive them of their beloved elephant. The Prince of Wales, and finally even Queen Victoria herself, backed up the children. John Ruskin sniffed that "England is not in the habit of selling her pets." Editorial writers went into overdrive. "No more quiet garden strolls, no shady trees, green lawns, and flowery thickets," wept the *London Daily Telegraph*. "Our amiable monster must dwell in a tent, take part in the routine of a circus, and, instead of his by-gone friendly trots with British girls and boys, and perpetual luncheons on buns and oranges, must amuse a Yankee mob, and put up with peanuts and waffles."

Not only were British children and aesthetes near-hysterical at the thought of the zoo's impending loss, Jumbo himself lay down in the street just outside the Zoological Gardens and refused to budge. When Barnum's London agent cabled this news to his employer, P.T. replied, "Let him lie there as long as he wants. It's the best advertising in the world."

Upon receiving word that Barnum was bringing Jumbo to the United States, Adam Forepaugh promptly began advertising *his* pachyderm, Bolivar, as the largest and strongest elephant in the world.

After a month of stubborn recumbency, Jumbo was persuaded to stand up and enter the cage in which he would be drawn through the streets by teams of horses to the waiting steamship. To bid him farewell, the animal-loving British public massed at the zoo gates and stood shoulder to shoulder all along the route to the docks. Among his scores of hand-tied bouquets, hand-knit doilies, stuffed toy bears, and other gifts was a trayload of oysters and champagne sent by a sentimental nobleman, and immediately scarfed up by the elephant.

After the procession at last got under way, Jumbo had one final trick up his trunk. Snaking that mighty appendage through the bars of his cage, he yanked the horses' tails. They bolted, galloping wildly, while the driver shouted and the public scrambled to safety. Order was at length restored, and Jumbo sailed for America on March 25, 1882, aboard the steamship *Assyrian Monarch*.

In London, Jumbo was replaced by Jingo, another African. When he, too, became difficult to handle, he was quietly sold to an American entrepreneur for only one-tenth of Jumbo's price. Alas, the transatlantic passage proved too much for Jingo, and he suffered horribly before expiring, it appeared, from sheer seasickness.*

Unlike Jingo, Jumbo seemed to have overcome his seasickness by sheer willpower. He debarked in Manhattan on Easter Sunday,

*His remains were heaved overboard that night, causing a great uproar the next morning among the crew of a passing ship that chanced upon the floating corpse.

let himself be paraded up Broadway, and put on his first show the following day. "In the next two weeks the receipts *in excess of the usual amount* more than repaid us the $30,000 his purchase and removal had cost us." (Barnum's italics)

A brief period of relative peace between Barnum and Forepaugh followed, and in the 1886 and 1887 seasons, the two shows temporarily combined. But Barnum's last years of elephant-related disaster and mayhem were scarcely at an end. In 1887, on November 20, fire swept Barnum's Bridgeport winter quarters, causing a $250,000 loss—the alleged destruction of everything but two elephants and a camel. Toung Taloung was safely led out, but later "charged back inside and stood there," writes circus historian Felix Sutton, "trumpeting and bellowing in terror as the flaming roofs and walls collapsed on top of him [and he was] immolated on a pyre of greed."

Years later, however, in his autobiography, Barnum wrote that thirty of his thirty-four stabled elephants escaped the flames. The next morning, "Grace was found in Long Island Sound, but died of cold and exposure" while being towed to shore. As for his white elephant, he had "committed suicide" by rushing back into the inferno.

Upon hearing this, Forepaugh had his "Light of Asia" washed off and reintroduced him to the public as "John L. Sullivan, the Boxing Elephant." For many years thereafter, twice a day, rain or shine, John L. "boxed" and then "knocked out" his unfortunate sparring-partner elephant, Willie.

A few years after that, Forepaugh died and Bailey bought his company. In 1906, the Ringling Brothers bought out Barnum & Bailey, and "John L."—now renamed "Old John"—became herd boss. He continued toiling for the Ringlings, as both performer and work elephant, until his death, at their Sarasota winter quarters, in 1932. In his obituary, the *New York Sun* recalled an occasion on which a famous "scientist" specializing in "metabolic research" claimed that an elephant was such a sensitive behemoth that a single peanut would alter its metabolism. With onlookers—and, of course, reporters—crowded around, the scientist produced a peanut from his pocket, rubbed off its papery red skin, and offered it to Old John. The elephant stared for a while, then reached his trunk into the man's coat pocket for the rest of the nuts.

For another view of Old John, here is the ever-alert Ivan T. Sanderson: "Some of the most gentle, reliable, and capable of performing Abu [the ancient Egyptian term for elephant, of either species] have been homosexual males, or asexuals like 'Old John,' the leader of Ringling's herd, who never once in a long life gave any trouble and died of old age." It is more likely that asexuality of this kind is a form of lifelong shock brought on by the rigors of captivity experienced by a wild animal.

One evening in 1885, at the close of Jumbo's fourth North American touring season, the circus was packing up after a performance in St. Thomas, Ontario, Canada. Thirty-one elephants had already been loaded back into the railroad cars when keeper Scott was walking Jumbo and a tiny elephant, Tom Thumb, back along the darkened tracks to join them. Suddenly they saw an unscheduled freight train bearing down on them at high speed. Too late, the engineer threw his locomotive into reverse and hit the brakes. Amid a shower of sparks, the speeding engine slammed full into Jumbo's head and derailed. The elephant expired of a massive skull fracture, the weeping Scott kneeling beside him.

When Barnum in New York got word of Jumbo's horrible demise, he immediately put out a story that Jumbo had "died heroically, trying to save the life of his favorite midget elephant, Tom Thumb." Then he called in the taxidermists. The following season, audiences were treated to a morbidly gratifying spectacle: Jumbo's 1,350-pound hide, realistically stuffed and mounted on wheels, followed by a second wagon bearing his immense reconstructed skeleton. Both were towed around the ring as the band played a funeral dirge. Behind them plodded Jumbo's "widow" elephant, Alice, veiled and shrouded in black, and she was followed by all the circus's regular elephants, each animal holding a black-bordered bed sheet in its trunk, and trained to wipe its eyes on cue. The economics of this arrangement meant that, since the stuffed hide and the skeleton ate nothing, gate receipts failed to decline after Jumbo's demise.

Alice, alas, perished by fire within her first year. Eventually Barnum presented Jumbo's skeleton to the New York Museum of Natural History and the stuffed hide to his alma mater, Tufts University, where it was exhibited until destroyed—again, by fire—in 1975.

In 1891, six years after Jumbo's death, Barnum died, worn out at last, at the age of eighty-one. Bailey died in 1906, of an infected flea bite. The Ringlings bought his show for $410,000, and more than made their money back in their first season. By 1907, they had become America's premier circus family and had two eighty-four-car circuses on the rails—the Barnum & Bailey show as well as Ringling Brothers—more than any other rail shows in operation. By 1911, thirty-two railroad circuses were crisscrossing the United States, ranging from small five-car shows to the two eighty-four-car giants. But in 1918, a terrible business year, due both to World War I and the influenza epidemic, Ringling Brothers and Barnum & Bailey combined forces at last.

The Depression ended the fifty-year "golden age" of the American circus, and indeed nearly wiped out the circus business altogether. John Robinson's show folded in 1930, followed by Sparks in 1931, Sells Floto in 1932, Hagenbeck Wallace in 1935, and Al G. Barnes in 1938. In 1932, John Ringling lost control of the big show to a candy wholesaler, and not until 1938 was the family able to wrest it back, under the leadership of John's nephew, John Ringling North. North ran the show all through the labor disputes of the late 1930s, followed by the terrible fire of 1944—on July 6 of that year, flames swept the circus's Hartford headquarters, leaving 186 people dead, and 487 severely burned, most of them women and children. Eventually $5 million in damages was paid. A series of acrimonious lawsuits continued. Finally it all became too much. The last show played under canvas took place on June 16, 1956, in Pittsburgh, after which America's circus tents were folded for good.

But then, phoenix-like, the great bird revived and again began playing "hard-tops," as it had in the early nineteenth century, before canvas tents were devised. Switching back to hard-tops cut running expenses by one-third or more, and the Ringling Brothers, Barnum & Bailey family tradition was able to continue a bit longer. By 1967, however, North had grown old and tired and was living mostly abroad, and a couple of New Jersey jazz, rock-and-roll, and sports promoters, Irvin and Israel Feld, were able to buy up the great old gaudy name. Appropriately, the contract of sale was signed in the Colosseum, in Rome.

CHAPTER 7

THE DISAPPEARANCE

SINCE OUR MOST popular zoo and circus animal has always been the elephant, it is not surprising that the life histories of the eight hundred or so animals brought to this country since the arrival of "The Elephant" in 1796 should have been exhaustively documented, as have the handful of elephant births. How odd it is, then, that the Portland authorities, at the time of Packy's birth in 1962, were so ignorant of the basic facts of elephant parturition. Still more peculiar, how is it that, before the advent of Packy, despite the presence in America of hundreds of mature and healthy animals, not one elephant birth was recorded in more than half a century?

We begin to glimpse the answer in the memoirs of the late F. Beverly Kelley, most respected of circus P.R. men:

> In the pre–Civil War period, elephants were as popular as rock stars are today and—since very few people had seen an elephant—size was the attribute which impressed them

> most. After that came dangerousness. The biggest beasts, box office–wise, had names like Hannibal, Tusko, Bolivar, Columbus, Tippoo-Sahib, Virginius, Romeo, Mogul, Siam and Pizarro—that is, most were aggressive-sounding males. Since size and dangerousness ranked high, the public was especially interested in each beast's homicidal potential.

A shrewd and lucky circus owner in nineteenth-century America could make very good money in the traditional ten-month touring season. But the hazards of life on the road were formidable. Add to the dangers of fire, flood, and other acts of God the ever-present problem of controlling the essential elephants, the most powerful beasts on earth, without benefit of steel bars, reinforced concrete walls, electric cattle prods, or the other refinements of modern zoo and circus life. Oldtime roustabouts and trainers could rely only on bull hooks, chains, and tent stakes, which had to be dug up and then restaked every time the show moved on. From time to time an elephant—most often a male in *musth*—would go on a rampage.

Under the conditions of circus life on the road, an 8,000-pound male in *musth* is a deadly nightmare, not only unreliable in performance but apt to charge the bleachers or attack his trainer, with murderous consequences, and the negative publicity inevitably generated could rarely be overcome. One berserk elephant could put an entire circus out of business.

What was to be done? The public's appetite for blood and the owners' dread of bankruptcy were on a collision course. In the end it came down to this: to advertise your show as a "circus," you must have an elephant. A trainload of tigers, clowns, ponies, and acrobats cannot replace one pachyderm. A circus without an elephant is merely a carnival. In the muscular prose of P. T. Barnum, "The elephant is the hook on which the circus hangs."

Between the end of the Civil War and America's entry into

World War I, as the range of traveling circuses extended into the smaller towns of the South and West, as well as north across the Canadian border, the number of such outfits increased, and yet—unnoticed—the total number of elephants on the road, and the big bulls in particular, slowly and quietly diminished. The circus owners themselves were responsible. They stamped out the male elephant in the United States because he was bad for business. And they did it efficiently, and in secret. Those who knew what was happening turned a blind eye, and no one else paid attention. When the show played the next town, the next day, its full complement of elephants might be down from nineteen, say, to eighteen, and no one the wiser. All circus elephants are traditionally called "bulls," all keepers are "bull hands," and, to the average observer, male and female elephants are indistinguishable. It was not difficult, therefore, during a show's final day in town, for hands and overseers to pass the word, "Boys, after the show tonight, we have to dispose of a bad elephant. Any volunteers?"

There were always volunteers. And in the ensuing sixty or seventy years, dozens of circus bulls, and some difficult females as well, were variously shot, poisoned, stabbed, clubbed, garroted, electrocuted, drowned, and even hung by the neck until dead. Humankind over the millennia has devised many ways to exterminate undesirables and—save for burning at the stake—I do not know of one of these techniques that has not also been used on an elephant. The grisly work was done mostly under cover of night and carefully hushed up afterward by a silent conspiracy of owners, trainers, and vigilantes properly fearful of the publicity. It was a kind of elephant genocide, or, more correctly, pachycide.

It is no easy task to kill, dismember, and bury an elephant overnight. In the early years of this century in central Kansas, for example, a circus elephant was ordered shot after he had stampeded and demolished a garage. The corpse weighed several tons, and the nearest wrecking crew was 200 miles distant, so two professional meat cutters were brought in, the circus owner having "conned them into believing that the meat and hide were valuable," writes Kelley. "After working seven hours, they had only one leg off, but were still going strong."

To keep the carnage secret was even more difficult. But do not underestimate the resourcefulness of Yankee showmen, nor the pull of market forces. Somehow, they managed it. By the late 1930s, not a single male of breeding age remained available. Not one. Hence the elephant birth rate in the United States was frozen at zero, and doomed to remain there until some time after Morgan Berry imported a young male, Thonglaw, as a pet for his children, in 1952.

I have used the term "available" in the previous paragraph to account for the infamous Ziggy, who spent the last miserable twenty-nine years of his life chained in one corner of his indoor winter quarters at Chicago's Brookfield Zoo. When finally he was winched out once again into the sunlight of summer quarters, he fell into the moat, and died shortly thereafter of his injuries.

The planned destruction of an elephant is rarely mentioned directly in old circus accounts, but sometimes one spots clues to what happened. A former director of the New York Zoological Park, William T. Hornaday, for example, writing in the long defunct *Mentor* magazine, recalled his early days as an Iowa farm boy. In 1861, he

> saw and can never forget Old Tippoo Sahib, of the Van Amberg show . . . that moving mountain of wrinkled gray hide, flapping ears, unbelievable trunk, and enormous white tusks [that] almost touched the ground. . . . Even the largest traveling shows of today have no such splendid old he-ones as "Tippoo" was. The showmen are afraid to carry on with them. They are too prone to go on rampages . . . kill visitors. . . . Today the standardized herd of show elephants, big or

> small, consists chiefly of modest and inoffensive spinsters, mostly immature, who . . . make no fuss about The Life.

Hornaday's article appeared in 1924. In 1934, the *National Geographic* allowed a discreet reference to the same subject matter to creep into an article, "Nature's Most Amazing Mammal," by Edmund Heller:

> Male Indian Elephants formerly were common in circus parades. Sooner or later nearly all male elephants become periodically dangerous at the recurrence of their "must" period, during which time they are uncontrollable and must be kept heavily chained. Frequently they take violent dislike to certain of their attendants and craftily await an opportunity to kill them unawares. So many men have been injured and killed by such treacherous male elephants that to-day the circus herds are usually made up of females only.

In 1841 in the small town of Algiers, Louisiana, outside of New Orleans, a near fight to the death took place between two mighty bulls, Hannibal and Columbus. Hannibal, imported in 1832, was the biggest elephant seen in the United States until the advent of Jumbo, fifty-eight years later. Columbus had arrived even earlier, on July 15, 1817, and was ballyhooed as the only male elephant in the United States. He was so popular that when he abruptly sickened and died, of natural causes, in Centreville, Maryland, in 1829, the news was hushed up and another bull, Mogul, was swiftly renamed Columbus in his stead. The fake Columbus toured the nation under that name until the sad day he, too, perished, in 1851, after falling through a bridge in North Adams, Massachusetts.

At the time of the fight, one bull was with a traveling menagerie, the other with a circus. But so much business was anticipated in New Orleans that it was decided temporarily to unite the shows. When the two outfits rendezvoused in Algiers, a contest immediately began between the two huge bulls, and trainers were barely able to separate them. As the caravan approached the outskirts of town, 10,730-pound Columbus, still enraged, suddenly whirled on his trainer, Crumm, and killed both the man and his horse. He then smashed up a llama cage, and attacked and killed a team of mules. Reaching his trunk over a fence, he grabbed the team's terrified black driver, a slave, and crushed him to death. The rampage left in its wake the two dead men and a dozen dead horses, mules, and cattle, and ended only when Columbus was shot three times in the head, beneath the right eye. He lived, though the bullet wounds remained running sores that festered twenty-four years, until his death. The show repaid the farmers for their dead livestock, and an extra $1,800 to compensate the slave's owner.

In 1880, in Charlotte, North Carolina, a John Robinson Circus elephant named Chief killed his keeper, John King, then ran wild through the streets. The herd leader, Mary, was turned loose to help corral him. Eventually Chief became so hard to control that he was given to the Cincinnati Zoo, where, in 1889, "he had to be shot." For years after, the John Robinson troupers and their circus band went out to John King's grave to pay their respects whenever the show visited Charlotte.

In the early 1880s, Barnum was touring his "7 United Monster Shows," one of the earliest of the three-ring circuses. Its other four elements were a museum tent, two menageries, and a half-mile hippodrome track on which "mounted Sioux warriors and harnessed giraffes and saddled ostriches competed against racing elephants." Women on foot dressed in jockey silks enlivened the contest.

The troupe of elephants, at least thirty in number, included the big bull Emperor. One day while being urged up a loading ramp into a circus car, Emperor became suddenly enraged, bolted from the railroad yards, and took off. He stormed a foundry and reeled into a trough of white-hot metal. Hot-footing it back into the street on his three good feet, he seized a man with his trunk and tossed him ten feet, breaking his leg. He scooped up a woman and pitched her through a plate-glass window. His rage spent, he "limped back to the circus car and submitted without protest to attendants who wrapped oil-soaked bandages about his blistered hoof."

In 1881, circus owner James A. Bailey was notified that while his show was on tour in New Zealand, one of his circus hands had been pounded to death by a rogue elephant, Mandarin. Unlike his flamboyant and open-handed future partner, Phineas T. Barnum, Bailey was a nervous, miserly misanthrope. But he was also a consummate businessman, deadly efficient, and possessed of a draconian sense of justice. He immediately ordered Mandarin crated and shipped back to New York, having privately arranged with a seaman to load up the crate with pig iron and push it overboard as soon as the vessel reached open sea. But before this could happen, Mandarin somehow ingested a load of sulphur matches and died. He was pushed into the Pacific uncrated, horrifying a shipload of incoming colonists who passed the floating corpse just outside Wellington Harbor.

Not long after, a big bull, Rajah, attempted to kill his keeper, and was sold to another show, which renamed him Samson. One day, a bull hand had unchained him and was leading him up to a wagon when the huge beast suddenly grabbed the man's arm and shook him to death. Samson then stampeded through the railroad yards, overturning a boxcar, and was splintering it into kindling when his rage subsided. He died a year later from a brain abscess, which on autopsy turned out to have been caused by an old gunshot wound that had left a bullet embedded in his brain.

In 1894, trainer Bill Emery had a hairbreadth deliverance from Tip, a big bull on the Barnum & Bailey show. Another elephant man, George M. Bates, fortunately came upon Tip just as he was attempting to crush his trainer to death. The bull had Emery pinned on his back, and had sunk his tusks more than two feet into the ground on either side of his body. Bates was able to beat back the behemoth with a sledgehammer and, at the end of the season, Tip was executed.

Another Tip, belonging to the Forepaugh Circus, was so huge and unruly that the management donated him to New York City's Central Park Zoo, where he killed three keepers before being "disposed of."

In 1898, in Racine, Wisconsin, a bull named Prince killed the show's beloved elephant boss Joe Anderson. Enraged, the other keepers destroyed the animal, very slowly, by inflicting multiple pitchfork wounds.

In 1901, in Peru, Indiana, a tusker called Big Charlie snatched up a keeper in his trunk, calmly strolled over to the banks of the Mississinewa River and held the man's head under water until he drowned. The owners revenged themselves on Big Charlie that night, when they succeeded in getting him to eat a poisoned apple.

The following year, 1902, "Another criminal elephant . . . was executed with a peck of poisoned apples in New Jersey," writes F. Beverly Kelley. Could it be that poisoned apples are irresistible to some elephants, despite the general rule?

A year later, an elephant named Topsy (or perhaps Tops) was electrocuted at the Luna Park amusement park at Coney Island, but only after attempts to hang it by the neck had failed. The owners claimed it had killed three children. In fact, it had killed its trainer in Waco, Texas, in 1900, and later that same year, in Paris, Texas, had killed his replacement. Two years after that, in Fort Wayne, Indiana, the same elephant destroyed a young menagerie visitor who'd had the bad idea of feeding it a lighted cigarette.

After some wrangling with the ASPCA, the execution of the

six-ton, twenty-eight-year-old pachyderm was finally set for January 4, 1903. The owners portrayed themselves as altruistic capitalists, willing to sacrifice a $6,000 elephant in the interests of public safety. Although the execution was officially advertised as "private," the owners had sold seats to the spectacle. Righteous-minded spectators gathered in a special, roped-off section of bleachers for invited, honored guests. Tall fences had been erected to keep out the merely morbidly curious, but the large crowds scaled them readily, and the executioners piously filmed the entire scene for posterity.

Plans originally called for Tops to be hung by the neck until dead, but at the last moment the animal refused to ascend the scaffold. Ultimately it was electrocuted, at ground-level, a job that required twenty-two seconds and 6,000 volts.

In 1916, in Elkton, South Dakota, a bull named Hero went berserk and overturned several railroad flat cars. His owners decided to stage a public execution, even though no loss of life had occurred. More than 2,000 rounds were fired before the big bull was adjudged *kaput*.

Nineteen twenty-six was the climactic year for Charley Ed, unofficial champion of truant circus elephants. The big bull had been named after the son of his circus's owner, Edward Ballard, and later renamed Cranbrook Ed in remembrance of his famous "French leave" that triggered a general stampede of the Sells Floto elephants one August morning in Cranbrook, British Columbia. Spoiled as a young calf, the mature Charley Ed had become increasingly difficult to handle. Then he fell in love with Myrtle and, if separated from her, bellowed nonstop until they were reunited. Finally, during a street parade, he led an escape. Vance, Barney, and Floto followed him, and all four elephants disappeared.

Indian trappers set out to recapture them; the roundup took three weeks. In the meantime, Myrtle caught pneumonia and died. Charley Ed's grief was so great that his unruly spirit subsided. But he and the other runaways were banished forever to winter quarters.

In another version of the story, told by Edward Allen and F. Beverley Kelley in *Fun by the Ton,*

> The real cause of the worst runaway in circus history was a fast freight engine letting off steam as it went past the herd at the unloading runs. Immediately they were off en masse . . . 15 circus elephants loose in the wilds of Canada! Twelve Indians were hired and offered $25 to the first man to sight an elephant. Tilly, one of the elephants, broke from the others and ran over a cliff and fell 1,000 feet to her death.

Circuses frequently used pairs of elephants to haul heavy wagons to and from the trains, and each wagon carried a two-man team—driver and brakeman—to handle its two-elephant team. Once in rural Wisconsin, a wagon's brakes failed, and the ten-ton vehicle started to roll downhill, slowly picking up speed. Circus personnel below could do nothing but run ahead of the juggernaut until all had reached level ground. The harnessed elephants sensed something was wrong and ran faster until pandemonium broke loose. One or two injured bulls started to run and crowd the others until they, too, started running. "Every man grabbed onto an elephant as the stampede progressed, trying to block the frightened beasts. But it was no good until Lizzie, the herd leader, sent in to 'sap' them as they tried to pass her on the narrow road, stopped the stampede."

Everything was in order again when, for no reason, two elephants chained together broke line and started running. Immediately pairs of chained elephants went pounding off in all directions. They were captured, and the circus was getting ready to load, when suddenly all the elephants swung around in unison, encircling two circus roustabouts, who "were knocked down, kicked and rolled around like a couple of soccer balls." They were not flattened, however, because an elephant is very careful where it places its feet. It will never step on any object it can walk around, unless intent on smashing it, in which case the animal is more likely to use its forehead.

The following day everything was under control again but the elephants seemed nervous. They were unloaded at Peru, Indiana, and during the three-mile walk to quarters, they made sixteen attempts to run off. They came to a big brick barn and bystanders scattered in all directions as the elephants headed for a small door in the side. One man took cover between the huge tusks of one of the bigger elephants and was thereby protected as the animal thrust its head through the door.

Tusko (formerly Ned) was a seven-ton Asian giant with seven-foot tusks who was exhibited around the country but never asked to perform, due to his notorious bad temper. A Mexican promoter booked Tusko into a bull ring in Juarez—the only occasion on record in modern times that a bull faced an elephant. The bull charged. The elephant slapped him with his trunk. The bull ran off, pursued by the elephant, who then kicked the bull until he was knocked senseless. Next he chased the matadors and tossed them among the screaming spectators. Finally, he seized the toreador's cloak and waved it triumphantly.

In retaliation, the Mexican promoter obtained a writ of attachment on Tusko for an overdue feed bill. That night, at his trainer's command, Tusko walked out of his holding cell, bringing the locked gate with him around his neck. He picked up his trainer with his trunk and swung him up on his head, and the happy pair set off down the road, leaving Juarez behind.

A passing motorist turned his car directly in front of Tusko, thinking he could stop him. Tusko bowled the car over and continued his stroll back to the circus lot.

Authorities ordered that Tusko be confined in a corral built of steel rails, and in addition loaded him down with an 800-pound network of chains. So many restrictions on his liberty were apt to put him in a bad mood, his trainer concluded, and he providently saved his life by quietly shipping him out of town.

In 1928, Ringling Brothers, Barnum & Bailey's big bull Rio was en route to New Haven when he

> threw [his handler] Shorty off his head and stampeded. . . . After quite a chase he was captured, taken to the circus ground and sentenced to die that afternoon. We erected an enclosure of canvas . . . Rio was marched inside and chained securely by all four feet to many wooden stakes driven into the ground. He was made to lie down on his stomach and another chain was passed over his back . . . so as to prevent him from rising again. . . . An elderly marksman from the Winchester Arms Company was given the signal that the rest was up to him. . . .
>
> As the lead struck, Rio got to his feet, snapping the chain over his back as though it were a piece of string.
>
> We all turned and looked at the executioner in alarm.
>
> "That's all right," he remarked. He aimed and fired again. This time the bullet entered Rio's head straight between the eyes and the base of the trunk, and he toppled over dead. . . .
>
> Rio died for stampeding and because he was a male, with the attendant nuisance of handling him.

While not with his regular handler, Black Diamond, the largest elephant in captivity after Jumbo, tusked a housewife to death in Corsicana, Texas, and tossed her husband over several railroad cars. The townspeople demanded vengeance. Diamond's longtime regular handler, "Slim" Lewis, says the death of this well-liked woman was "a turning point" in the history of male elephants in America. Elephants had been executed as murderers before, but generally only if they had killed somebody other than a circus roustabout. The death of an itinerant bull hand could readily be hushed up. Often, the party line was: "We warned him not to treat the animal that way. You couldn't really blame the animal for striking back. . . ." Switching sympathy to the elephant tended to avoid lawsuits or public outcry. But you couldn't pull this with the entirely innocent and popular Corsicana housewife. After her death, says Lewis, circus owners redoubled their efforts to get rid of male elephants, "selling or giving them to zoos if they could, or shooting them after the slightest misbehavior."

Texas newspapers took up the cry for retribution. Owner John Ringling assured the townspeople that the elephant would be killed in some humane way. The Chamber of Commerce of Corpus Christi suggested that tons of lead be tied to Diamond's feet and that he then be dragged by tugboat into the Gulf of Mexico. A rumor next circulated that the animal would be strangled to death by his fellow pachyderms. But circus people would have no part in such gratuitous cruelty. Several electrocutions had taken place successfully and humanely, they claimed, making reference to Topsy's death at Coney Island and the killing of another bad bull in Little Rock, Arkansas, where the voltage required had left the city in darkness for ten seconds. Accordingly, says "Slim" Lewis, Black Diamond, covered in chains, was led with three anchor elephants to the place of execution. Twenty or so men had been selected as the firing squad.

> Diamond's chain block had been delivered ahead of us. . . . Jack had him put his front feet on it, and chained them securely to the ring in the center. The three leg chains were fastened to trees on each side. . . .
>
> Peanuts had been removed from several bags and their shells filled with a deadly, tasteless, odorless poison. They were then put back in the bags with the rest of the peanuts,

> and all the bags, including unpoisoned ones, were placed in a wicker basket of the kind used by circus candy butchers.
>
> The basket was placed where Diamond could reach it with his trunk. He eyed it suspiciously for a moment, then he deliberately selected a bag. He put it in his mouth, sack and all.
>
> He ate two or three bags. He took up another, hesitated, and tossed it aside. He groped around and picked up another bag to stuff in his mouth.
>
> How he knew which bags to eat and which bags to skip is something nobody can answer.
>
> Next he was offered poisoned oranges. Like all elephants, he liked oranges, but these he politely refused. . . .
>
> We were told later that more than one hundred and seventy rounds were fired into Diamond before he was dead. . . . Diamond died without making a sound or fighting his chains.

In the early 1930s, a circus bull named Major was shot and killed in Lancaster, Missouri. In 1938, Ringling Brothers, Barnum & Bailey presented a troublesome bull named Sammy to the Detroit Zoo, which decided to execute him as "too mean to live." After Sammy had been securely chained between a row of pilings and a tractor, two men climbed up onto a platform and fired seven bullets into him. A taxidermist was retained to make four novelty waste baskets from Sammy's feet, and the rest of him was sent to a "rendering plant."

In 1940, at the Los Angeles Zoo, Billy Sunday was "euthanized" for "bad temper." The same year, in Baldwin Park, California, another former Ringling Brothers, Barnum & Bailey elephant, Joe, was shot dead. The following year saw two more executions: Danny was killed by the Pittsburgh Zoo, and Romano met the same fate in San Antonio, Texas.

In the 1950s, at a Texas military base, an Air Force psychiatrist killed an elephant inadvertently. The late Louis "Jolly" West, M.D., had ordered the creature delivered to his lab by my old friend Morgan Berry, the Seattle animal dealer. The doctor was curious about an elephant's reaction to LSD, which he suspected might be similar in chemical makeup to temporal gland fluid. He injected what he calculated was the proper LSD dose for a four-ton animal, and was surprised when death ensued within half an hour. On hearing this story, several people surmised that perhaps the beast died because elephants already live in a hallucinogenic world, and any amount of LSD for such a creature is much too much of an already familiar thing.

Since the bad behavior of rogue female elephants cannot be blamed on *musth,* I shall list the executions of females separately. Soon after the Coney Island snuffing of Topsy, or Tops—almost surely a female—came the 1909 or 1910 killing of Empress in Frankford, Pennsylvania. Originally known as Queen in the Adam Forepaugh Circus, this elephant's first victim was her keeper, whom she killed by wrapping her trunk around his neck and squeezing. After this, Queen was sold to the John O'Brien Circus, and her billing was changed to "Empress, The War Elephant." Under this name, she killed at least five men. O'Brien sold her to the W. H. Harris Nickle Plate Circus, then playing on an empty lot on Robey Street, in Chicago, where her name was changed again, to Mary. Mary's next victim was her new keeper, known as "Jimmy the Bum."

From here on, the story grows more complex. According to *Facts on File,* "She was condemned to death, but Col. George ("Pop Corn George") W. Hall secured her [a] stay of execution. It almost cost him his life. Hall was feeding a peanut to Palm—a baby elephant standing next to Empress-Queen-Mary in the menagerie—when the older pachyderm went jealously berserk, slammed Hall to the ground, and attempted to crush him. Barney ("Elephant Fat") Shea, their new keeper, diverted the maddened beast by sticking his thumb in her eye; but Hall's hip was already broken in two places and he was left crippled for life.

Mary was renamed Queen, and leased to one circus, then sold to another, and sold again to a former bull man with the

Forepaugh show, John "Blue Jay" Durham. Queen remembered him, and was very peaceful under his command. But in the spring of 1906, Durham sold out and left. Although Queen missed him and ran away from the lot whenever possible, she otherwise remained calm for the season.

The following spring, however, she tried to kill her new keeper while the show was still in winter quarters. "Only a short foot chain held her back. When a spring snow snapped the quarter pole in her top, she broke her chains and demolished several cages and most of the menagerie before being brought under control."

Later the same season, during the show's parade into Buffalo, New York, a little boy tried to dash across the street in front of Queen. In a flash, she had swatted him flat with her trunk, knelt on him, and killed him. The show was able to hush up the story and move on, but at the close of the season, in Columbia, South Carolina, Queen pulled the same trick. An assistant boss canvasman was repairing a sidewall outside the menagerie when a sudden gust of wind lifted the canvas flap he was working on. In one movement, the elephant saw, swatted, knelt, and crushed. The man died in the hospital the following day, her thirteenth victim.

Queen was kept in chains thereafter, until the show was able to sell her to another outfit. But her new owners found her so difficult to manage that they decided to stage a public execution, and began selling tickets to her electrocution, scheduled to take place at Tattersall's Pavilion, in Chicago. The Humane Society managed to put a stop to the event, however, after which Queen was sold again, and thereafter disappears into the fogs of circus history.

In 1914, the good people of Hartsville, South Carolina, rid themselves of an obstreperous female pachyderm, peppering her with over a hundred shots from squirrel rifles, shotguns, and revolvers.

In 1916, "Murderous Mary" was hung by the neck from a railroad derrick in Erwin, Tennessee, after she had killed three people. This was a true lynching. The thirty-year-old Mary, an enormous creature who for fifteen years had been billed as "the largest land animal on earth," was one of five elephants performing for Sparks World-Famous Shows, and was valued at $20,000. A couple of days earlier, in Kingsport, Tennessee, Mary had killed her trainer. The provocation remains in dispute. Some say he had treated her with particular cruelty, others say he merely refused to give her the piece of watermelon he was eating. Still others insist she was crazed by chronic pain caused by abscessed teeth.

Rumors spread that Murderous Mary had killed between three and eighteen people in the past and, despite the lack of evidence, her owners decided to accede to the rising tide of blood lust among the rural citizenry and stage a public hanging rather than risk what seemed a sure drop-off at the box office. The noose was chosen rather than the firing squad because of doubt as to whether the marksmen could fell the giantess quickly enough.

On execution day, Mary was chained and dragged to the CC&O Railroad yards and a 7/8-inch chain wrapped a couple of times around her neck. She was lifted only five or six feet in the air when the chain snapped and she crashed to the ground. "In a stupor, Mary offered no resistance as another chain was secured. She was hoisted a second time, gave a twist and a sigh and died."

As the writer Harry Crews tells the story, which he first heard in rural Tennessee as a young boy, the elephant, whom he calls Alice, had killed a five-year-old girl in Erwin, Tennessee, and then beat the floor with her, holding the small body in her trunk like a bunch of weeds and horribly mutilating her corpse. The town put the child's remains on display, then decided to retaliate by lynching the perpetrator. They walked her to a stretch of track that had a portable railroad derrick used to hoist steel sections of track into place. The townspeople put a steel logging chain around Alice's neck and started lifting her up. "She didn't understand,

and stood on her hind legs, and started shitting, and they kept hoisting and Alice kept shitting until she was dead."

The most notorious rogue female was probably Boo, imported from Germany in 1903. She got her name because people noticed that if they offered the little girl treats, and then pretended they weren't going to give them to her, she would make a peculiar sobbing sound, "like a bass horn: Boo-Boo." Boo hit her first man within two months of her arrival in the United States, probably because he was teasing her. The next provocation came from a young keeper who offered her a red apple, then pretended to eat it himself. Catching the young man off guard, Boo grabbed his wrist with her small trunk, pulled him to her, forced him down by leaning on him, and stuck her small, pointed tusks through his body. His lungs were punctured and he died, but Boo was saved because circus hands knew that her behavior had been a response to her keeper's taunts.

At age two her training began, but she drew an inept trainer, a "nervous type" who abused her. She struck back, and soon was tagged by circus men "as a hardened criminal." Man was her enemy. Her pattern was to do her tricks well, wait patiently for an opportunity to catch a trainer off guard, then pin him against a wall or wagon and squeeze hard. She seemed "diabolical" in first gaining the men's confidence; she was in fact herself an elephant con woman. As a performer she was perfect, punctual, and always obedient. Until . . .

One short-term trainer decided to teach her a lesson. He heated a long metal bar white hot, and then, knowing Boo hated him, walked over to her and waited until she tried to grab him, whereupon he "thrust the hot iron into her trunk." Trumpeting in agony, she tossed the iron bar back over her head . . . but made no immediate attempt to attack the man.

For several days she neither ate nor drank (one wonders if she could) until someone, a "little fellow," taking pity, began hand-feeding her with hay, and then put the water hose in her mouth.

The elephant seemed grateful; the man seemingly expected good behavior in return. "We reckoned without the beast's deep-seated hatred for mankind and without respect for her native cunning."

Trunk healed, Boo returned to her circus routine and, for a long time, did her act as though nothing had happened. Then one day her abusive trainer arrived at her barn in winter quarters with a hangover, and again decided to put her through her paces. The "little fellow" tried to stop his abuse. Everyone could see trouble brewing. When the trainer threw caution aside and began to "work out" on Boo, she struck, grabbing his arm in her jaws. He fainted, and when the "little fellow" ran to help, Boo dropped the trainer and crushed her benefactor against a concrete wall. Before she could trample the trainer, others armed with pitchforks drove her off. But the "little fellow" was already dead, and the trainer died of blood poisoning soon after.

Another trainer, Ed Allen, came upon Boo holding a man gripped in her "vise-like jaws" and shaking him as a cat would a mouse. The only way Allen could get Boo to drop the victim was to leap upon her head and "get her by the eyeball and with all the strength I could muster in my fingers and thumb, try to pull it out."

Now branded a killer, Boo wound up in a cellar in Lancaster, Missouri. The locale was Bill Hall's "sort of circus salvage establishment," or "circus boneyard," which leased out both livestock and rolling stock, suitably repainted and renamed, to would-be showmen eager to cash in on the new money-making business. It was a magnet for the bankrupt, the place where old circuses, railroad cars, battered cages, and so on went to "die" after shows had failed.

Boo remained chained up at Hall's place for five years without any exercise at all. This was around 1924. Five years later, Hall acquired two more middle-aged female elephants, and since Boo appeared more or less happy to see them, he decided to try working Boo with them, and rented out the trio to independent circuses and county fairs. This went well for several seasons, but then a new, less understanding trainer took over the act. The showdown came in Chicago, in 1929. All three "bulls" were kept in a holding pen, and had to walk underneath the city's elevated railway to get to the fair site. One day as a train was rumbling overhead, the elephants started to stampede, and the trainer at once tried to "abuse" Boo, although by what means I do not know. She immediately maneuvered the man into a narrow alley and mashed him against a wall. He died in the hospital. Boo was sent back to the farm, again chained up and forgotten for another five years. Then she was put on the newly organized Cole Brothers and Clyde Beatty Circus, along with two companions. They became part of a performing herd of twenty elephants until, in 1935, after a year or more of good treatment and good behavior, Boo again killed her keeper, and was given to the San Diego Zoo, where, in 1937, she was executed.

In December 1976, *The New York Times* reported that the Central Park Zoo had been forced to destroy its thirty-year-old elephant Julia because she attacked her keeper. But also, the zoo vet claimed in his pre-euthanasia press conference that Julia had "a mental disorder," adding that "if she were a person, we'd probably put her in a sanitarium." Sadly, no such facility was available, but "she has been exhibiting hostile behavior for 11 years, not only to her keepers but to her roommate, Tina. I feel terrible about killing her, but it would be irresponsible of me to permit further risk of her killing some little child, or another keeper, or an adult." Tina would "thrive and feel relieved," he added. "She has been pushed around and beaten up by Julia, and lives in terror of her."

So saying, the vet injected two quarts of a barbiturate and later, he performed an autopsy. The *Times*'s reporter, Edith Evans Asbury, ends her story by reminding readers that, a year earlier, the Society for Animal Rights had filed suit to close the zoo, alleging

DOUG BEGHTEL, *THE OREGONIAN*

Morgan Berry, "The Man Who Loved Elephants," father and grandfather of captive elephant breeding. In his heyday, Berry ruled Elephant Mountain, his one-man wild-animal sanctuary in Oregon, where dozens of elephants, and more than seventy other wild species, roamed at large while awaiting sale to U.S. zoos and circuses. Berry and his sons also built this ark-like homestead for his large family.

Belle was the first pregnant elephant recognized in the U.S. in half a century. In 1962, toward the end of her twenty-two-month confinement, she developed cravings for freshly dug dirt and for black coffee, which I often fed to her, cup and all.

A rare photograph of Packy with both parents: his mother, Belle, and his father, the mighty Thonglaw.

MARSHALL LOCKMAN/BLACK STAR

OREGON ZOO

OREGON ZOO

Packy weighed 225 pounds at his birth, which I attended, in Portland, Oregon, in 1962. Today he weighs about 15,000 pounds, stands more than 11 feet tall, and is almost certainly the largest Asian elephant anyone has ever seen.

PATRICIA MABERRY

Packy's dedicated obstetrician was "Doc" Maberry, D.V.M. I still visit him whenever I get to Portland, as here, and at Christmas he never fails to send me a package of his unbelievably good homemade cookies and preserves.

PERSONAL COLLECTION, STEVE COHEN

Eloise Berchtold, partner of Morgan Berry, trained their favorite elephant, Teak, the son of Packy's father, Thonglaw, and "little" Pet. Not long after this photograph was taken, Teak, in heavy *musth,* tusked Eloise to death in front of 10,000 circus fans in Toronto.

RANDALL MOORE

The evil-looking Buddha, chained between two trees atop Elephant Mountain, was Morgan Berry's favorite elephant. He was also the animal that ended Berry's life in a most bizarre fashion. Note that I am standing well clear of the brutal behemoth.

SANDRA SHOSHANI

Dr. Jeheskel Shoshani, elephant anatomist extraordinaire, with his pet hyrax, Shafti. Zoologists classify the hyrax as the animal kingdom's closest relative to the elephant, because of the similar skeletal structures of their toes.

PERSONAL COLLECTION, RANDALL MOORE

As a teenager, Randy Moore shoveled dung for Morgan Berry; later he managed the family circus act and came to regard Morgan and Eloise as his loving grandparents. After Morgan's murder, Randy decided to repatriate his boss's African elephants. Here they are in Mexico, awaiting passage to South Africa. Today Moore is the millionaire proprietor of the luxurious Abu's Camp in Botswana, which offers ten-day elephant-back safaris to other millionaires.

PFENING ARCHIVE, COLUMBUS, OHIO

Breeder Fred Alispaw and his wife, Lucia Zora, eventually trained Snyder to stomp around the circus ring on his hind legs, mouth open, with Lucia covered in rhinestones, standing upright on his tusks. But Snyder, by then, had fallen hopelessly in love with Alice.

CIRCUS WORLD MUSEUM, BARABOO, WISCONSIN

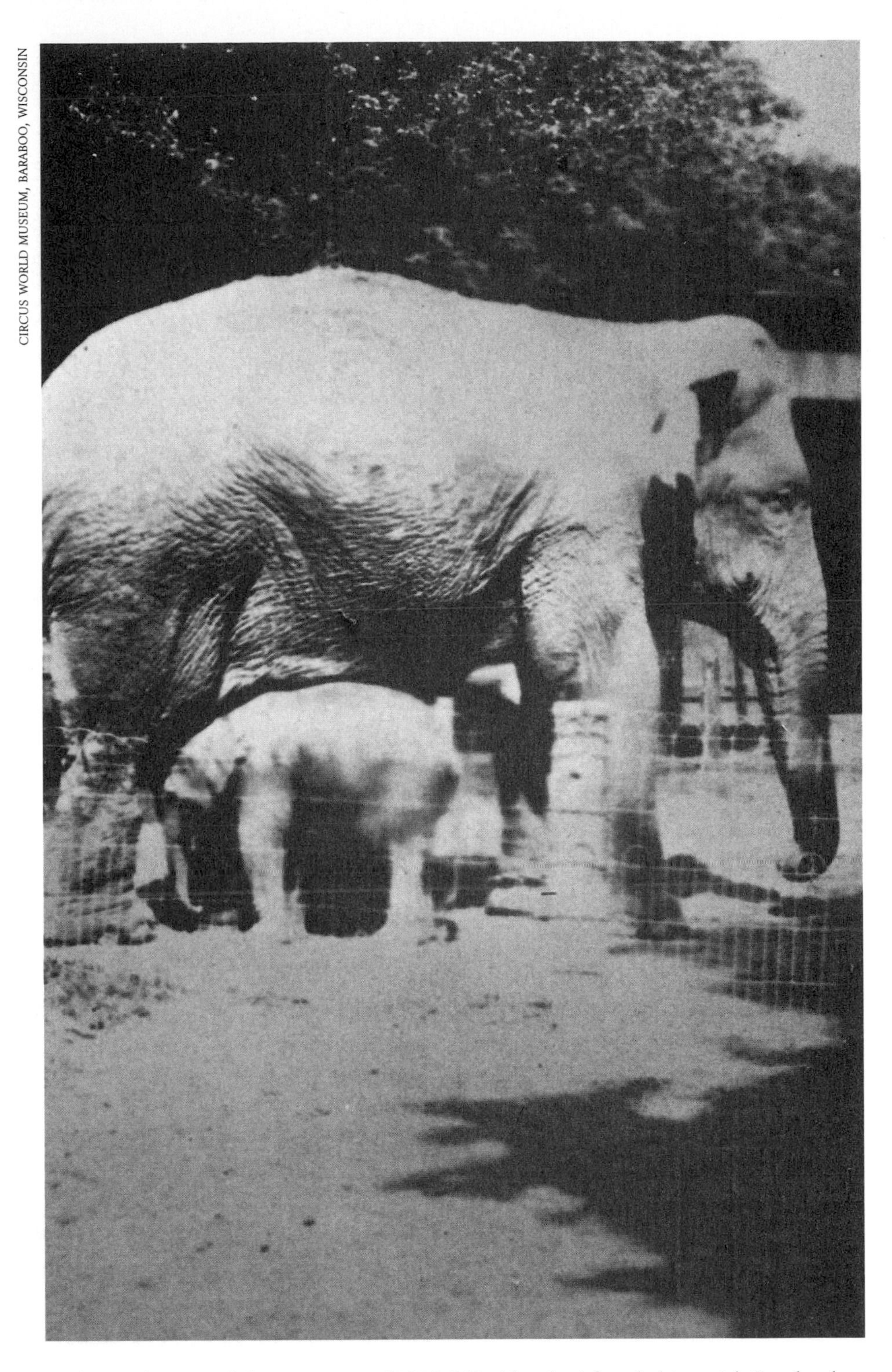

In the peak years of their romance (1912-18), Alice had four babies with Snyder, her sometimes-beloved mate. Prince Utah, the last of the four, lived eleven months.

PFENING ARCHIVE, COLUMBUS, OHIO

By 1928, Mighty Tusko, an Asiatic, weighed more than seven tons and wore more chains than any animal ever exhibited. During *musth*, he was kept for three months in a crush cage too small to permit him to lie down or turn around.

JOYCE POOLE

Oria and Iain Douglas-Hamilton, at home in their Kenya farm, are pioneer researchers on African elephants in the wild, and known worldwide as "Mr. and Mrs. Elephant."

ORIA DOUGLAS-HAMILTON

Dr. Joyce Poole has spent hundreds of hours alone in the African bush observing wild elephants. She was the first scientist to discover that sometimes female elephants, like males, secrete a fluid from their temporal glands. Poole and her mentor, Cynthia Moss, were first to note and describe "green penis syndrome" in *musth* bulls.

DR. TERESA HOWARD-CARTER

Raman Sukumar, world-class expert on the Asian elephant, advises the Indian government on how best to save its 25,000 or so remaining wild elephants. Dr. Sukumar led our extraordinary 1997 tour of Indian elephant sanctuaries.

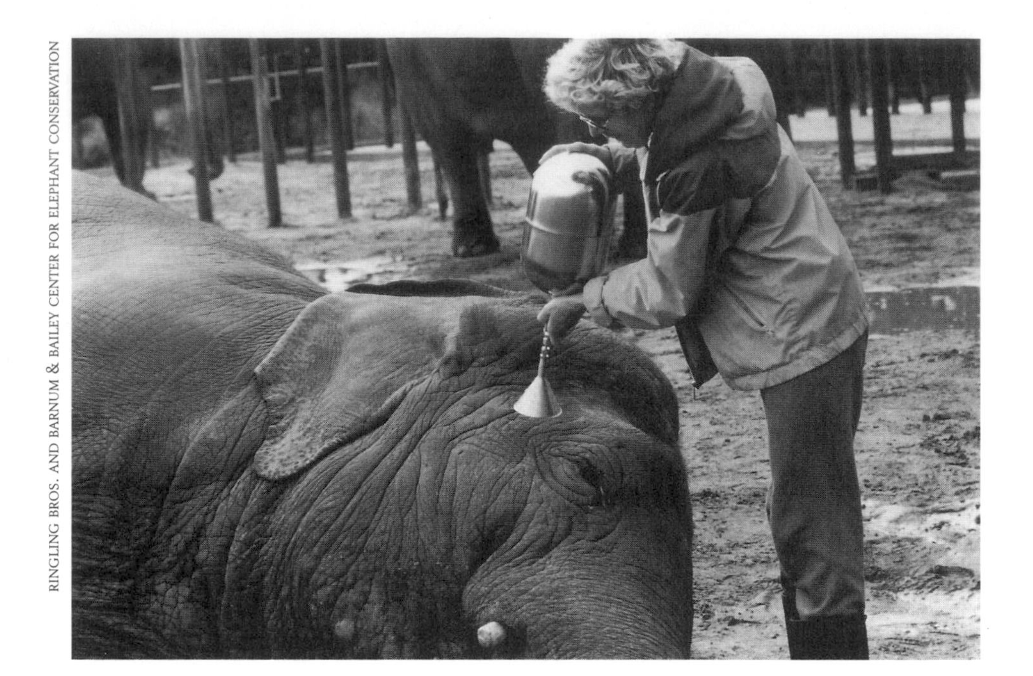

RINGLING BROS. AND BARNUM & BAILEY CENTER FOR ELEPHANT CONSERVATION

Dr. L.E.L. "Bets" Rasmussen and her husband, Rei, are co-inventors of steel vacuum storage bottles capable of collecting and storing pure samples of all a creature's bodily secretions: urine, blood, breath and (as here) temporal gland secretion during *musth*. A chemist and molecular biologist, Bets spent a decade analyzing 11,000 gallons of elephant urine.

JEHESKEL SHOSHANI, SAN DIEGO WILD ANIMAL PARK

Elephants very rarely breed in captivity. If this mating should prove successful, a calf will be born twenty-two months later.

NATIONAL ZOO, SMITHSONIAN INSTITUTION

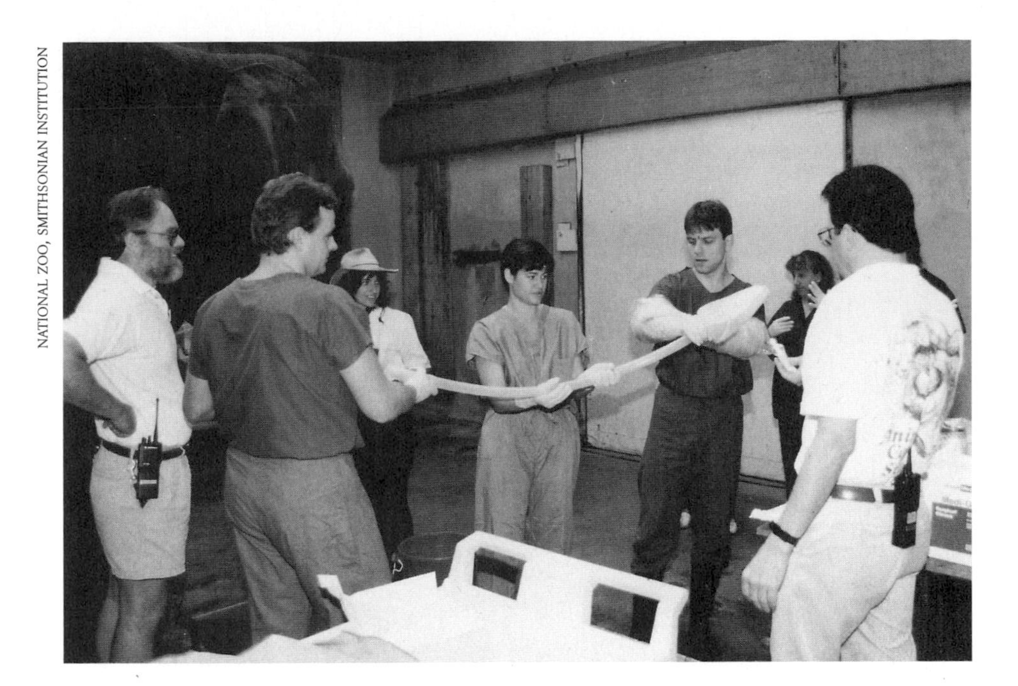

The crack research team at Disney's Animal Kingdom eventually taught themselves to artificially inseminate elephants. Here they adjust a vital balloon catheter. Left to right: Disney chief John Lehnhardt, Dr. Frank Göritz, National Zoo head keeper Marie Galloway, Dr. Nancy Pratt, Dr. Thomas Hildebrandt, inventor of the A-I procedure.

DR. NANCY PRATT

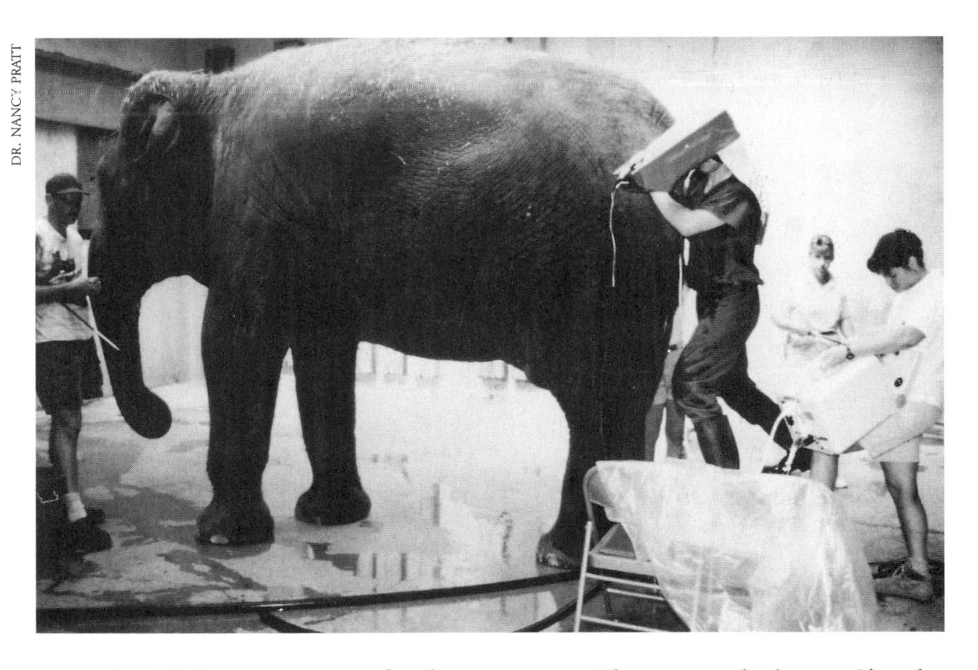

An early (1995) attempt at artificial insemination. The patient elephant is Shanthi, at Washington's National Zoo, and the hooded man is Dr. Thomas Hildebrandt, maneuvering his "swan-neck probe" into position.

STEVE COHEN, OREGON ZOO

Mike Keele's first job in Portland was cleaning the zoo's rat and armadillo cages. In 1997 he was made Assistant Director and Curator. "Little" Pet, born in 1955 in the jungles of Thailand, came to the zoo as a seven-year-old, the youngest of Maberry and Berry's four original females.

JEFF GLAZIER

Veterinarian Dennis Schmitt worked more than ten years to achieve his goal: the world's first elephant created by artificial insemination. Haji, here three days old, weighed 278 pounds at birth on the Sunday after Thanksgiving 1999 at the Dickerson Park Zoo in Springfield, Missouri.

that "the mental, physical and emotional health" of the elephants and other animals "was being threatened by noise of blasting for a subway extension." No true New Yorker can fail to sympathize with the animals' plight.

By the mid-1930s, U.S. owners had succeeded in virtually eliminating male elephants from their zoos and circuses. In 1936, the noted animal physiologist Francis G. Benedict published the first complete metabolic study ever performed on an elephant. He had done all his work on Jap, a mature Asian male, and his results so intrigued him that he launched a search for other captive elephants on which to do comparative studies. He found only sixty-four animals available, and sixty-three of them were females.

Records are scant, but in the following season the Cole Brothers and Clyde Beatty Circus advertised that they carried a herd of thirty-seven elephants. They did not disclose that only one of their animals was a male. "Sidney," "Louis," "Tommie," "Tony," and virtually all the others were, in fact, females.

In 1952, *Billboard* published a revised U.S. elephant census and counted 264 animals, most of them young, and only six of them males. According to a 1985 census, there were still well over 250 elephants in American circuses, and the importation of baby Africans—heretofore thought too wild to be trained as circus animals—was becoming more common. But despite the pronounced, ongoing imbalance between male and female circus elephants, all the animals continue to be referred to as "bulls," and their keepers and handlers are all "bull hands."

In consequence, the birthrate for captive elephants in the United States had declined virtually to zero by the time Packy was born. At my request, the dean of U.S. circus historians, Stuart Thayer, recently made a meticulous search of all circus records, and came up with two other infant pachyderms, Bibbitt and Ellie, both of them born shortly before Packy. But before *that,* not one baby elephant had been born in this country since the World War I nativity of Prince Utah, whom we shall meet in the next chapter.

Bringing our tale of death and destruction more or less up to date, in the early 1990s, Tyke, a panicked and fleeing African circus elephant was cut down in a hail of bullets fired by a squad of pursuing police officers in downtown Honolulu. Earlier, Tyke had trampled her trainer to death before a large crowd of spectators at a performance of Circus International. (An autopsy revealed the presence of alcohol and cocaine in the man's body.)

In May 1993, newspapers worldwide reported that the internationally known elephant trainer Axel Gautier had been "stomped to death while visiting the Ringling Brothers, Barnum & Bailey Circus elephant breeding farm." Elsewhere in Florida, at about the same time, an 8,000-pound twenty-year-old Indian elephant named Janet suddenly went berserk. She was in mid-performance with the Great American Circus in Palm Bay, Florida, just outside of Titusville, and five small children and their mother were riding around on her back. Without warning, Janet smashed a cage in the center ring, threw her trainer to the ground, grabbed at a rope with her trunk, tried to bring down the tent, then trampled her way through the toppling canvas to the outside, where she knocked down a cop who was trying to help. A second trainer astride a second elephant was finally able to get close enough to remove the screaming children and their mother. The cop, having recovered, opened fire on the animal, at the show's owner's urging. The mortally wounded elephant nonetheless turned and tried to charge the bleachers as terrified patrons ran in all directions.

The entire episode lasted less than twenty minutes. When an autopsy was ordered to try to determine the cause of Janet's sudden savage, uncharacteristic behavior, the procedure proved impossible to carry out. More than fifty rounds of police gunshots had completely destroyed her head. Like Tyke in Hawaii, Janet's carcass was unceremoniously hauled off to the town dump.

"These elephants are trying to tell us something, I think," said one of the police officers later, appalled to find that he had personally fired forty-seven of the fatal shots. "Zoos and circuses are not what God created them for.

"But we have not been listening."

CHAPTER 8

LIEBESTOD

THE FOREGOING GRISLY accounts notwithstanding, the history of circus elephants in America is far from an unrelieved horror story. It also has its *Liebestod.* I speak of the tragic, true-life World War I romance of the teenaged Alice and mighty Snyder, her five-ton Romeo—parents of four of the last baby elephants born in the United States until Packy's arrival a half-century later.

During the long weeks when I was hanging out in the back room of the Portland zoo's elephant house, waiting for Belle to give birth, someone recommended I look at "The Elephant Is Slow to Mate," a poem by D. H. Lawrence then considered so erotic that the city's public library kept it behind locked doors. Reading it today, the lines seem tame enough, and eerily descriptive of Alice and Snyder, whose story the poet could not possibly have known about when he wrote.

> The elephant, the huge old beast
>   is slow to mate;

he finds a female, they show no haste
  they wait
for the sympathy in their vast shy hearts
  slowly, slowly to rouse
....

Oldest they are and the wisest of beasts
  so they know at last
how to wait for the loneliest of feasts
  for the full repast.
They do not snatch, they do not tear;
  their massive blood
moves as the moon-tides, near, more near,
  till they touch in flood.

Alice and Snyder were German-born Asian elephants whose fourteen-year romance was not only chronicled but to a large extent orchestrated by Fred C. Alispaw, menagerie superintendent of the Sells Floto Circus, and his flamboyant wife, Lucia Zora.

Elephants in those days were not known to breed in captivity. Then, in 1902, a small-time Denver outfit called Otto Floto's Dog and Pony Show decided to upgrade itself to "circus" status by adding elephants, and imported six elephants from the famed Hagenbeck Zoo in Hamburg, Germany. One of the new arrivals was Snyder, a healthy but unschooled five-year-old male born in Hamburg in 1897. In circus parlance, he was "hook-wise"—conditioned to fear the bite, in tender groin or armpit, of his keeper's steel-tipped elephant hook—but he did not yet perform tasks or tricks. Under Alispaw's diligent direction, Snyder became not only an ace working bull, hundreds of times helping to raise and lower the canvas and pull the clumsy, top-heavy circus wagons out of muck and mire, he also developed into the best-trained, most admired show elephant in America. At the dazzling finale of the family act, the magnificently tusked Snyder rose up onto his two back legs, his trunk and forelegs high in the air, mouth agape. With the befeathered and spangled Zora standing upright astride his huge tusks, her own eyes, arms, and rhinestone-handled whip pointing heavenward, the beast stumped slowly out of the ring on his back legs while the crowd went wild.

Alice, also born in Hamburg, in 1888, arrived at Luna Park, Coney Island, four years later, and began her professional life as a "howdah bull" performing in the spectacle "The Durbar of Delhi." In 1904 she was sold to the newly organized Sells Floto Circus and brought to its winter quarters in Denver, Colorado. It was here, under the sun-struck peaks of the Rocky Mountains, that the lovers first met. Snyder was now seven, Alice a demure sixteen-year-old. Soon after Alice joined the show, keepers began to notice that she and Snyder would not leave each other's side.

Fred Alispaw, like Noah, preferred his animals in pairs. His self-styled "hobby" was breeding difficult wildlife specimens, and his experiences with Alice and Snyder—the only breeding pair of elephants in circus history—were exotic indeed. After his retirement, he wrote them up in the early 1930s for a small circus publication, *White Tops*. Earlier, Lucia Zora had told her story in her autobiography, *Sawdust and Solitude*. To them both I owe a great debt of gratitude.

Whether or not Lucia Zora had the pipes to make it as an opera singer—the career for which her parents had trained her—must remain a matter of speculation. But certainly she had the temperament. At nineteen, she ran away from the theological seminary in Cazenovia, New York, to which her "well-fixed" parents had consigned her for safekeeping, and joined the Sells Floto Circus. A year later she married the show's new menagerie manager, Fred C. Alispaw. Theirs may have been the only courtship in history to take place on top of an elephant's head. Lucia said yes while the affianced pair sat side by side on the head of Old Mom, another of the Hagenbeck-Hamburg elephants, who nightly led the Big Parade. Mom's original name had been "Mutter Mary," and she spoke only German. For the rest of her life, on the rare occasion when someone addressed her in German, she appeared to become overjoyed, and answered back with guttural sounds of pure delight.

The night of the nuptials, Old Mom was preceded into the ring by clowns dressed as comedy bridal attendants and carrying bouquets of cabbages. The audience erupted with cheers and jeers. A string of old shoes had been tied to the elephant's tail, JUST MARRIED banners draped her flanks, and the band broke into "Here Comes the Bride." As soon as the parade ended, the sinister clowns kidnaped the groom and held him prisoner for three days. Even the fortune teller couldn't find him, said Lucia.

Upon marrying Alispaw, the bride's circus expertise broadened. She learned to administer paregoric to ill elephants, and helped her husband apply a mustard plaster to a 400-pound tiger down with pneumonia. Then a pair of year-old, yard-high baby elephant twins arrived from Ceylon, and when their keeper grew homesick and took off, Lucia took over. Her description of the twins' training underscores the elephant's innate intelligence. Getting an elephant to lie down on command—the essential lesson number one, says Mme. Zora—requires the use of block and tackle, as well as elephant hooks. Once the canvas sling is in place under the animal's belly, forelegs and hind legs are pulled in opposite directions until it topples over. Learning to lie down on command took the twins three weeks, during which Lucia daily sat on the elephants' quivering thighs, dispensing lump sugar and encouraging words. Once the beasts had gotten the knack, they loved it, voluntarily crashing to the tanbark and squealing with joy at Lucia's approach.

In lesson number two, the headstand, the same tools were used, hauling the hind legs skyward after getting the trunk out of the way by lashing it down between the forelegs. By the time spring arrived and the circus was again ready to take the road, both twins were able to stand on their hind legs as well. They also knew how to stand on a drum on their forelegs and "dance" to the tune of "Turkey in the Straw," accompanying themselves on sleigh-bell bracelets in different keys that trainer Zora had attached to all eight legs.

With gigantic Snyder, the show's biggest bull, Zora reached her zenith. She warmed up the herd by having them form a pyramid over her supine body, then break up the formation, then pyramid themselves backward, all of it leading up to the act's heroic exit with the spotlit Zora balanced on Snyder's huge, upraised tusks.

A few years later, Mme. Zora reckoned she had performed before one-sixth of the population of the United States and had survived every type of circus catastrophe: fire, flood, train wreck, stampede, and tornado. She had nursed sick chimpanzees, fought "blood-maddened tigers," raised lion cubs on the bottle, and trained all manner of elephants. Her medical history included three fractures of the arm, more than one hundred claw marks, two broken ribs, a fractured collar bone, a dislocated hip, a compound fracture of the ankle, a fractured jaw, and a fair number of new teeth. Midway through World War I, the Alispaws decided it was time to retire, and threw themselves into the work of raising food for our doughboys overseas.

In the circus, male and female elephants are treated alike, both in and out of the ring. They work side by side performing acrobatic routines, hauling heavy wagons out of the mud and plodding trunk-to-tail into a new town for the next day's show. But whenever a circus moves by rail, the elephants are segregated by sex, and the more troublesome males are kept together in a doubly reinforced "bull car." However, the watchful Alispaw was quick to note that once the cars were unloaded, Snyder stood beside Alice at every opportunity, his sexual interest in her hugely apparent. Intrigued, Alispaw arranged for Alice and Snyder henceforth to travel together in their own private boxcar.

Climate appeared to play an important role in the developing attraction between the star-crossed lovers. Alispaw reported that Alice and Snyder spent May and June gently getting to know each other, standing close together, exploring and patting each other with their trunks, and communicating in low, throaty rumbles. Not until July and August did the affair heat up. Particularly in the sultry, muggy hours that preceded big electrical storms, whenever thunderheads boiled up on the horizon and heat lightning flashed through the heavy skies—then Alice and Snyder struck out for the nearest swamp or bog or muddy wallow; even a water-filled roadside ditch attracted them. Alice usually led the way, careful to look back over her shoulder to be sure that Snyder was following. Sinking into the delicious mud, rolling and lolling in the ooze, squirting water and mud over each other's backs, stroking each other all over with their trunks, they engaged in long, teasing, joyful bouts of sexual foreplay. The brief act of mating, however, took place under cover of darkness, and in the privacy of their railroad car.

Alispaw was surprised to find that, despite Alice's probable pregnancy, the animals continued playing and mating with each other for another ten months or so, particularly in soggy, steamy weather. Then, little by little, Alice lost interest in Snyder's advances, and began to show increasing signs of irritation at his approach. Perhaps her behavior reflected her gradual realization that motherhood was imminent. During the first year of her pregnancy, she continued working in the Big Act, but her disposition worsened, her mood became flighty, her behavior undependable, and her very presence stirred up trouble among the rest of the herd. Surprisingly, her nature reversed in her second year and she became more tractable than ever before.

As her time drew near, Sells Floto cabled back to the Hagenbecks in Hamburg for guidance. Old Carl Hagenbeck warned that if Alice were indeed pregnant, the rough road conditions—one night stands and insufficient rest—made miscarriage the most likely outcome. If things went well, however, he advised occasionally separating the expectant mother from the other animals to accustom her to the isolation she would have to endure when her time came. Being herd animals by nature, elephants prefer the company of other elephants at all times. But, on the road, the only way to control a three-ton beast in the throes of labor would be get her away from the others, lest her thrashings trigger a general stampede, and further, to minimize the rumpus and danger by chaining each leg to a stout wooden stake. No one knew how long a labor to expect, but once the calf dropped, it would be important that the newborn begin nursing as soon as possible. Other than that sort of broad, general advice, the Alispaws were on their own.

At the start of the 1912 fall season, in Albuquerque, New Mexico, Alice was put on maternity leave, and relieved of her duties in the Big Act. All went without incident until early one morning the following April. The circus train was unloading in Salinas, California, when Alice's behavior suddenly changed dramatically. She refused the customary long drink of water that was always offered after the herd was unloaded. She emitted a series of low, throaty rumblings that seemed to say that she wanted to be alone. As soon as the big top was raised, Alispaw moved her away from the other animals, rigged some spare canvas to provide her with a private enclosure, and chained and staked all four of her legs.

For the next two hours, Alice bellowed, strained, and labored mightily against her restraints. Then, without warning, the newborn crashed to the ground between Alice's hind legs. Its mother was too hobbled to move, and the baby could not yet stand. Keepers pushed the infant onto a sheet of canvas and dragged it alongside its mother's head. Alice took one look and furiously tried to squash it with her forehead. At each murderous maternal thrust, the baby, still unable to stand, bounced several inches into the air before collapsing again to the canvas. Alice changed tactics, and tried to rake the creature toward her with one chained forefoot in order to destroy it by kneeling on it. A keeper was working frantically with his bull hook to rescue the infant, when suddenly Alice wrapped her trunk tightly around the man's foot, seemingly thinking she'd caught hold of the baby, and broke several bones. Others dragged the bleeding infant out of Alice's range, and began to rub it briskly with burlap to get its blood flowing and keep it warm.

The newborn was a 180-pound male, twenty-eight inches high, with an absurd-looking twelve-inch trunk and a coat of two-inch-long coarse black hair. The keeper somehow escaped, but Alice continued to fight her chains, and was gradually loosening them, even though each one was attached to a six-foot stake driven five feet into hard ground. Alispaw summoned every man on the lot to assist him in driving more stakes and adding more chain, but after an hour it appeared that the men were losing ground to Alice's fury. Then she got one rear leg free.

By now the baby had wobbled to its feet. Alispaw grabbed it in his arms, commandeered a passing taxi, shouldered in with his precious cargo, and told the startled driver to rush at top speed several miles out into the countryside. And indeed, when Alice could no longer catch the baby's scent, she quieted down.

But that night things grew worse. The circus had added an extra car intended as a private place for the new mother and child. Once Alice was inside it, still chained by all four legs, her newborn son was brought to the opposite end of the car. At the sight of him, Alice went into another storm of protest, crashing into the sides of the car, straining against her chains, attempting headstands. She was so violent that five men could not restrain her and it looked as if she might well demolish the railroad car and probably kill someone. Alispaw got the baby out of sight, ordered one of his big bulls brought up, chained Alice to the bull, then walked them both back to the bull car and ordered the train to start up.

Alice was now sufficiently quiet for her keeper to milk her. He got about three pints, which he put into an oversize milk bottle with a rubber nipple, of the kind used to feed newborn foals and calves. The now six-hours-old elephant gulped it all down. Alispaw was overjoyed. Elephant milk looks watery but is in fact extremely rich in both sugar and fat and contains less water than cow's milk. Nursing young gain twenty-two to forty-four pounds a month on this diet exclusively. They suckle more frequently than human babies, but take only a small amount each time.

It was decided to name the infant Baby Hutch, in honor of the show's general manager, Fred B. Hutchinson, and the name stuck despite vociferous objection from several California newspapers, which felt that the name "Native Son" was more appropriate for the nation's first homegrown pachyderm.

Despite concerted efforts to milk Alice, she yielded less each time, and within three days had completely gone dry. Cow's milk was offered as a substitute, but Baby Hutch refused it. The attempt to synthesize elephant milk has a history as rich and strange as the milk itself. When the king of Siam received the gift of an orphaned elephant calf considered to be a semi-albino, which automatically conferred sacred status on the beast, he ordered the young women of his realm to present themselves at the royal palace daily in groups of twenty-four for the purpose of suckling the baby. The procedure was not discontinued until the holy roly-poly little fellow was five years old.

After some frantic experimentation, Alispaw invented a concoction of boiled rice, cow's milk, and Eagle Brand condensed milk that seemed to provide the needed laxative qualities in addition to proper nourishment. The baby appeared to thrive, and soon was making daily trips to the circus lot for exhibition purposes. When not on exhibit, he was housed in a little mobile van, specially padded, heated, and ventilated, with a keeper always on watch. Every time Alice caught sight of him, she lunged in dangerous fury. By now the Big Blessed Event had been heavily promoted, and Baby Hutch was earning his owners $1,000 a day. Alice was carefully kept out of sight, and twice a day her baby was placed in a glass box—a former snake exhibition cage—and tenderly pushed around the ring by reliable Old Mom wearing a blanket banner proclaiming THIS IS MY BABY! while the circus band played "Mammy's Lullaby."

Audiences went crazy. Sells Floto attempted to take out a $100,000 life-insurance policy on Baby Hutch, but underwriters refused, doubtful that he could survive so far away from his natural habitat and under such unusual circumstances. As usual, the actuaries had it right. California's hot, dry weather seemed to make the baby extremely uncomfortable, and water was poured over him daily from a bucket, as Alice would normally have done with her trunk. Baby Hutch relished the baths and squealed with delight. A new special railroad car was built, with screened sides for greater ventilation, and during the nightly "run" between towns, he nestled happily against the screens.

One night, just as the baby was enjoying his 2:00 A.M. feeding, the train's engineer unexpectedly slammed on his emergency brakes, and the little fellow was flung the length of the car, rendering him severely dazed, badly bruised, and totally terrified, though no more so than the engineer, who had just noticed that the fully loaded "stock" car, adjoining the elephant cars, was on fire. Roustabouts awoke to the worst sound a circus hand can hear, as shouts of "Fire!" swept the train. Six of twelve horses in the burning car had been led to safety before the conductor shouted "Cut!"—a signal to sever the flaming death trap from the rest of the train and tow it to the nearest water tank, two miles down the track, while the six screaming horses inside were burnt alive. In the interim Baby Hutch's screen-sided car had filled with dense, acrid smoke, and the infant appeared to be choking.

There was no place to put the six rescued horses except in Baby Hutch's car, which increased his terror and need of fresh air, but no relief was in sight until the circus train pulled into Pendleton, Oregon, at nine the next morning. For the first time ever, the baby had refused his 6:00 A.M. bottle, and when he could now be examined by a convocation of local veterinarians and animal men, it was seen that his eyes had been dreadfully inflamed by the smoke, and his body badly bruised. His keeper administered a large dose of castor oil, but the little fellow failed to rally, sank to his knees and finally, lying in a pitiful crouch position alongside his beloved screens, died.

He had lived exactly six weeks, and gained just over one pound a day during that time. Alispaw performed an immediate autopsy, and found his stomach filled with a pasty, milk-like, semisolid mass that could evidently pass no further, and would likely have killed him in a week or so even without the trauma of the sudden stop and the fire. The circus's owner, Henry Tammen, ordered Baby Hutch's remains sent to a Denver taxidermist. This necessitated prior embalming by a professional undertaker, an operation that was successfully performed, for ninety dollars, after the required four gallons of embalming fluid was obtained from another bereavement specialist in faraway Walla Walla, Washington. Then American Express refused to accept the cadaver until it was packed in a double box and surrounded by an eight-inch-thick ice jacket.

In Denver, the three Jonas brothers, world-famous taxidermists, went to work. After much trial and error, they found the correct blend of tanning fluids to soften the hide, which had been rendered stiff and unwieldy by the unusual quantities of embalming fluid employed, and mounted it on a remarkably lifelike, 150-pound plaster cast of the corpse. He was posed standing on three legs, with one foreleg slightly lifted, mouth open and trunk raised in an attitude of friendly expectation. In due course this ingenious simulacrum of Baby Hutch was returned to the circus, where he was reinstalled in his pony-drawn glass case for the Big Parade with Old Mom, and also exhibited as a sideshow attraction between performances.

Henry Tammen was also a part owner of the *Denver Post,* and when the circus season ended, Baby Hutch was stationed in a corner of Tammen's newspaper office so that notable visitors could have their pictures taken alongside "The First American Bred Baby Elephant."

Fred Alispaw, stunned by his swift success and heartbreak, now set his heart on achieving a second American-bred baby elephant. Once again hot, muggy weather played a role, seemingly encouraging Alice to accept Snyder's renewed advances as the heavens opened and showers poured. Together, the lovers wallowed in deep, warm, springtime mud, but their sharp-eyed keeper concluded that their matings were not fully consummated until the heavy midsummer downpours arrived. Then Alispaw saw that the temporal gland vents in Alice's head had opened, and she began showing unusual affection for Snyder, allowing him to mount her every other day for two weeks while the vents remained open and the wet weather held. This early reference to temporal gland secretion in a female is highly unusual, a testament to Alispaw's acuity. A closed, or inactive gland is all but invisible, just another wrinkle in the skin between eye and ear. That female elephants also at times secrete fluid was not generally known until the pioneering work of Cynthia Moss and Joyce Poole in Africa fifty years later (discussed below, in chapter 9).

Alispaw became certain during Alice and Snyder's two weeks of warm, wet weather that impregnation had taken place. Winter was uneventful; in the cold, dry air, even Snyder lost interest. By spring, Alice was back at work, again growing increasingly resistant to Snyder's advances and, by September, treating him with utter disdain. That December Alispaw noted that Alice's breasts had begun filling with milk. This time, he prepared for the unpredictable cravings of pregnancy by scooping up several yards of swamp soil, enriched with such soggy delicacies as bulrush and cattail roots, and soon was feeding the mess to Alice at a rate of about fifteen pounds every other day.

Alispaw's other preparations included encasing Alice in a heavy chain halter that when the time came could be quickly snapped

hands pulled the little creature out to what they thought was safety outdoors, but Alice crashed into the door, and got momentarily wedged in the frame. By the time she emerged, door frame around her neck, the men had thrown the baby underneath a heavy wagon and covered it with canvas. Alice overturned the wagon.

Alispaw had run for dependable old Mama Mary, and now pushed her between the wagon and Alice, shouting to his men to drag the baby out. Once the little one was out of sight, Alice quieted down. Several men were gently massaging the inert baby with blankets in an attempt to get circulation going. Soon they noted feeble movement. "It's a miracle she's alive at all," said one, and on the spot Little Miracle became her name. Word of the struggle had spread, and now the circus owners arrived, accompanied by the mayor of Denver, the chief of police, and a small squad of veterinarians, physicians, and reporters. The medics concluded that the calf probably had a broken back, plus internal injuries, and was as good dead. It was near dawn when they went sadly home.

A couple of hours later, Alispaw and his patient both felt better. Incredibly, he began carrying her back to chained-up Alice. But when he got near, the little elephant began bawling and wriggling in terror, and Alice started trumpeting and lurching toward her offspring. Ultimately, Little Miracle had to be entirely hand-raised, using a feeding formula slightly different from that fed to her late brothers.

The weather on the road was again foul, but Little Miracle lived in a well-heated, well-ventilated cage, under constant supervision. As soon as the weather warmed up, she was given a daily bucket of water with which to squirt herself. All went well until the day her leg joints unaccountably swelled up mightily. Alispaw decided lack of exercise was the problem, and gave her a football, which she much enjoyed kicking around her yard for hours every day. Her legs improved, but the new teeth coming into her lower jaw were painful and she attempted to use the football as a teething ring. Fearful she might choke, her trainer substituted a length of garden hose.

At sixteen weeks her milk teeth were in, and roughage in the form of young corn stalks could be added to her daily gruel ration of two pounds of rice boiled in three cans of sweetened, condensed milk. At age three months, Little Miracle made her circus debut as a member of Lucia Zora's troupe, eagerly draining a nursing bottle held by Zora, who was costumed for the occasion as a Red Cross nurse in a fancy cap and floor-length white uniform.

In September came a sudden cold snap. The heavy swaddling wrapped around the cage, and more around the baby herself, proved useless. Little Miracle shook with chills, stopped eating, refused even warm water, and within ten hours quietly died. A few wheezes at the end made Alispaw suspect fatal lung congestion, a finding confirmed at autopsy. At the time of her death, in Spokane, Washington, Alice's third baby had lived twenty-one weeks—longer than either of the others—and weighed 240 pounds. Her remains were given to a local university. Everyone on the circus was depressed and disheartened.

A month before Little Miracle's death, her canny owners had quietly managed to get rid of troublesome Alice. They had got wind that in Salt Lake City a new zoo was under construction, and that the city fathers longed for an elephant, if only they knew where to get one, and how to finance the purchase. Tammen let it be known he might be induced to part with Alice. Zora's other four elephants had grown so huge that there was no longer room for Alice in the act, he explained. Furthermore, Alice was a "breeding elephant," and might indeed be with calf at present. Nothing could have pleased the family-minded Mormons more, and somebody dreamed up the "Princess Alice Dollar Club": for every dime contributed by a Salt Lake City schoolchild, the Mormon elders would throw in a matching dollar. In its blend of sentiment, thrift, family values, and healthy sex, the scheme appealed to Latter-Day Saints on many levels, and a deal was struck, for $3,250, with appropriate hoopla, on August 26, 1917.

"Queen Alice" might have been a more appropriate name for her than "Princess," as nine months later, in April 1918, she gave birth to her fourth calf, a strong, 170-pound male covered all over with soft, mole-like fur, and swiftly named "Prince Utah." Once again, the long-suffering Snyder was the father. Once again, Alice had struggled to destroy the newborn, who once again was rescued by keepers, returned to its angry mother, once again beat up . . . but somehow the little fellow managed to struggle to his feet. Whereupon Alice flipped. As Alispaw later put it, "For the first time there dawned upon her the miracle of motherhood! and placing her trunk about him she gently drew him to her breast and thus was her fourth offspring accepted by her with show of deepest affection and maternal concern." Indeed, her old trainer had predicted that once she recognized that the newcomer was another elephant like herself, her relief from loneliness would be so intense as to soften her great, dark heart.

Alice nursed readily, her son suckled greedily. Mother and baby thrived, and Prince Utah grew into a healthy, playful, energetic youngster much beloved by the city's children and appreciated by their parents as a money-making tourist attraction. The Pantages vaudeville circuit offered $50,000 to send mother and baby on tour, and the Orpheum Circuit offered $70,000. But the elders decided the pair would bring in even more revenue by staying at home, and for a time all went well. By fall, teeth began to appear, and Prince Utah was able to eat hay and other roughage. Then the cold weather hit. For two weeks he shivered and refused food, and on March 15, 1919, the little fellow simply lay down and died. This time the death was attributed to "a vegetable growth in the heart."

Whatever the true cause of the death of Prince Utah, another elephant would not be conceived and carried to term in the Western Hemisphere for forty years. Alice lived out her life uneventfully until, at age seventy-eight, she became seriously ill and was mercifully and humanely put to sleep.

Let us return now to Snyder's story. Gradually, as spring 1917 came on, the circus folks cheered up. The herd leader, Mama Mary, was clearly pregnant and hopes were high that her greater age and sagacity, steady temperament and agreeable disposition would make her a better mother than the wretched Alice. During the latter half of her pregnancy, Old Mom was relieved of her customary duties in the Big Act, in which she was the centerpiece of the show's "Great Elephant Pyramid Finale." Her replacement was Trilby.

As for Snyder, he continued greatly to mourn the loss of his beloved Alice, his rightful and chosen mate. He had shown no interest in Old Mom, her substitute, nor she in him. But after Snyder made it clear that he at least preferred Old Mom to Trilby, the former stood still for his advances. Was it not ever thus?

News that Sells Floto again had a pregnant elephant spread up and down the circus route, and little towns began competing for the honor of becoming the infant's birthplace, and thereby "making history," by publishing laudatory stories in their local newspapers. On the night of June 16, 1917, in Elgin, Illinois, Old Mom remained good-natured, but seemed newly reluctant to enter her private railroad car, causing Alispaw to suspect that she knew better than he did that motherhood was very near. The following day, Sunday, they were due in Milwaukee, where *accouchement* facilities, and medical help if needed, were assured. At 5:00 A.M., at a rural stop forty miles outside of Milwaukee, it looked as if Old Mom might deliver momentarily, so Alispaw ordered her car cut loose from the train and parked in the railroad yards, while the rest of the first section lumbered on to its destination. He did not want his patient to have to contend with the normal rocking of the train, which would mean trying to keep her balance and delivering her baby at the same time. Two hours later, nothing had changed, however, so when the second section arrived in the yards, Alispaw had Old Mom's car towed on to Milwaukee.

At 10:00 A.M. on the morning of June 17, 1917, in Milwaukee, Wisconsin, Mom began laboring in a difficult "dry" birth. She ate little, drank less, and strained until nightfall, with no result. At dawn, she began to try again. At 10:00 A.M. she stopped, exhausted. A veterinarian said an unprecedented cesarean section was the only solution. Alispaw believed that the risk of infection was too great and surmised that—as often happens when medical science confronts the mysteries of the world's largest land mammal—the man was overeager to experiment.

It was now necessary to allow the train to proceed to Oshkosh, where a veterinarian pronounced the baby still alive, and Old Mom capable of delivering it. That afternoon, she was permitted some mild exercise in the yard; that night, the train moved on to Sheboygan, where another veterinarian pronounced the baby dead. But Alispaw had learned of a new drug just developed for pig breeders that promised relief for farrowing sows, whether the piglets were born alive or dead. He persuaded the vet to obtain a quantity of the serum sufficient for forty 200-pound sows and himself injected two giant syringes of the stuff into a vein in Old Mom's neck. He then ordered Old Mom to stand up. She began violently beating her flanks with her tail and, twenty minutes later, a handsome, well-developed male calf was born dead.

Old Mom was a wreck, so exhausted and sick that she hardly noticed the baby, but instead twined her trunk around Alispaw, as if seeking comfort from a friend. The placenta remained unexpelled and for the next two weeks the trainer lived in mortal fear of losing Old Mom to septic poisoning. He used gallons of potassium permanganate in an effort to stave off blood poisoning, until he was certain the battle was won. It was many weeks before the old lady recovered her strength, and Alispaw formed the habit of letting her out of her car at every opportunity to roam untethered through nearby fields to graze on the fresh grass that he hoped—correctly—would restore her.

That winter, Alispaw decided to resign from the circus. The deaths of four such carefully tended baby elephants in less than seven years had been too heartrending to bear. As a prelude to his departure, he himself skinned Old Mom's unnamed infant, sent the hide to professionals to be cured and tanned, and afterward took it home with him as a treasured memento.

Meanwhile, in another part of the tent, Snyder was not faring so well. The trouble had begun when the show played Riverside, California, where chilling rains succeeded by blistering sun seemed to make all the elephants wild and crazy. Then, across from the circus lot, a cigarette ignited the exposed tanks of a gas station and fire broke out. Snyder ripped a huge opening in a canvas sidewall and plunged away, followed by Floto and Frieda—and then, Troby, dragging his chains behind him. Snyder was found by his trainer in an orange grove enjoying an impromptu marmalade feast. Troby, meanwhile, had become involved with a chicken coop. Floto had taken off in the opposite direction, leaving a blood-stained trail behind him. He was ambling through an orchard when a woman saw him and threw a chair at him. Angered, he hurled her to the driveway and, now mad with fear, crashed through a fence and charged down the street, causing a horse to rear and overturn its wagon. Frustrated at finding the wagon in his way, Floto kicked and gored the helpless horse, and ran down the highway. When the trainer caught up with Floto, he was entertaining himself by overturning other wagons. Eventually he found a bag of feed. His rage appeared to subside, and a trainer led all three elephants back to the lot.

The circus was billed for $17,000 in damages. Snyder was blamed for leading the stampede, and the injured parties strongly suggested the circus get rid of him. The manager argued that Snyder had done no harm; Floto had caused all the damage. The orchard owner countered that Floto was just a dope, or a dupe, but that Snyder had ruined his good name. Snyder was blacklisted as "unsafe," and a public demand arose that he be got rid of.

The show could not go on without community approval, and it was decided Snyder must be sacrificed to restore public confidence. By the time the day of execution was set, the circus had moved on to Salina, in the Kansas wheat belt. That morning the doomed elephant seemed somehow to know that all was lost. He broke from his place in the picket line and charged Floto. In the fight that followed, Snyder got in a few slashes at Floto with his trunk before turning tail and taking refuge behind the hippo den. Ten men plus the boss trainer were needed to corner him and get him back to his place. When the trainer hurled a poisoned apple at him, the elephant tossed it on to Floto, who was just about to chew it up when one of the bull men knocked it out of his mouth. Mr. H. B. Gentry, the boss of the show, sent for thirty-two grains of potassium cyanide and offered it to Snyder in a marshmallow. Snyder ate it but was not brought down. Cyanide only made him more vicious.

Government rifles finally arrived—but without bullets. By the time the ammo got there, Snyder had run off into a field. A dozen volunteers closed in on him, but at the first volley Snyder charged and the men fled. One witness later pointed out that elephants are said to be especially sensitive to the sound of their own names, and each time Snyder charged the ring of "bull men" who were trying to get him back under control, his charge was deflected by one of the hands stationed behind him calling out his name. Thus distracted, his attention would sometimes wander to one of the heavy circus wagons parked nearby, and he would lift it with his tusks and trunk and hurl it twenty or thirty feet through the air, much to the delight of the 8,000 spectators standing around laughing at the spectacle of the big, clumsy brute attempting to "amuse himself."

After several hours of this, the men maneuvered Snyder away from the crowd to an empty corner of the lot, where a marksman with an express rifle—one of the cowboys in the show's sharpshooting act—was able to knock the elephant off with a single shot through the eye. Snyder was only nineteen years old when he died, and is still the only elephant in the world ever capable of walking a decent distance on his hind legs while carrying a full-grown woman on his tusks.

Lucia Zora and Fred Alispaw got word of Snyder's death at their ranch in Colorado, the patriotic venture they'd originally launched to help feed U.S. troops during World War I.

"Snyder the magnificent, killed because they said he had 'gone bad,' " wrote Zora in her memoirs. "But we who knew thought differently—that he had fretted and grieved and was misunderstood, that he had died because he loved and remembered."

PART III

SAVING THE ELEPHANT: LOOKING FORWARD

CHAPTER 9

THE FOUNDING FOREPERSONS

MORE THAN THIRTY-FIVE years have passed since I stood on tiptoe in the Portland elephant house and saw the newborn Packy drop to the hay beneath his mother's belly. Today Packy is almost certainly the largest Asian elephant in the world and, in the words of one observer, sorely needs "not a bigger room but a bigger planet."

My own approach to elephant-watching has not changed in all that time. I remain an informed *amateur,* a word rooted in "lover." But our understanding of elephant biology and behavior has changed profoundly. Back in Morgan Berry's heyday, the little that was known of the abilities and habits of elephants was a rag-bag of lore and anecdotes handed down by unlettered circus hands, trainers, zoo keepers, mahouts, *oozies*, ranchers, historians, and not a few fabulists. The systematic study of live elephants was impossible. They were too big and too dangerous in the wild, too scarce and dangerous in captivity.

Only in the past few decades have zoologists and field and laboratory biologists begun to study in detail the physiology, chemistry, natural behaviors, breeding patterns, reproductive biology, and social relationships of elephants. I have been fortunate in meeting and observing at their work many of the founding fathers of the exploding field of elephant science—an astonishing number of whom turn out to be founding mothers. I'd guess that almost half of today's leading researchers, and their students, are American women.

Curiously, the new crop of elephant scientists all began their work at roughly the same time, between the years of Packy's birth and Morgan Berry's demise—that is, between 1962 and 1980. I sometimes think of them as modern phoenixes arising from Morgan's ashes. Each started independently, often working with tools and techniques unavailable a decade or two before. Taken together, their work offers some hope of preserving both species of elephant from what otherwise would seem to be certain extinction.

• • •

Without doubt, the "founding grandparents" of modern elephant science are the intrepid Scottish zoologist Iain Douglas-Hamilton and his brave and radiant wife, Oria. In 1965, Douglas-Hamilton went directly from his Oxford studies in zoology to Tanzania, determined to write his Ph.D. thesis on elephant behavior in the wild, and on the animal's prospects for survival in a rapidly changing Africa. To do this, he literally had to live among elephants. He chose for study the 450-strong herd living in Lake Manyara National Park, near the Kenya-Tanzania border. He built himself a tiny house, and learned to fly a plane, first an eighteen-year-old Piper Pacer with a 150-horsepower engine. Numerous crashes and hairbreadth escapes later he was piloting a 1961 Cessna.

After two years with the herd, Douglas-Hamilton had learned to recognize 130 individual animals by sight. Three years into his study, African-born Oria Bruno, the earthy, exotic daughter of an

Italian big-game hunter and a French mother, came to Manyara to join the project, and eventually to marry Iain. Their observations, published first in scientific journals and then, in 1975, in the best-selling *Among the Elephants*, are the pioneering study of elephant social order. It established that elephant society is matriarchal, and founded on the family unit. A herd is a group of closely related cows and calves led by a mature matriarch. The unusual gentleness, tenderness, and affection within each group is unique in the animal kingdom. A young elephant gets a reassuring touch from its mother, or another close relative, every few seconds. On the move, or stopping to browse, herd members stay within eyeshot or earshot of the matriarch. They listen when she listens, stop when she stops, and when she moves, they usually follow. If smaller ones straggle, they are nudged forward by older siblings or cousins. An infant elephant's relationship to its mother is a nonstop petting, stroking, correcting touch-a-thon. In nature, daughter elephants never leave their mothers, nor the family into which they have been born. They spend their entire life as part of a group, taking care of their offspring and one another.

Before Douglas-Hamilton actually moved in with his elephants, government rangers, big-game hunters, and advanced zoologists all believed that the herds were led by wise old bulls. Iain and Oria worked tirelessly to sort myth from fact, and eventually established that elephants tend each other's wounds, stand watch over their sick, and sometimes bury their dead. They assist as midwives. In times of drought the ones with the longest trunks use them to dig wells, which keep alive not only the herd, but many other thirsty species on the baking savanna.

"Here is an alien intelligence tantalizingly like our own when it comes to family ties, loyalty and love," writes Iain. The first herds he saw appeared to number eighty to a hundred animals, but he soon realized that these large groups were conglomerates of smaller stable family clusters averaging ten or twelve animals each. A healthy elephant population increases at about the same rate as a healthy human population, approximately 5 percent per year. But throughout Africa in this century, human population pressures inexorably increased until the elephants' only safe refuge was a park or game reserve, and "the range of elephants is now confined to islands of wilderness lapped by seas of humanity."

Thanks in great part to more than twenty years of struggle by the Douglas-Hamiltons, by the early 1970s the world had begun to awaken to the dubious survival status of African as well as Asian elephants. The price of ivory had soared, and poaching thrived. The biggest bulls, which carry the heaviest ivory, had already been wiped out. The widely respected Dr. Joyce Poole said in an official report on East Africa that she doubted there were enough males left to fertilize the females.

The massive illegal ivory exports of the 1970s and 1980s reflected the slaughter of something like 700,000 elephants. Most of the ivory was finding its way to Japan, where the booming economy had spawned a nationwide, nouveau riche craze for *hanko* made of ivory, rather than wood or bone or horn or stone. Commonly called "chops," *hanko* are signature seals with which businessmen stamp their correspondence. All official documents require the stamps to be legal, and each one is registered in a central government office. By 1981, status-seeking Japanese were buying new *hanko* carved from solid elephant ivory at the rate of two million per year.

Restrictions on the lucrative international trade in elephants and elephant products had become imperative. In 1973, the Asian elephant had been added to the international endangered-species list. Two years later, the CITES (Convention on International Trade in Endangered Species) treaty, signed by the United States and more than a hundred other nations, barred any animal on the list, and its parts and products, from being imported or exported for commercial purposes. In 1976, the U.S. Department of the Interior added the Asian elephant to its own endangered-species list, underlining the urgency of the earlier CITES agreement. But thirteen more years would have to pass—years of corruption and bribery at the highest levels in virtually every African government, years in which an incredible 700,000 tons of ivory, and perhaps much more, were smuggled out, years during which half the remaining elephants in Africa were slaughtered—before the international ban on all ivory trade was finally agreed upon in 1989, and celebrated six months later with President Moi's sky-high Nairobi bonfire.

The ban posed a major threat to U.S. zoos and circuses. How would they now replenish stock lost to death and disease? Ringling Brothers, Barnum & Bailey responded by buying up 200 acres of Florida land between Orlando and Tampa, and setting up a five-million-dollar experimental breeding center, not open to the public. Soon they had hired staff, and stocked the place with twenty-eight healthy females and four bulls. Clean and scrubbed but treeless under the pitiless sun, and—inexplicably—lacking a mud wallow, its expensive acres of concrete and reinforced steel pipe suggest a gulag for pachyderms. Shade is provided by free-standing metal roofs like those in gas stations. Without one curved line, one warm color, one melodic note, a less sensual breeding place is hard to imagine. Nonetheless, nine healthy babies have been born so far, all by natural breeding, not "assisted reproduction"—as artificial insemination is sometimes called—and the females continue getting pregnant. So perhaps I am guilty here of just the kind of sentimental anthropomorphism so despised by serious scientists.

At about the same time, Arthur Jones, an American businessman and adventurer who had made a fortune with Nautilus weight-training apparatus, decided to make history by assembling the world's largest elephant breeding herd. He began by flying nearly a hundred young African elephants to his ranch near Ocala, Florida. All were recent orphans, a consequence of the infamous culling policy at Kruger Park, a model South Africa elephant reserve about the size of New Jersey. Jones's breeding venture lasted two or three years before enthusiasm and funds ran out.

To supervise the deal, and manage the farm, Jones contracted with my old friend Randall J. Moore, the man who had got his start in the elephant world as a teenager shoveling dung for Morgan Berry. Later Randy served as road manager for Morgan and Eloise Berchtold's elephant act. After their deaths, he had tried to keep Morgan's herd together and, when that proved unworkable, he decided that, as a kind of memorial to Morgan, he would personally escort Morgan's three remaining young Africans, Tshombe, Durga, and Owalla, back to their native continent. He even persuaded ABC Television to underwrite, and film, the adventure.

Randy remained in Africa after that, always working with his beloved elephants, and occasionally sending me a postcard about his newest undertaking. One of these was the Florida deal. By the mid-1990s, Randy was a millionaire biologist-entrepreneur in Okavanga Delta, Botswana, where his major enterprise was Abu's Camp, a luxurious elephant-back safari outfit for other millionaires. Handsome, dashing, and mustachioed, Randy had also become something of a film star, and screenwriter, on several elephant movies, and a producing partner of Clint Eastwood. Tshombe perished from salmonella. Durga and Owalla thrived as matriarchs in a model South African game reserve where they now tend growing families of their own. Randy visits them as often as he can.

• • •

After two years at Oxford writing his Ph.D. thesis, Iain returned with Oria to East Africa. In their absence, the price of ivory had soared tenfold. Not one of Manyara's older bulls or matriarchs remained. All had been illegally shot for their ivory, and the danger of extinction appeared acute. When Iain flew over Tsavo, Kenya's largest park, he saw more dead elephants than live ones.

Whole families had been mowed down by ragged poachers with Kalashnikovs, and the stench of death was overpowering even at five hundred feet. As Oria later wrote,

> With its curved magazine and stubby barrel, the AK-47 was the most deadly weapon of destruction ever used in the long history of the African elephant. Its inventor was Mikhail Kalashnikov, a 28-year-old Red Army sergeant who dreamed up this formidable but easy-to-manage assault rifle while lying badly wounded in a hospital bed in 1941. The Second World War had ended by the time the first *Avtomat Kalashnikova* began to roll off the production line in 1949; but soon, spread by Russia and China in the name of world revolution, they poured into Africa . . .

. . . literally by the millions.

Drought and the AK-47s reduced the elephant population in East Africa by 75 percent. Their numbers dropped from 45,000 to 6,000 in only eighteen years. Many of the surviving animals became extremely dangerous, hated humans, and charged any vehicle on sight.

In 1976, the Douglas-Hamiltons began the first aerial census of all elephants in Africa, country by country. Counting elephants from a low-flying plane is extremely difficult, as the animals on the plains tend to take refuge in tree shadows, and in wooded areas they disappear completely. (Under the tree canopy, they create soft, luxuriant forest paths on which one can walk barefoot for miles.) The Douglas-Hamiltons were the first to make accurate counts, and have updated them over a quarter-century. In that time, they survived numerous harebrained adventures in the jungle, raised two daughters, published two worldwide bestsellers, as well as numerous scientific reports by Iain, and spectacular wildlife photographs by Oria, while becoming known around the world as "Mr. and Mrs. Elephant."

Oria is not only a gifted photographer but a particularly observant writer. Here she describes an official government elephant cull in Zimbabwe:

> Already the spotter plane was up. The guns were gathered, the men were dressed for action; yellow overalls for the meat cutters, blue for the scouts in their sinister black truck. The capture cars with their crates were waiting. So were the hunting cars in which the gun-bearers lounged, cartridge pouches strapped around their chests; and the hunters, swashbuckling figures weighted down with ammunition belts and holstered knives, some with radios in khaki backpacks, others holding camouflaged FN rifles. . . . Their legs were brown and muscular, crammed into soft leather "hot pursuit boots." . . .
>
> We crept downwind to where the elephants were feeding. Unaware of our presence, they ambled along, plucking at leaves. . . . The killing team fanned out, guns at the ready. . . . Suddenly Clem began a fast, crouching run . . . straight for the elephants. Then all hell exploded. . . . Another gun-bearer ran with me. The scene was indescribable: dust rising, branches breaking, elephants falling everywhere. One bull screamed in pain. He had been hit in the spine which immobilized his hind legs. On the right flank a cow ran straight into a lethal fusillade and went down as if pole-axed. . . . There was no escape.
>
> The gunmen moved fast now, jumping onto the quivering corpses to deliver rapid brain shots for any that were not quite dead, running over the warm, soft, yielding bodies. . . . The stricken bull instantly collapsed onto his sternum, and from his head a wine-red jet of blood pumped onto the dry ground. His amber eyes were open and seemed to be watching everyone. . . .

> The only survivors were two small babies. One was pushing into his mother as if trying to raise her to her feet. . . . Five men pounced on him. A rope was slung around his leg while they . . . tied him to his dead mother's foot. . . .
>
> Hardly had the last shots died away than the men in blue were running in to cut the throats. The researcher, with his chalk, carefully wrote numbers in a white circle on each grey forehead. Then the men in yellow arrived with meat hooks and knives. Each group chose an elephant. A slit down the middle of the back, and with rapid flicks of the knife they pulled off the heavy grey slabs of skin. Then the cutters set to work, hacking and chopping. Ears were peeled off, tusks wrenched out and trunks rolled away until one by one the massive bodies were reduced to nothing but a bloody wreckage of bones.

Between bouts of census-taking and book work, the charismatic Oria traveled the world gathering aid from wildlife and ecology groups, and even from the U.S. Congress. At home, she and Iain had begun radio-collaring family groups and following them over several seasons. Elephant family connections, they learned, are far more wide-ranging, stable, and long-lasting than even they had suspected. Kinship ties may endure for a century.

In 1993 the couple founded Save the Elephants, an organization aiming "to secure a future for elephants, to sustain the beauty and ecological integrity of the places where they live; to promote man's delight in their intelligence and the diversity of their world, and to develop a tolerant relationship between the two species." Save the Elephants promotes "green hunting," in which bull elephants are tranquilized instead of killed. It has also done groundbreaking research on elephant migration through the deployment of the new GPS (Global Positioning Satellite) radio collars, first tested in North America on moose and bears. These record the animal's exact location once an hour, enabling researchers to calculate the speed at which the wearer moves, and how much time is spent where.

The collars have also produced evidence of Abu's remarkable adaptability to habitat extremes. Generally speaking, the animals' range varies in inverse proportion to the rate of rainfall: in lush Manyara, one female never moved out of the same six square kilometers of forest, whereas another cow, in drought-stricken Namibia, foraged over a range of 80,000 square kilometers.

Reaffirming the extraordinary adaptability of the species, the Douglas-Hamiltons' latest GPS data suggest that modern elephants plan their moves with what *The Economist* has termed "guerrilla-like precision," sprinting from the safety of one game reserve to another under the cover of darkness, and spending as little time as possible in the poacher-infested areas between.

I'd met Iain and Oria first in Long Island, brought to my house by Peter Beard, and next in Kenya. Best was a visit to their home on stilts in a little forest in Langata, not far from Nairobi. I remember exotic plantings and hammocks and a small stream running through the house, and a section of one of their wrecked planes mounted on a wall like an abstract sculpture, but not much else. So I e-mailed Oria, and she wrote back:

> We live in a two-storey sort of wood and slat house which I built 20 years ago. . . . On the ground under the dining room floor the warthogs live. . . . Sometimes they dig, and puffs of dust come up through the wooden boards under our feet—other times the males have great fights and bang their noses on the floor. . . . Big windows upstairs and downstairs look out onto the Ngong Hills and often at night we see the head of a giraffe peering into our rooms. . . . At night, we have tree hyraxes scratching from the trees and are woken by a serenade of birds at dawn.

To such an alluring couple, enemies would be inevitable, and over the years the Douglas-Hamiltons have been branded variously as "stars," amateurs, tyros, alarmists, self-promoters, dreamers, exploiters, "academically challenged," full of charisma, rank propagandists, shameless avatars of jungle derring-do, and "flakes."

For all that, their life story is so adventurous, romantic, and fine that it inspired one senior literary critic to write, "The Douglas-Hamiltons lead a life that makes me suspect I may have wasted mine."

• • •

In 1967, two years after Iain had begun work at Lake Manyara, a young American woman, Cynthia Moss, visited his camp. Soon she decided to abandon her job in Manhattan, move to East Africa, and dedicate herself to saving wildlife. By the time I met her, she had lived in Africa seventeen years, much of that time alone except for the companionship of elephants. For her first four years, she worked on-and-off as an assistant to Iain, becoming adept at his homemade identification system. He had taught himself to recognize individual animals by their tusks, and by the notched, tattered edges of their enormous ears, and the pattern of bulging veins on their reverse sides. No two elephants are alike, and tusks plus tatters plus veins identify an animal as unerringly as a thumbprint does a human being.

In 1972, Cynthia was urged by a group of ecologists to study the elephants at Amboseli National Park, a protected 150-square-mile area in southern Kenya, at its border with Tanzania. Melting snows from the adjacent Mount Kilimanjaro, an extinct volcano 19,000 feet high and snow-capped all year round, feed underground springs that ensure a perpetual water supply, lush woods, and grasses, even permanent, all-year swamps and mud flats—an ideal setup for Amboseli's 600-odd elephants to pursue a normal, natural existence, undisturbed by the sudden rise in poaching that was decimating other African herds.

As a mnemonic aid, Cynthia decided to give each animal its own name. The task required her to work her way methodically through four *What Shall I Name My Baby?* books, before moving on to dictionaries of saints. She grouped the elephants into alphabetically arranged families—Teresia was the mother of Trista, who was the mother of Tallulah and Tim. The system helped to make each animal immediately recognizable to Cynthia, and the alphabetical groupings helped her remember their many, multi-entwined relationships. At the time, she never dreamed that, a quarter-century later, she would still be reporting on the lives of the same elephants. Moreover, each Amboseli elephant knows and recognizes Cynthia, a blond and clear-eyed 4-H Club poster child–type, now grown into confident middle age. Today she knows more than 900 elephants individually. She has published four books and many scientific papers. She is on the board of the African Wildlife Foundation and helps raise money by giving popular lecture tours in the United States and making TV documentaries. Her latest activity is serving as an advisor to the world's newest and finest wildlife display, Disney's Animal Kingdom, in Florida.

When she first came to Africa, Cynthia Moss was on a leave of absence from her job as a researcher at *Newsweek*. Born in 1940 in Ossining, New York, she is the daughter of a legal secretary and a small-town newspaper publisher. At Smith College she majored in philosophy. By her sophomore year, she had lost the three people she loved most in the world—both of her parents and her grandmother. She later told friends that these early losses made it easier to cut herself loose from human society and live in a tent or trailer with only elephants for company.

At *Newsweek* Cynthia specialized in stories on religion and theater and kept in touch with the outdoors by joining the Sierra Club. Her African visit was the result of a long correspondence with a school friend with similar interests. But within a week of her arrival, "I had this overwhelming sense that I'd come home. I felt, this is where I belong. This is where my body belongs."

It was not, at first, the wildlife that drew her so powerfully, but some mysterious combination of landscape and light. When she told me about it, I knew just what she meant. I'd had the same overpowering feelings when I first lived in the desert, north of Reno, in 1950. I was there for only six weeks, establishing residence for a divorce, but found it extremely difficult to tear myself away.

I'd first met Cynthia at her home in Nairobi in 1985, and felt immediate kinship with this round-faced, cheerful woman. Tan and serene, she was the same age I had been when spellbound by the strange, bare, bonelike beauty of the desert. And I, too, was once a *Newsweek* staffer. Could I have done what Cynthia has? Not a chance. The solitude would have defeated me. But Cynthia doesn't feel solitude; she feels the close companionship of hundreds of elephants. At night, she has a special appreciation of the animals "moving on spongy, soundless feet, their ivory glowing in the dark."

When the time came for the Douglas-Hamiltons to return to Oxford, Cynthia carried on, working at various wildlife-related jobs, until the arrival of another young American woman, referred to her by Iain. This was Joyce Poole, who soon became Cynthia's closest associate. Daughter of a former director of the African Wildlife Foundation, Joyce was a nineteen-year-old college student on vacation in 1975, when she first worked with Moss. She later earned an M.A. in animal studies at Cambridge University, and wrote her Ph.D. thesis on "*Musth* and Male-Male Competition in the African Elephant." *Musth* had never been well-understood, especially in African elephants, and Poole was the first scientist to establish that females, too, have active temporal glands and that, although females do not experience *musth,* their glands may secrete when excited, lost, sick, or stressed. These findings, at first ridiculed by older animal experts, have by now established Poole in the foremost ranks of her profession.

Over the years, Joyce has become a passionate believer in the self-awareness of elephants. "The elephant is *more than* the sum of its very large parts." She is certain that they have a sense of humor, a well-developed emotional life, and strong emotional attachments to one another. These feelings enhance their awareness of mortality, she says, and account for the many observations of elephants picking over and fondling the bones of their dead. For fifteen years Joyce worked alongside Moss to unravel the mysteries of *musth.* In 1975, Moss published her first book, *Portraits in the Wild.* It received excellent reviews and helped her establish an ongoing relationship with the African Wildlife Foundation. In 1988, her second book, *Elephant Memories: Thirteen Years in the Life of an Elephant Family,* became an international best-seller. Her documentary films are stunning. In one, a group of elephants go to sleep, collapsing like huge balloons. In slow-motion, the collapse turns fluid and Pavlova-like. They become dying swans, and for an hour or two sleep deeply, even snore. Their slow-motion awakening suggests the beginning of life itself: groggily at first, intellect and dignity emerge from the primal slime and reach heights of physiological complexity and elegance. When the hard rains come, they walk through their world of water with shining grace. After the rains, the savanna looks as clean and pure as a child's dream of Paradise before the flood. Another film shows a fierce fight between stately old Dionysus and a young challenger. The proud disdain of the old bull as he accepts victory, trunk upcurled above his pursed Louis XVI lower lip, is unforgettable. Some frisky young elephants dashing full-tilt toward the camera, their fringed, frilly, ever-flapping butterfly ears ruffling in the wind, are at once funny, awkward, funky, and sublime.

• • •

After Amboseli, I felt better grounded in *Loxodonta africana.* But *Elephas maximus* was a species I'd seen only in zoos and circuses. Although India had always fascinated me, its well-advertised poverty and human wretchedness had kept me away. Then I heard about a proposed tour of Indian wildlife sanctuaries, to be led by the foremost living authority on the Asian elephant, the renowned Dr. Raman Sukumar. He is considered that species' best hope for survival; by some, its only hope. After six or seven thousand years of being central to Indian life and culture, *Elephas maximus* is literally being crowded out of existence, both on the Indian subcontinent and in the twelve other Asian range countries. The human population of India has quadrupled in this century and approaches one billion. Elephant poaching for meat, not ivory, has been reported. Hindus are forbidden to eat meat, and regard the elephant as semi-sacred, but some people in remote areas are simply too hungry to resist.

Sukumar's tour was sponsored by Wildlife Preservation Trust International, a modest and highly effective organization founded by Gerald Durrell. Its credo: rather than send Western scientists to "save" Third World countries, motivate and teach local people to look after their own wildlife. Concentrate on lowering death rates and raising birthrates, and on creating veterinary manuals for field use. For most endangered species, including elephants, no such manuals exist. WPTI has by now trained field biologists in more than fifty countries. The organization also specializes in preserving those endangered but non-showy species known in the trade as "LBJs"—little brown jobs.

In 1992, the Indian government had launched Project Elephant, and put Dr. Sukumar in charge. He viewed his assignment as threefold. *Habitat conservation* was the first problem, since wild elephants require large stretches of deciduous forest, and today less than 20 percent of India's land remains wild. In Dr. Sukumar's words, "The rest has been sacrificed to the paper companies." Of the wild elephants that remain—22,000 to 28,000—

"Maybe we can save fifteen thousand in the long term." To halt the rampant habitat destruction, all logging and wood-cutting in India have been banned. But the majority of rural people are "subsistence farmers," families that grow just enough food to feed themselves, and they cook with firewood, as they have for thousands of years. As a result, the law exempts firewood.

Sukumar saw his second problem as *human-elephant conflict:* How could subsistence farmers protect their crops from destruction by hungry elephants living in an adjacent sanctuary? Ringing the sanctuaries with trenches seemed a promising idea because elephants can't jump; an animal with a maximum stride of six feet cannot cross a six-and-a-half-foot-wide trench. But sometimes the elephants filled in the trenches with dirt and branches after dark and walked across to the delectable bananas and melons growing on the other side. By day, farmers sometimes crossed the same "bridges" in the opposite direction to collect firewood.

High-voltage electric fencing was tried, but the big males soon learned to tear out the fences using their tusks only, ivory being a nonconductor of electricity. Sometimes hungry animals simply trampled down the fences with their spongy feet, which are relatively poor conductors of electricity. If the crop is an unusually delicious one—sugarcane, for example—elephants have been known to push over trees so they fall across the wire and then get across themselves by clambering over the fallen tree trunks.

India had begun converting its quaint, British-built railway system from narrow to standard gauge, and the latest elephant-containment scheme was to weld the old track into stout fencing for the one hundred of India's four hundred sanctuaries that contain elephants. But it is a massive job; encircling only Nagarhole National Park (where our tour would spend three days and nights) would require welding 155 miles of track. Whether fencing or trenching or some combination was decided upon, the big problem was sure to be maintenance. Having learned to bridge trenches and short-circuit electric fencing, elephants would probably figure out how to demolish railroad track-fencing as well.

The third problem was in some respects the most difficult, requiring a truly colossal judgment call. *How should limited conservation money be allocated?* In his characteristically understated way of putting things, Sukumar says, "It is not worth saving a five-thousand-dollar crop with a ten-thousand-dollar trench."

The tour was set for spring 1997, and could accommodate eight travelers. With some trepidation, I signed on. Modern India is a mosaic of literally hundreds of different peoples and cultures, and we saw most of it. We began in New Delhi, visited the Taj Mahal and a few other essential tourist stops, then spent seventeen days crisscrossing the vast, teeming, troubled subcontinent—mostly by bus, train, plane, and motorboat, but on occasion by foot, ox cart, horse *tonka,* canoe, and elephant-back. Only one element appeared common to all the peoples of India, and that was an eye for embellishment, an overpowering compulsion to *decorate*. Even from a bus window, one could see that anything that could possibly be ornamented *was,* extreme poverty notwithstanding. Geometric patterns adorned the omnipresent roadside stacks of dung used for fuel. The belly fur of gaunt camels hauling two-wheel carts was incised in zigzag designs. The humblest farmer tinted the horns of his bullock two different colors, and sometimes tipped them with gilt balls. In southern India, where most of the wild elephants live, commercial vehicles were so gussied up in swirls of pastel paint they seemed the work of a pastry chef on LSD.

Banners fluttered everywhere in celebration of modern India's fiftieth year of independence. Whether the new India had become too modern to insure the survival of its age-old friend the elephant was what I most wanted to discover.

Raman Sukumar, age forty-two, was an unusually tall, slender man with thick spectacles, dark skin, and a serene, graceful bearing. He hopped aboard our bus at his university, the India Institute of Science, in Bangalore, and we drove on together to Nagarhole National Park. Much of the funding for his research, we learned en route, especially support for field surveys and distribution studies, came from the MacArthur Foundation. He was also supported by the Indian government, among others.

It was late afternoon at the park when we climbed into three jeeps and set off, Sukumar in the lead. Many Indian wildlife sanctuaries were formerly the private hunting preserves of princes, and much of Nagarhole's 250 square miles once belonged to the Maharajah of Mysore. Narrow dirt trails threaded through it, and the vast, amoeba-shaped lake at its center—created by damming up the maharajah's trout stream—was now a spectacular haven for water birds, fish, and crocodiles. As in many parks, the forest encircling its shores had been cut back to make the animals easier to observe when they came down to drink and bathe. But teak is impervious to rot, and jagged teak stumps protruded like broken-off dragon's teeth from the shallows.

We boarded a little motor launch, and soon Sukumar pointed to a small elephant herd on a far distant slope and said, "Eight females, two calves." How could he tell?

We spent the next three days in the jungle in jeeps and boats, and our nights in modest comfort at Nagarhole's Kabini River Lodge—rustic cabins, part-time hot water. We dined in a well-screened lakeside gazebo with good food and touchingly eager service. The Indian-born boss of the lodge, "Papa" John Wakefield, was a gruff, savvy man in his eighties, formerly the director of Tigertops, the famed wild-animal camp in Nepal. He had managed logging elephants on teak plantations in the 1930s, served in the Indian Army, and survived imprisonment by the Japanese in World War II. On our twice-daily game drives, Papa drove the lead jeep, with a park ranger stationed on his tailgate as a spotter. "Samba deer at two o'clock," the man said quietly, and forty clones of Bambi stepped daintily out of the forest, back-lit by sun rays filtering through the tree canopy. "Wild boar up ahead!" A family of five approached a salt lick. Once he whispered, "Big leopard, in bamboo . . ." but I saw only dappled shadow. Amid such an abundance of wildlife, it seems churlish to complain. But though we saw hundreds of elephants, they were usually too far away to see very well.

When I mentioned the possibility of breeding by artificial insemination, Sukumar erupted. "A-I has not succeeded *once* in ten or fifteen years of experimentation!" Reducing the high death rate by providing proper health and veterinary care would achieve a stable elephant population at far lower cost. It was obvious that Doctors Sukumar and Schmidt, the Portland, Oregon, veterinarian, ran on very different tracks. Eastern tradition and Western technology do not mesh well. I mentioned Portland's vaunted crush—in reality a modern, hydraulic-powered adaptation of the ancient Indian squeeze-cage built of bamboo poles—and Sukumar dismissed it as being "of very limited use." Why not invest those thousands of American dollars in elephant sanctuaries in Asian and African countries? Yet, with the fondness for paradox so common in Asia, Sukumar consistently maintained that, "If I see a hope for elephants anywhere, it is in India. . . . A very strict conservation policy is now in force. Shoot a sparrow in the jungle, and you can be prosecuted. Much as the bison was wiped out in the U.S. and then came back, the elephant too can come back."

A combination of different strategies would work best, he thought. First, a modest amount of "population control." Translation: kill the few, most destructive males that are responsible for nearly all the crop damage. "They plan their nighttime raids kind of like a stag party." A farmer might spend a hundred sleepless nights a year sitting in a treetop trying in vain to protect his crops. Firecrackers are useless; birdshot or buckshot work best. "But most Indian farmers are very tolerant. They don't *want* to kill elephants."

Fortunately, the problem of marauding elephants gobbling up

every green thing in sight is not quite so acute as it was a few years ago when a column of hungry wild pachyderms got to within thirty miles of Calcutta before anyone was able to turn them back.

In 1980, Indira Gandhi put through the Forest Conservation Act, which gave more authority to the federal government, while taking a corresponding amount away from the states. One now needed federal permission to clear a plot of more than fifty acres. Although this sounds good, "Often good policies mandated by the central government are not carried out by the state." In the beginning, federal officials had asked state officials where their worst problems were, and visited these areas. Such was the unfriendly climate, however, that when a visitor asked a villager to see elephant damage, he was likely to respond: "All right, but how do I get compensation for *my* time, if I take the time off from my work to show you?"

On our last morning at his camp, Papa Wakefield parked in the shade of a banyan tree and summed up what he had been telling us quietly every time Sukumar was out of earshot. One, no elephant research is being done in India. Two, no money for, nor interest in, elephants exists on the part of the Indian government. Three, some resistance to present elephant conservation efforts is coming from the Forestry Department itself. A devastating indictment, it left me sad and depressed.

We went on to visit a half-dozen other sanctuaries all across India, and Sukumar and I talked daily on the bus and over nightly feasts of strange and wonderful Indian foods. But I could never dismiss Papa Wakefield's gloomy forecast from my mind. At our last dinner I told Sukumar the crusty old Colonel's cynical conclusion: saving the elephants is already a lost cause. People take priority over wildlife. Nobody in India cares about elephants.

When I got home, a fax from Dr. Sukumar in Bangalore was waiting for me. It refuted, point by point, everything the Colonel had said. That no Indian government agency is directly involved in elephant research was only technically correct. The federal government funded elephant research by universities and other private institutions. It had invested $10 million in the past five years to assist the states in elephant conservation.

"The problem . . . is [the] gap between relatively sound policies being laid out by the centre and their implementation by state government agencies," Sukumar wrote. "I would agree with the colonel's statement that for most politicians the elephant (or wildlife, for that matter) is a low priority. There is resistance from the state forestry departments to implement wildlife policies based on mere scientific considerations. . . . Usually the easy options are taken, and these are not necessarily at all relevant."

Perhaps we should leave the last word on all this to the ancient sage, Palakapya, whom Sukumar had told us about late one night on the bus. In the sixth century B.C., the great king Romapada had asked his mahatma what to do about the elephant problem. "There *is no* solution to the elephant problem, Your Highness," the wise man replied. "I would suggest you let your 5,000 palace elephants return to the jungle and be free."

CHAPTER 10

SEX AND THE SINGLE ELEPHANT

WHEN PORTLAND'S NEW zoo veterinarian, Dr. Michael J. Schmidt, first arrived at his post in 1973, fresh out of veterinary school at the University of Minnesota, the breeding of farm animals via artificial insemination (A-I) was commonplace. But the entire subject and science of elephant A-I was *terra incognita*, the extreme difficulties and hazards of research being at least partially responsible. The one artificial insemination effort I knew of had occurred the previous year in South Africa's Kruger National Park. One day Dr. Russell Jones, a research fellow at the Wellcome Institute of Comparative Physiology in London, flew into Kruger by helicopter, bringing with him a twelve-volt car battery, some tanks of liquid nitrogen, a large custom-built aluminum probe, a supply of animal tranquilizer, and a bunch of enormous sun bonnets. He began his experiment by hovering above a herd and eventually knocking down a couple of likely-looking bulls with tranquilizer darts. He then landed and tied a sun bonnet onto each fallen behemoth. (Because of their great mass and lack of insulation, all elephants are extremely vulnerable to heatstroke.) Next, the ardent zoologist hooked his huge probe to the car battery and inserted it deep into the rectum of the nearest unconscious elephant. It took about fifteen minutes of experimental shocks per animal to make him ejaculate into a beaker. Each resultant liter of semen was diluted with egg yolk to preserve it, frozen with liquid nitrogen, and flown back to London. There it was thawed and fired up the four-foot vaginal canals of the zoo's female elephants, using a sort of blowgun. I was rather pleased to learn that this experiment with *Loxodonta africana* had been a complete failure.

Today it is well known that captive elephants rarely reproduce. However, "they do breed fairly regularly in the semi-natural conditions of an Asian lumber camp, where they are turned out every night to find their own food and where they feed on natural foods when resting in the off season," reported Sanderson in 1962. "In effect, the animals are only domesticated eight hours out of twenty-four." As a result of this relative liberty—choosing their own forage, gathering it themselves, and enjoying a large measure of time in the company of wild, jungle elephants, with no human beings around—the birthrate of the logging herds of Myanmar (formerly Burma) has been maintained for two hundred years.

The elephant is the only working animal that has never been fully domesticated. A portion of each succeeding generation of logger elephants must therefore be captured in the wild. In India today, logging is a thing of the past; the forests have all been cut down. Myanmar, however, still has nearly 3,000 working elephants, about half of which were born to captive females released temporarily into the wild to breed. This long-established, farsighted policy does much to maintain the herd's diverse genetic makeup. The other 50 percent of the animals are captured in the jungle between ages twelve and eighteen. Thereafter, each is trained and cared for by its own individual *oozie* (in India, mahout) until it reaches working age, eighteen to twenty years. Man and beast then work a nine-month year, with three months off to rest during the monsoon season, until the animal's retirement, at age fifty.

A working elephant, though immensely powerful, has limitations. The animal is far more effective dragging and pushing heavy loads than it is as a beast of burden; this is especially true of the Asian elephant, with its sloping hind quarters and shorter back legs. To give some idea of the animal's strength: a trained elephant can push over a telephone pole by leaning on it, or can grip one in its trunk and uproot it with ease. But it can carry only one-tenth its own weight. One elephant can do the work of six ponies, but a single truck can carry as much as several elephants. However, elephants can work on narrow jungle paths and ledges where no pony or truck dare venture. Still, an elephant can work only five hours a day before tiring, and must have frequent rest periods. Indeed, under the rigorous climatic conditions of the Burmese forest, the average elephant works only 150 days a year.

• • •

Before he came to Portland, the young Dr. Michael Schmidt had scant interest in elephants. But by the time he got there, two things had happened that dramatically changed the elephant *Weltanschauung* for all time. One, the pachyderm population of Portland's Washington Park Zoo had exploded. Twelve more calves had been born since Packy, and in Schmidt's first year on the job, four more infants arrived. Moreover, the adult population had swelled to six breeding females and two bulls; Thonglaw and his seventeen-year-old son, Packy, were both in prime condition. In response to the worldwide publicity, several other zoos in Europe and the United States had attempted to launch their own breeding programs, but none had bred more than three calves.

By the time of Thonglaw's death, in the mid-1970s, his progeny would total fifteen elephants, including Packy, who is himself the father of seven more, his own firstborn having appeared in 1975.

In the mid 1990s Packy was temporarily, and probably permanently, retired from stud duties. The risks of early inbreeding—which had actually occurred during Thonglaw's time at stud—were now understood to be too great. Thonglaw's bloodline is still the most represented of any elephant in the Managed Breeding Program that today governs captive elephant reproduction in the United States.

Inbreeding leads to a condition known as "depression," which is characterized by decreased immune function, decreased fertility, and poorer general health. More genetic defects are apt to appear, and more stillborn babies occur, as the population becomes steadily less viable. In a captive population, additional issues of diet and exercise also come into play that increase the likelihood of infertility. Hence the objective is always to maximize genetic diversity.

The second dramatic change was in the field of elephant studies. By the time of Schmidt's arrival, the rapidly declining numbers of wild elephants in both Africa and Asia had become a matter of worldwide concern. A more complete understanding of the elephant breeding cycle was urgent, lest the two remaining species of Proboscidea were to go the way of the 164 other species of that order that were already extinct.

Thus, despite Mike Schmidt's prior lack of interest, it was apparent that his top job priority would be to make Portland's remarkably fertile elephants the basis of a study of pachyderm reproduction, and then to develop an artificial-insemination program. Being by nature sure of himself, outspoken, and highly opinionated, the young Dr. Schmidt quickly earned the mistrust of Portland's conservative, old-school elephant men, people like Doc Maberry and Morgan Berry. They had no use for newfangled, expensive "safety" devices like the $200,000 hydraulic crush.

They believed in dealing with zoo and circus animals hands-on, as had always been done in the past. Most important, they considered any use of zoo animals for private research or experimentation to be highly unethical. Since zoos are supported by tax money, they averred, their sole purpose should be to exhibit animals and educate the public.

Schmidt and his six-man crew of elephant keepers knew they were venturing into uncharted territory, and that the problems they faced in developing reliable techniques for elephant A-I were formidable. Breeding an animal in captivity first requires a complete and detailed mapping of the female's estrous cycle. After that, one must develop reliable methods of semen collection, of sperm freezing and thawing, and of insemination.

By the early 1980s, having spent nearly a decade doing "sniff tests" and charting Thonglaw's and Packy's thunderous responses to Portland's various females (described above, in chapter 2), Schmidt knew that a healthy cow ovulates every sixteen weeks, or about three times per year—a far less frequent cycle than that of any other mammal. Furthermore, within each cycle she is "hot" for only a brief period, forty-eight to seventy-two hours. Since gestation takes twenty-two months, and is followed by at least two years of nursing, a minimum of four years must pass before she can become pregnant again. Thus the largest of land mammals has a window of opportunity for mating that is unbelievably tiny, and remains open for only two or three days.

Breeding elephants by A-I presents other unique problems. In most ungulates—deer, wildebeest, moose, and so on—all the females come into estrus at the same time, triggering the males' annual rut. But each female elephant cycles individually, according to her own biological clock, and calves are born throughout the year. Nor are her cycles as regular as those of most other mammals.

Furthermore, it is well-established that, left to themselves, elephants travel and live in sex-segregated and extremely stable family units. A herd is composed of grandmothers, mothers, daughters, great-aunties, aunties, and their mixed-sex offspring. As a young male approaches breeding age, however—ten to twelve years—he gradually detaches himself from female society. Henceforth he will lead a solitary existence, or perhaps join a small bachelor band of four or five. This arrangement is probably nature's way of avoiding inbreeding between mothers and sons, or sisters and brothers, which could damage the gene pool.

Males define their position in the dominance hierarchy through ongoing tests of strength. While their sisters play at being mothers, young bulls joust and fence with each other with their tusks, and the sharp clack of ivory on ivory is often heard in the jungle, just as it is in a pool hall.

A couple of other special problems remain. To a greater degree than in any other animal, each elephant is a unique individual, and a would-be breeder must know enough about his own particular animals to judge which pairs of elephants are likely to mate. Often they bypass the opportunity, even when they are stabled together and left in privacy for some time. More so than horses, cattle, sheep, or dogs, a pair of captive elephants must actually "like" each other. If they don't, breeding them is impossible. As Dr. Bets Rasmussen, elephant scientist extraordinaire, once phrased the matter to me, "All she has to do is cross her legs and he can't get her. He can kill her, but he can't get her."

The biggest problem of all is that any successful A-I program will result in 50 percent male calves. As Schmidt himself put it in a 1982 paper, "Since A-I would be used *because* male elephants cannot be kept in most zoos, the birth of every male calf presents a future problem. We suggest that this might be solved by castration . . . of . . . young males."

But because an elephant's testes are internal, suspended from the dorsal body wall in a fold of peritoneum and connective tissue just behind the kidneys, and each one weighs up to three kilograms, removal requires not one but two invasive surgical procedures, with anaesthesia. Until recently the mortality rate from the surgery approached 90 percent. In anticipation of developing successful A-I techniques, Schmidt teamed up with several other veterinarians to perform experimental castrations on six circus bulls already marked for execution because maturity and *musth* had rendered them useless or uncontrollable. In the course of these experiments, Schmidt and colleagues learned substantially more about elephant abdominal surgery, as well as about administering anaesthesia, and a few years ago he told a reporter, "We have yet to lose a bull."

• • •

By the time I returned to Portland, in 1980, to inquire into the circumstances of Morgan Berry's death, Dr. Schmidt was well along in his research on ovulation. Step Two was finding a means to collect and store the sperm necessary for an artificial insemination program. A mature male elephant ejaculates about a quart of semen, and can do so six or seven times a day if he is so minded. To collect it, Schmidt had devised an artificial elephant vagina, or A-V, similar to the ones that have been routinely used in cattle and horse breeding ever since the technique was invented in 1922 by a Russian scientist. Today nearly all cattle, both beef and dairy, are bred by A-I. Schmidt determined to find a way to make breeding elephants as easy and practical as it already was with large farm animals.*

When I went back to Portland the next time, in 1996, Schmidt was no longer a kid. The brash young vet had matured into a balding, brainy, quiet-spoken visionary. Although newly laid back in manner, he remained a highly opinionated scientist, well en-

*For some years Schmidt and his wife, Anne, a biologist, had owned a farm on an island north of Portland where they bred Hanoverian horses. Whenever Mike got discouraged, Anne would remind him that Colorado State University, which had done vast amounts of horse-breeding research, fully expected its frozen sperm to last 10,000 years.

dowed with the healthy skepticism of the breed. And Step Two in his breeding program had virtually been accomplished.

"It's a purely voluntary, cooperative procedure," he told me on the morning I dropped into his book-lined office in the zoo's fine new animal hospital. "You basically take a heated, lubricated cylinder that simulates the female reproductive tract. The bull gets the same stimulation he would from a natural mating, and ejaculates." I said it sounded a lot better than the battery and electrodes in use a quarter-century ago when Packy was a pup.

But each elephant is a unique individual. Rather than be "electro-ejaculated," one 13,000-pound Portland bull broke each successive steel door installed in the crush until he forced the zookeepers to abandon their quest. Yet another animal was electro-ejaculated more than 130 times without incident.

Step Three had been to find enough elephants. "We didn't have 300 fertile elephant cows in all the zoos of the world," Dr. Schmidt said sadly. Then, in 1992, he heard from a Burmese woman, Dr. Daw Khyne U Mar, a Stockholm-trained veterinarian who had been named manager of research for the Myanmar Ministry of Forestry. The post is an important one, as timber is a primary export and source of foreign exchange, earning about $100 million a year.

Although the present government is politically repressive in the extreme, Burmese conservation and forestry policies have long been, and continue to be, models of enlightenment. Meticulous records of the Burmese timber industry, animal by animal and even tree by tree, date back to 1808. Dr. Mar sought Schmidt's advice on elephant breeding. Her country was the largest in Southeast Asia, about the size of Texas, and three-fifths of it remained richly forested. Despite its large force of working elephants, 200 to 300 animals a year were being lost to injury and old age, and its wild population—perhaps another 6,500 animals—had dwindled to the point where it could no longer be relied upon to make up the difference.

Myanmar appeared to offer the lock to fit Schmidt's key. He now foresaw a possibility not only of saving at least the Asian elephant from extinction, but extending its existence as a viable, healthy species "for a thousand years, perhaps much longer."

The Myanmar timber industry could readily see the value of A-I. The elephants would no longer have to stop working in order to drift off into the jungle and mate haphazardly—that is to say, naturally—as they had always done. Furthermore, Schmidt told me, "Wild elephants herds are unlikely to survive much longer. There is no room left." Not only was the wilderness shrinking fast; the composition of the jungle was changing. The teak and other valuable hardwoods had been logged out in many forests. Tree plantation, done by machine, had begun to supplant the kind of one-on-one selective jungle logging that requires elephants. Unless something was done soon, tractors and bulldozers would replace Myanmar's elephants in a very short time. This had already happened in Thailand: its forests were almost all gone, and its 1965 elephant population of 30,000 working animals was, by the 1990s, down to 2,000. Logging in Thailand now was mostly illegal, done surreptitiously with animals doped with amphetamines.

India still had 20,000 or 30,000 elephants, wild and domestic, a greater number than any other country, but its problems, too, were greater. Myanmar, said Schmidt, offered a far better survival opportunity than India, "where the elephants have to compete with the paper industry for the grass. An elephant is a very expensive item to maintain, unless it's a high earner. Otherwise, it eats too much."

Today, many Asian countries have sad, hungry, homeless elephants wandering the cities and countryside along with their owners in search of employment. The situation is somewhat comparable to the problems of homeless people in large U.S. cities. In Thailand, where the elephant for millennia was the holy symbol of Buddha, even more divine than the emperor, one could now see gaunt and sickly elephants rummaging for food in garbage dumps, reported the *New York Times* in 1996. About fifty mendicant elephants roamed the streets of Bangkok seeking handouts. In the garish nightclub districts, wealthy people paid the equivalent of $1.60 to "walk under [an elephant's] belly for good luck, or 80 cents to buy a handful of bananas or sugar cane, which they then feed back to her to earn Buddhist merit."

Together, the two veterinarians Dr. Schmidt and Dr. Mar figured they had twenty years to get their program into operation. By 1997, they had crossed the Pacific a total of twenty-eight times and believed themselves very close to attaining their objective. Myanmar had a breeding center in operation that matched Portland's own. Each center had an A-V, and male elephants trained to use it. Each had female elephants trained to accept a five-foot, flexible pneumatic insemination tube in return for a bunch of bananas. Each had a computerized semen freezer. The freezer was vital because careful control of freezing and thawing rates appeared to determine the sperm's viability.

The money to pay for Myanmar's freezer came from private contributors at fund-raisers held at the Portland zoo, events known as "Packy Parties." Myanmar and Portland were the only two places in the world that had such devices, and both were experimenting with rates of timing, rates of freezing, how much and what kind of "antifreeze" is necessary to protect the sperm from damage by ice crystals, and so on.

But a few problems remained. In Myanmar's monsoon season, rivers overflow and logging stops. Since weekly and sometimes daily blood samplings are necessary for precise assays of a cow's hormonal level, human swimmers were being used to ferry blood samples across flood waters that cut off jungle logging camps from the Medical Research Institute in Yangon (formerly Rangoon). Nonetheless, Schmidt believed he was "close to success. We now have the ability to freeze elephant semen so that 25 to 40 percent of the sperm survive when we thaw them. Our goal is 50 percent survival. This would mean viable, fertile sperm."

The goal remained elusive, he said, "strictly because of numbers. We've got a method to collect it. We've got a method to preserve 35 to 40 percent of it." But only 25 percent of the sperm that survived freezing recovered motility, and hence potency. Schmidt didn't yet know why, but eventually he would. "With every species, you have to write your own cookbook." In human beings, the semen of one out of every ten men cannot be frozen without destroying the sperm. No one knows why. Something equally mysterious happens with elephants. On the other hand, one male elephant Schmidt tested had a 60 percent sperm survival rate after freezing, yet had not achieved one pregnancy. "So we know motility is not the only answer.

"When venturing into the biological unknown, one expects to make many false starts," he added. "With Dolly, the sheep, they tried three hundred times before they had success in cloning." Dr. Schmidt's level of enthusiasm remained high. Since thousands of elephants would be available to the sperm collection center in Myanmar, "you get the benefit of the genetic diversity of these animals. You *capture* it, for all time! All you need is one sperm collection headquarters, and who knows what we'll be able to do in ten years, or a hundred, or three hundred years? We could breed smaller elephants, or bigger cows. The Burmese see this as a window of opportunity, something they'd like to pass on to their grandchildren."

I could not share Dr. Schmidt's cheery optimism. It reminded me of something Dr. Shoshani had written when *he* was trying to look on the bright side:

> Perhaps it will adapt. In some places, elephants are already changing their habits; they are becoming crepuscular—active mostly during twilight and at night when they are safe. A vision I sometimes see has haunted me . . . a different kind of elephant may develop: a stealthy, tuskless animal which will communicate in a way that humans cannot hear, never

> announcing its presence. Perhaps it will be smaller, and not require as much food, or perhaps it will move to remote areas, away from dead elephants and their dry bones, and be wary of its only natural enemy, man.

Schmidt said he was pleased with the progress of his breeding program, "but the most intriguing thing going on right now with elephants" was not breeding but the fact that all up-to-date zoos were moving to a new style of dealing with the animals. "We call it *protected contact.*" Men and bulls are never in direct contact; a fence or electrified wire always separates them. The Wild Animal Park north of San Diego, run by the San Diego Zoo, was the pioneer in this new approach. Next they planned to "switch over" the downtown San Diego Zoo itself. Other zoos that were making the same changes included the Brookfield Zoo, in Chicago, and the municipal zoos of Toronto, Tacoma, and St. Louis.

In these zoos, as in Portland, the entire animal population had been divided into "hands-off animals" and "contact animals." Elephant cows are contact animals, but all bull elephants are hands-off, whether in or out of *musth.* It is a matter of safety. The Bureau of Labor Statistics lists elephant handling as the most dangerous of all occupations in the United States, about a third more deadly than hang gliding, which is about double the risk of the third-most dangerous job, coal mining.

In plain fact, too many keepers were getting killed. Some members of the various animal-rights groups, one of this nation's best-organized and most vocal lobbies, claimed that this was because the elephants had begun "striking back" at the cruel terms of their confinement. Whatever the reason, these days one was seeing a more frequent use of crushes and other safeguards, and far less direct contact with the animal. "If you're *in,* and the animal gets upset, you're limited in what you can do, because you're not safe," Schmidt emphasized. So many zoo directors were coming around to his point of view that soon "protected contact" would be "the only way you'll see elephants handled in the future."

As its contribution to greater safety in the management of captive elephants, Portland issued "The Elephant Restraint Chute Owner's Manual" (available to other zoos free of charge). Stock men and dairy farmers have long relied on a restraint device known as the "cattle hugger"; but the Elephant Restraint Chute is of a different order of magnitude. Visualize the terrifying mechanism Edgar Allan Poe describes in "The Pit and the Pendulum," in this instance constructed of vertical, six-inch-diameter round steel bars. Placed on twenty-four-inch centers, the bars have seventeen inches of open space between them, and each one is removable, giving medics and keepers ready access to "feet, tail, legs, ears, mouth, trunk, tusks, etc." Each bar weighs 300 pounds, and requires three men to move it.

At the time of the manual's publication, early in 1991, 3 percent of captive elephants in the United States and Canada had already been involved in at least one human death. Of the eighty-five U.S. zoos that were accredited members of the American Zoo and Aquarium Association, thirty had subsequently installed chutes of some kind, and at least a dozen more were under construction. Chutes can cost anywhere from Portland's formidable $200,000 installation to the $3,000 spent by the Dickerson Park Zoo in Springfield, Missouri, for its first homemade but quite serviceable contraption.

Portland's manual reminds zoo people that "the ultimate animal you are building [your] chute for" is

> particularly dangerous and aggressive (if a bull, you assume he's in *musth*), it weighs 15,000 pounds, and exerts the applied force of a 15,000 pound mass; it is 13 feet tall at the shoulder and can reach upwards another seven feet with its trunk; it is 15 feet long (including tusks); it is six feet wide; it can reach as far as seven feet out to the side through a bar-

> rier; it can stand on its hind feet and raise its head to 20 feet above the ground (unless prevented from doing so); it can undo many types of fasteners, such as nuts on bolts.

The pamphlet's authors were Dr. Schmidt and the zoo's four senior keepers, led by Roger Hennous. Although recently retired, Hennous was still the acknowledged dean of U.S. elephant handlers. "Working with a male elephant," Hennous once told me, "is like jumping off a forty-story building." But he didn't blame the elephants, being always first to point out that the killers are "victims of hormonal changes not under the animal's control."

• • •

Determining the size and makeup of elephant populations has always been a tricky business, fraught with difficulties political, geographical, statistical, and equivocal. By 1997, some authorities already were claiming that it was too late to save either species. In January 1999, Dr. Jeheskel Shoshani estimated in the respected journal *TREE* (*Trends in Ecology and Evolution*) that "Of the 164 species and subspecies of *proboscideans* that lived in the past only two or possibly three survived, and of the approximately 1.5 million elephants that lived in the wild in the 1970s only about one-third of them remain."

Having read all sorts of figures myself over the years, I telephoned the World Wildlife Fund on reading this and asked for their current best estimates. They conferred, then called back to say they'd put the remaining number of Africans at "somewhere between 280,000 and 600,000. . . . No one can be sure." The WWF put the number of surviving Asian elephants as "between 45,000 and 50,000. . . . But this figure, too, is somewhat speculative." Although Africans were far more numerous than their Asian cousins, the two species were considered equally imperiled, Africans mostly by the threat of poaching, Asians primarily by loss of habitat. I recalled putting the same question to the top authority I knew, Dr. Mike Schmidt, the last time I saw him, and remembered his long silence before offering me this carefully measured response: "I'm not sure it's not already too late. Even a five-hundred-elephant herd in a national park is a dead group, genetically."

• • •

More than fifteen years after I'd first met the Douglas-Hamiltons, and through them Cynthia Moss and Joyce Poole, and Mike Schmidt and Raman Sukumar and the others, Cynthia and I met again. It was a snowy afternoon in Princeton, New Jersey, where she had gone to do some research on the same question that most vexed me as an elephant amateur: the size, growth, density, distribution, and vital statistics of elephant populations. Again I found Cynthia's companionship extraordinarily comfortable. It was 1998, and her Amboseli Elephant Research Project, now in its twenty-fifth year, was the longest-running elephant study in the world, containing an unprecedented body of knowledge on the biology and behavior of *Loxodonta africana*. The park now had 900 elephants, and the matrilineage of 72 percent of them was known. A sure way to determine an animal's patrilineage is to do a DNA analysis of its dung, and this tedious but crucial project was now under way.

The *New York Times* had recently termed Cynthia "a Joan of Arc for elephants," but I could not see her as a martyr. A *heroine* she certainly was, but a heroine whose life had grown and broadened and become richer, more challenging, and I suspect more pleasant with each passing year. She maintained two permanent residences, a tent in Amboseli and a house in Nairobi, and had three excellent research assistants, all African women, two in their thirties, and one in her twenties. All were born as tribal Masai, which bodes a bleak future in today's world, especially for a female. "The one thing I've done that I'm most proud of is bringing those girls up," Cynthia told me.

Over lunch, I learned that she agreed completely with African Wildlife Foundation founder Russell Train that the most important element in elephant conservation "is that the future of Africa must be in African hands." To that end, the AWF had created the College of African Wildlife Management, which teaches elephant education, gives courses on species and ecosystems, and on "commerce"—the best way for nations and institutions to earn tourist dollars from their wildlife.

For my part, I had noticed a big change in the demeanor of elephant experts over the years I'd been interviewing them. Many had become extremely wary and guarded, much like wild elephants overexposed, or wrongly exposed, to mankind. One of the fearless few who still spoke her mind was Cynthia Moss, and at our lunch she did not hold back.

On zoos? "I'm not against all zoos. I just wish they were fewer and better. Some eastern European zoos have truly terrible conditions."

On the elephant's chances of survival in the long view? "Depends which day you ask me. The Asians will have the hardest time surviving. There are vast areas of Africa which are okay for wildlife but not good for humans. Too much thick bush and tsetse flies. As for the far, far future—a thousand years on—I dunno. Dunno if *we'll* be here either, of course.

"I'm encouraged that tourism today has become bigger business than ever. This alone acts as a powerful force for conservation. Furthermore, as the planet shrinks, and populations increase, our human need to experience wilderness seems to be growing. And you can't have wilderness *without* elephants. They are the architects of the savanna.

"All elephants today are clearly living on borrowed time. But they are so much more adaptable and resilient a species than I'd had any idea. Because of their amazing ability to adapt, we still have reason to be optimistic about their survival. They can adapt to desert, adapt to swamp, adapt to temperature extremes. An elephant carcass was found on Mt. Kenya at 16,000 feet. They can even adapt to human beings. But they'll never adapt to our weapons.

"Another thing—as with humans, elephant behavior must be *learned*. It takes time. They're not like a bird, born with instinctive knowledge of how to fly from one continent to another. It takes a newborn calf about six months to learn to feed efficiently. Earlier it spills and slops its food and water, cannot readily coordinate its movements, cannot find its mouth with its trunk-tip. This is why the destruction, for ivory, of mature bulls and cows is so disastrous for the future."

On attempts at captive breeding? "Captive breeding programs alone will never save the elephant. The only way to save the elephant in the long run is to save its habitat."

CHAPTER 11

7,000 GALLONS OF URINE

IT WAS 1980, Dr. Michael Schmidt's eighth year at Portland's Washington Park Zoo, and he was escorting a visiting scientist through the zoo's newly refurbished grounds. She was Dr. L.E.L. "Bets" Rasmussen, a biochemist and expert scuba diver who had spent the previous two decades studying the reproductive biology of sharks. Dr. Rasmussen had great respect for Dr. Schmidt's accomplishments. "He did the pioneer studies on the estrous cycle of elephants in the late 1970s," she reminded me later. Schmidt and Dr. David Hess published their signal paper in 1983. "His work fundamentally changed our understanding of female reproduction."

On that long-ago afternoon, the then teenaged Packy, one of Portland's nine resident elephants, was sunning himself in the zoo's open-air patio and sniffing with unusual interest at a spot in the sandy yard. He repeatedly dabbed it with his trunk-tip, then curled his trunk into his mouth. Bets asked Mike why he was doing this. The vet said Packy was tasting some urine left in the enclosure by one of the previous visitors, a female. Bets and Mike looked at each other for a beat, each of them wondering the same thing: "Could there be a chemical in the urine that the bull recognizes—maybe a sex pheromone?"

Bets later understood that what they had witnessed was really a "flehmen response" to a pheromone. The term "flehmen" was introduced, around 1900, by the German zoologist who first studied this phenomenon. (The word's origins are unknown; it is not to be found in any German dictionary.) The same response is readily observable in tigers, wombats, pigs, seals, and an immense variety of other mammals, including my own two poodles, a mother and son. The flehmen is a grimace, more often performed by males, although females on occasion flehmen as well. Cat flehmens resemble a Cheshire Cat grin. In hoofed mammals, the animal lifts its head, opens its mouth, and curls back its upper lip. A bull elephant that detects the pheromone in female urine not only flehmens, he often exhibits a highly visible erection.

The flehmen response has been observed for millennia. Pliny and Aristotle both describe flehmen in deer: "Head back, teeth bared, upper lip raised." Twenty thousand years ago, Bets told me, Cro-Magnon artists had included an antelope flehmen among the animal images they painted on the cave walls at Lascaux, in southwestern France. Astonished, I realized I had seen this myself. In 1970, while in Europe, I'd rushed to Lascaux after reading in a newspaper that the famous caverns were about to be closed to visitors forever; the artificial lighting and the carbon dioxide exhaled in human breath were gradually eroding and destroying "*le calcite*"—the cave artists' pigments.

I was a member of the last batch of tourists admitted. Waiting in near-darkness at the center of the big cave while our eyes became accustomed to the gloom, I felt like a midget Thumbelina standing on the bottom of an unbelievably vast French casserole, staring up at the underside of the lid. Then briefly the lights brightened, revealing a masterful illusion: a mighty swirl of graceful, lifelike, *life-sized* beasts seemed to be dashing at full gallop around and around the curved interior walls of the cavern. One antelope was flehmening.

In 1813, a Danish anatomist, Ludwig Jacobson, discovered an inconspicuous and hitherto unknown organ in the heads of a wide variety of mammals, including horses, pigs, rodents, and some carnivores. For a century and a half it was known as "Jacobson's organ." More recently, scientists have termed it the "vomeronasal organ," or just VNO. It is buried deep in the animal's skull, just above the hard palate. Ducts lead to a pair of small, inconspicuous openings in the roof of the mouth.

For a long time the VNO's function was poorly understood. But today we know that many kinds of mammals, reptiles, and even amphibians use this organ, which is loaded with sensory receptors, to detect faint odors of biological significance.

The afternoon she saw Packy's flehmen, Bets Rasmussen drove directly from the zoo to the Oregon Graduate Institute, a small research "think tank" where she maintained a modest lab to pursue her unpaid shark studies. On this day, however, she headed for the laboratory of her friend and mentor Dr. G. Doyle Daves, chairman of the Institute's chemistry department.

Dr. Daves, an organic chemist, had scant knowledge of elephants. But Bets told him about flehmens, adding that female elephants about six weeks prior to ovulation release a "signaler molecule" in their urine. Bets was almost positive that Packy's flehmen was a physical response to that very specific chemical signal, a pheromone. The signal is species-specific, she added, and incredibly powerful; bull elephants can detect it at a concentration of less than one part per million.

Daves sat up straight. "You mean you can *see* him do it?"

"You can't possibly miss it," Rasmussen replied. "And not only that, you can *count* them."

His eyes brightened. Her meaning was clear: a chemist guided by a bull elephant would be able to search for and identify an extremely minute but biologically active compound in female urine, then be able actually to quantify it, and even eventually to produce it synthetically.

"Drop everything else, Bets," he advised. "This is the opportunity of a lifetime!"

She started work the next day, quite unaware that she had embarked on a quest that would ultimately take her fifteen years and 7,000 gallons of elephant urine to resolve.

By the time I caught up with Dr. Rasmussen, in 1997, she was a middle-aged professor of biochemistry and molecular biology working at the very frontier of her sciences. For fifteen years she had spent almost every waking moment in dogged pursuit of an extremely rare, unknown chemical compound that she could neither see nor smell, nor even define. The problem was worse than trying to find the proverbial needle in the haystack, she told me. "It was like you're up on Mount Hood looking for one particular flake in a hundred years of snowfall."

Fortunately, Rasmussen has the energy of a volcano, the concentration of a whirling dervish, the focus of a laser. She was fortunate, too, in having access to a veritable Niagara of elephant urine. But urine "has thousands of components," she explained. "It has proteins, it has acids, it has phenols, it has hormone byproducts, it has salts, it has esters. You name it, it's in there. And *elephant* urine is positively the worst! They're indiscriminate eaters, you know. They'll eat anything they can get hold of—rubber tires, plastic caps, tree bark."

Not knowing what she was looking for, the only way to start was to collect a supply of urine, begin breaking it down in a variety of standard chemical ways and, at each step of the game, bring a sample back to Packy and see whether he flehmened. Only his behavior, not her lab results, could tell Bets if she was on the right track.

Her work is considered critical to the survival of the species. The difficulty of a male and a female finding each other within the minuscule seventy-two-hour window of opportunity that in nature usually occurs quadrennially at most, is made worse because elephants are migratory, their range is vast, and the sexes live separately. So how do they manage it? Before Bets, no one really knew.

As soon as I read about Dr. Rasmussen's work, I called her. She told me she had now broadened her study to include many kinds of chemical communication between elephants. "The elephant is kind of like a smokestack," she explained. "There are at least four ways it can give off chemical signals—in urine, breath, temporal gland secretion, and blood." She was trying to measure all four compounds, in both males and *musth* males, estrus and nonestrus females. "Because that's what the elephant is doing in nature. That's what the other elephants are picking up on."

Her experiments had stimulated a range of other, related studies. She had concentrated primarily on female-to-male signals conveyed by the cow's urine. But now her doctoral student Nancy Scott was working on bull-to-bull signals. And Dr. Bruce Schulte, in Rhode Island, a behaviorist interested in male-to-female signals, was trying to find out "which sex makes the choice to mate." Barbara Slade's graduate studies at Portland State University had revealed that chemical signals in urine tell females which other females are in estrus, so now she was looking for evidence of estrous synchrony. Her studies paralleled the amazing work of Dr. Martha McClintock at Smith College, who discovered a few years back that when two or more young women—previously strangers—were assigned to room together, their menstrual cycles began to synchronize, due to unconscious mutual pheromone exchange.

Meanwhile Dr. Rasmussen herself became involved in two further mysteries: First, how, precisely, does the male elephant receive the pheromone message? What are the mucus-to-mucus chemical pathways between female urine and the male trunk-tip and VNO? Second, What are the chemical signals that males send out during *musth*? "We know that other animals, both male and female, alter their behavior when they encounter *musth* bulls." What causes these alterations?

Since "pheromones may be made in the liver or reproductive organs, and then spill into the blood," Bets collects blood and the gaseous compounds from it, and compares the *musth* and non-*musth* males. "But other elephants don't have access to the blood—only to urine, breath, or temporal gland secretions. So we collect all three and analyze these volatiles also." She has already identified compounds that she can demonstrate are *musth* male signals. Some are intended for females, others for *musth* males.

• • •

In spring 1997, I flew back to Portland. Bets met me at the airport—a small, Peter Pan–ish woman in rumpled plaid pants, Nikes, and an elephant T-shirt. Her nature was sunny and her body strong and wiry, toned by the one-hour swim with which she begins each twelve-hour working day. A fringe of blond hair like that of a Franciscan friar surrounded her beaming visage, much creased by the sun, and radiant with her love of her work and her surpassing love of elephants.

Did I mind if we drove straight to the zoo, she asked. Packy was in *musth* and she was avid to get hold of some *musth* urine before closing time. Later we would visit her main lab at the Oregon Graduate Institute, and her smaller lab at the zoo's new animal hospital, down the hall from Mike Schmidt's office. She also sometimes works at home, she told me, and, in all, maintains six large freezers, each one crammed with containers of elephant urine in different stages and phases.

I found Portland's newly modernized zoo almost unrecognizable, though not so unrecognizable as the monster Packy. Now thirty-five years old, he weighed 14,500 pounds, and stood 11 feet high at the shoulder. He was confined in the crush while keepers waited to collect a fresh urine specimen. They had been waiting several hours.

Imprisoned as tightly as a man in a broom closet, all four feet secured, his domed head scraping the ceiling, heavy wire mesh interwoven between the crush's three-inch-thick solid steel bars, and no room to move anything but the bottom third of his trunk and the flapping, speckled ears high above my head, he appeared to loom even larger than massive life in the fetid gloom of Doc Maberry's old elephant house. Often Bets or one of her young students would be waiting for the urine. But Bets was kind and unselfish and exceptionally sensitive to the feelings of others, traits that won the adoration of zoo directors and broom-pushers alike, and the keepers had been happy to stand in while she went to the airport to meet me. For four hours now the youngest one had been sitting just outside the crush on a three-legged stool. He held a long pole across his knees with a hook at one end, from which dangled a maple syrup bucket. If he left his post to visit the men's room, another keeper sat in.

"WHAM!" Louder than a gunshot, forceful enough to make the entire building tremble . . . "WHAM!" It must be the mighty hydraulic mechanism, I thought, but Bets said no, it was just Packy smashing his head full force against the massive steel bars—"his signal that he wants attention."

She and the keepers were quick to assure me that Packy was not injuring himself. His skull is a honeycomb of bone, a lightweight battering ram virtually impervious to harm. "He's like a kid banging on his high chair with his spoon," said elephant keeper Fred Marion as he forked a bale of timothy hay beside the behemoth's left forefoot.

The crush is the sole passageway between the indoor concrete elephant enclosure and the pleasant outdoor patio, which now had been sand-floored and sculpted into a "natural rock" formation. The bulls know this; else there would be no sure way of getting them into the crush. If a bull were tricked into entering, he would then attempt to batter his massive head through the sliding steel-and-concrete door only inches in front of him. One time another bull, Hugo, got through the door—literally—and emerged into the patio with its punched-out frame hanging around his neck.

Packy is long-legged, like his father Thonglaw, but unlike Thonglaw he has no tusks, only "tushes," overgrown incisors five or six inches long. The tush is more fragile than the tusk, which is truly hard ivory.

"WHAM!" Packy was two weeks into his annual *musth.* If he consented to urinate before closing time, Bets would also collect a sample of his breath, which she does by pressing a vapor-collecting vacuum container against the tip of his ever-mucus-dripping trunk. Midway into her study Bets had learned how to capture elephant breath, and has since analyzed the breath of twenty-five elephants throughout the United States. She studies the gaseous compounds in breath exhaled directly from lungs via the trunk. "Trained elephants—or even *annoyed* elephants—will readily exhale at you, which makes the sample easy to obtain." In addition to the chemical signals, she hopes to find better ways to diagnose early pneumonia and tuberculosis. "These respiratory diseases do in many elephants, you know."

At the same time, a keeper would collect some of the blackish temporal gland secretion that was dripping down Packy's cheek, and the zoo's junior vet would take some blood from one of the bulging veins in the back of his ears. Bets needed all four substances, and they had to be collected on the same day. "But if I can't get the urine, it isn't worth getting the rest." Collecting the temporal gland secretions was particularly difficult, "since Packy doesn't like to turn his head."

I wondered how Packy *could* turn his head in the crush, and wondered, too, about possible danger to the vet. Some years ago, when Packy was in a barred room and a keeper got too close, the bull casually put his trunk through the bars, then suddenly grabbed the man's arm, pulled him close, and employed his forehead to squeeze the arm against the bars, splintering the bone. But I kept these thoughts to myself, aware how reluctant elephant people always are to acknowledge that any "accident" is ever the elephant's fault.

"Whew! It sure stinks in here!" I said instead.

"Hugo's smell in full *musth* is much worse!" said Keeper Marion.

"Elephants react differently to *musth,*" said Senior Keeper Roger Hennous. "Packy becomes disoriented. Hugo gets very restless." Roger is a slender, sly, salty-talking man who has been at the Portland zoo as long as Packy. He once was a truck driver, but his innate facility with elephants is precious and rare. Hugo was "wild-caught," he said, which might account for the difference.

"There's so much we still don't know," said Bets. Does the urine-dribbling of a *musth* bull indicate a loss of control? Or is he deliberately spreading his urine around? Remember that long before the bull's temporal glands begin to secrete, a whole continuum of chemical changes has begun inside his body. What are they? Remember, too, that he may breed best in early *musth.* By late *musth,* his metabolic changes, some of them caused by his lack of appetite, may have worn him out. But we need more new studies.

Packy may have failed to urinate, but he now let fall sufficient dung to fill a wheelbarrow. Instantly the young fellow was on his feet sweeping it out of the crush. Roger grinned. "If this job wasn't so glamorous, I'd have given it up long ago." It was one of his oldest gag lines.

We moved from the crush toward the large interior elephant enclosure where the females were kept. The young fellow with pole and bucket remained behind. "Blood you can take!" grumped Roger. "Urine they gotta *give* you!"

"WHAM!" The concrete walls shook although we were now all the way across the building from the crush. "You can't really judge Packy's size until you see him breed," Roger told me. He was at least three times the size and weight of any of the females, and a mighty breeder.

In between her bouts of breaking down urine, Bets has carried on Jacobson's work with elephant anatomy, conducting marathon dissections all over the United States. She has extracted the vomeronasal organs, trunk-tips, and palatal pits of eight elephants, and from them mapped the precise anatomy and histology of the VNO system. She once worked seventy-two hours straight alone in a refrigerated room dissecting an elephant's head.

The VNO of a hamster is tiny, and a serpent's is tinier still. But an elephant has a VNO "the size and shape of paired cigars." What's more, she can now locate its exact position in the skull, and trace the huge nerve that leads back to the brain.

The skull of a newborn elephant has the classic mammalian shape, Bets explained. "If you split it down the middle, it would look more or less like the skull of a rat, or cat, or opossum." But as the animal matures, the mouth and jaw begin to bend downward at a ninety-degree angle. At the same time, the top part of the skull rapidly expands, bulging upward and outward until its entire anatomy and configuration alters. This is what makes the VNO so difficult to find. It now lies buried deep in the bone, "back between the teeth—probably the most protected organ in the body. And of course its massive sinuses already give the elephant the best protected brain of any animal."

We were standing in the back doorway of the big concrete indoor enclosure, watching my old friends Belle and Pet, who had been tied up to await their twice-daily medicated foot-soaks. The elephants' trouble affects primarily the front feet, which do more of the weight-bearing. Both Belle and Pet wore sandals, handmade leather-and-chain contraptions strapped onto their forefeet in an attempt to protect them. Belle suffered chronic foot infections: either her soles cracked, or pus accumulated in the sweat glands between her toes. The following week she was due to have foot surgery for another bone infection.

"A lot of Packy's offspring have bitten the dust," Fred Marion said. "It could be a matter of bad genetic traits." Rosy had died of foot infections. Thonglaw's feet got so bad that it was deemed necessary to tranquilize him in order to work on them. But determining the proper drug dose for an elephant is always tricky; this time the vet had guessed wrong, and Thonglaw expired.

A few years ago, when Rosy died from her foot infections, Roger Hennous wept, Bets said. Certainly the concrete floors of the elephant house—easy to hose down but hard on the animals' feet—contribute to the problem. OSHA, the federal agency that regulates working conditions, considers concrete floors so tough on human feet that factory workers are not permitted to stand on naked concrete.

What no one said is that all these foot problems are directly related to the confinement of the elephants. They don't ever get to really exercise, or even to walk much, which is what elephants in the wild do about 75 percent of the time. As somebody once said, denial is not only a river in Egypt. *All* these people denied that Pet's and Belle's and Packy's and the late Thonglaw's and Rosy's foot problems were due to the terrible terms of their confinement, just as thirty years ago Morgan and Matt and all the others had denied that the fatal "accidents" of elephant keepers and owners were ever the elephant's fault.

We were joined now by Dr. Mitch Finnegan, the zoo's clinical vet, who had brought a hypodermic needle to take Packy's blood sample, provided he urinated. The foot problems were also causing a form of anemia, Finnegan told me, known as "the anemia of chronic disease." For example, Pet's hematocrit, a standard measure of anemia, had lately fallen from 35 to 22 percent.

We had now been waiting two hours for Packy to urinate. "He's gotta whiz pretty soon," said Roger. "I've primed him with a sixty-gallon barrel of warm water."

But it was getting late, and Bets reluctantly decided to give up. After we'd climbed into her Jeep I said, "What *is* a flehmen, exactly?"

"It's a chemo-sensory response to a biological signal, and has mainly been studied in cats, goats, deer, and pigs." Many mammals do them, but some, such as certain rodents and some marine mammals, do not.

"Do humans have a VNO?"

An area of VNO cells in the human nose was described "about ten years ago, and we have some evidence that it is active. It responds to relaxants . . . but we don't yet know if or how it functions. It's a teeny patch of tissue up your nose. You can stick your finger up to about where it is."

The flehmen response had been well investigated only in the past twenty years, she added, led by Dr. Dietland Muller-Schwartz's study of antelope and deer. He established that one function of the VNO is to detect the evanescent chemical signal that causes the flehmen. The organ has billions of receptor cells, and its single nerve is wired through a cribriform (sieve-like) bony plate to an accessory olfactory bulb of the brain, similar to the olfactory nerve that serves the nose. A flehmen makes it easier for the VNO to pick up chemical signals.

Packy is very interested in urine, Bets said. He positions his huge trunk-tip directly above the urine he is about to sample. "The inside of the trunk is loaded with mucus glands, and I am reasonably certain that the mucus plays a chemical role in transporting the signal. Basically, mucus plus urine would produce a blend of pheromone plus maybe protein." When Packy puts his trunk in his mouth, this mixture is conveyed by trunk mucus to the VNO ducts, where it meets more mucus from the VNO itself. "It's a mucus-to-mucus trail."*

What's more, an elephant's trunk is perfect for flehmen study. "A horse or rhinoceros or a giraffe first licks the urine, using its tongue the same way the elephant uses its trunk-tip." But the elephant's trunk-tip is not only uniquely visible. It is one of the most

*"Signal transduction"—another problem Rasmussen is currently working on, thanks to a recent NIH grant—is the term for how the chemical message gets into the cell, through its outer membrane. The biochemical changes that ensue help the nerve cells send the message directly along its own nerve, "as if through a subway, to the brain."

supersensitive, nerve-filled areas known, bristling with literally billions of nerve endings and special receptor cells. It is in constant motion, exploring every aspect of the animal's environment, and it is especially eager to investigate secretions and emanations like the urine, saliva, mucus, breath, and so on of other elephants. What's more, an elephant's flehmens are easily countable, and there's no question whether it's a flehmen. "You can clearly see that he's not eating, and not drinking; he's pressing his trunk tip to his VNO." A "hot" female may cause a bull to flehmen thirty-five times in one hour.

One advantage of working with elephants is that they are a trainable, highly intelligent animal that can be taught to cooperate with the researcher. Mindful of this, Bets has always taken care never to "become friends with Packy," never even to feed him a banana, lest she imperil her scrupulous scientific objectivity.

When an Asian elephant curls his single-fingered trunk-tip into his mouth, his nostrils fit the paired VNO openings like a key to a lock. The African's two-fingered trunk-tip is more prehensile, like man's thumb and forefinger, and hence has a slightly less snug fit.

Another advantage of working with elephants is the extreme tactile sensitivity of the trunk, and the animal's hyperacute sense of smell, far superior to that of a dog. It is so sharp that Bets found she could dabble a sample of female urine on the sandy floor of the elephant patio during a rainstorm, and four hours later, Packy could still detect it. "He walks with his trunk waving from side to side, like a mine detector, and can zero in on it from one trunk-length away," she said.

Finally, "the elephant VNO is as thick as my finger, and as long as my shoe, so I can get plenty of tissue out of it," for molecular and fine structural studies.

Bets's husband, Rei (Dr. Reinhold Rasmussen), joined us for a restaurant dinner, after which both Rasmussens returned for a few hours to their respective Oregon Graduate Institute labs, as is their nightly custom. Rei is a tall, slim, fair-haired Dane, by profession a student of atmospheric gasses—an air scientist. He is also an inventor, with avid curiosity about absolutely everything known or unknown to science. In the early 1970s, Rei devised a way of collecting and preserving 100 percent pure gas and vapor samples at room temperature, using vacuum-sealed, airtight stainless-steel bottles that enable a scientist to "trap a chemical at a moment in time." The Rasmussens now manufacture these collection vessels at home, in twenty varieties from minuscule to gallon-sized, and sell them to scientists from Japan to eastern Europe.

Early the next morning, Bets picked me up at my motel and we drove to her lab at OGI. En route, she talked about how elephants of both sexes are forever tasting and testing one another's secretions with their trunks. This is due, partly, to their hypersensitivity to odors and aromas of every sort, and partly it is because all elephants are endowed with what Kipling famously called " 'satiable curiosity." Packy is a nonstop sniffer, and apt to flehmen two or three times at *any* novel compound Bets sets out, a predilection that considerably slowed her rate of progress.

Dr. Rasmussen's OGI lab suggested the domain of a movie "mad scientist." Liquids and vapors of many colors gurgled through complex architectures of glass tubing. Cabinets filled with flasks of mysterious substances lined the walls; dials and gauges trembled. The dominant structure was a connected lineup of vertical glass columns of varying heights—the slow separators—which Dr. Rasmussen designed herself.

The difficulties of urine purification are mind-boggling. One reason the work took so long is that "I didn't even know what I was looking for," says Bets, and her only confirmation that she was on the right track were Packy's sometimes capricious responses. She started with column chromatography, to separate the mix of about 500 different compounds. In separating, "you keep refining and refining and refining, to get rid of the inactive stuff."

She built an extractor that holds twenty liters of urine, and set it to run for one week. "It had to be done very *gently*, so as not to create emulsions. It's particularly hard to get things out of urine, because it's such a *mess*, chemically. The only thing worse is elephant feces."

Solvents dripping down through the urine in the columns picked up pheromones and other compounds, "pheromones plus garbage." She took samples of each fraction down to the elephant yard and dabbled it about, then called for the hydraulic doors to be opened and watched Packy's reaction. In the great majority of her tests, she got no response. "He responded to it as if to regular urine, not estrous urine. He didn't flehmen."

Next she tried high-pressure chromatography—a horizontal version of column chromatography—which eventually reduced her twenty-liter samples to two milliliters, about fifteen drops. She brought hundreds of such samples down to the elephant yard, put them out on the ground in groups of three to fifteen—"the maximum number I could watch at one time"—and monitored Packy's reactions to her display for one hour. Her rule was that his trunk-tip had to pass within eighteen inches of the sample five times for her to be certain he'd smelled it. One reason it took so long is that "I was looking for an *unknown*!" Had she known what to search for, she might have found it in six months.

Then one day, in among the thousands of compounds in the urine, a blue molecule turned up, related to indigo dye, that behaved chemically as if it might be the active pheromone. It appeared in one of the tall glass columns as a blue band, which turned out to be composed of the blue molecule plus the active pheromone. "So when they were separated out, they came out together. This meant in future I could use the blue molecule as a marker. The blue compound gave me a way to separate large amounts of the pheromone to test on elephants without wasting time."

After months more of separating, purifying, and testing, she was down to running one-hour separations, each of which produced perhaps twenty compounds. Then a huge blip, or peak, indicating tryptanthrine, appeared on the bottom line of her graphs. But it was the tiny blip just preceding it that would turn out to be important.

By 1992, Bets had found and purified the active compound, although she still could not identify it. At this time, however, her mentor, Dr. Daves, was working with Dr. Terry Lee, of the prestigious Beckman Research Institute, which specializes in the study of immunology, at the City of Hope Hospital, in Duarte, California. The two chemists were searching for a way to use small protein molecules in the treatment of cancer, and had developed the new analytic equipment necessary. Together, they were able to identify the compounds Bets was finding.

One of these was a yellow compound related to Bets's blue molecule. Once they had learned how to make it in the lab, synthetically, they could test whether it would cause the elephants to react in the same way as the natural substance in urine. Bets made some, dissolved it in urine, and went to the zoo; nothing happened. It was "a real low point" in her study. She decided that the only way to solve the problem was to enlarge the original urine sample a hundredfold, in order to increase the fallout of pheromone to an amount she could detect. It was at that point that she installed her six large freezers. It would take another four years to collect sufficient urine for Doctors Daves and Lee to analyze the tiny blip.

Then came a truly serendipitous moment. One day her sons' school called: her seventh-grader was running a high fever. "Get down here right away!" Before taking off, she attached a very large test tube to catch whatever else might come out of the chromatograph while she was gone. But in her haste to leave, she forgot to turn off the ultraviolet detector.

"When I came back, three hours later, I saw this *huge* blue peak. It had taken two hours or more to come out; the peak came off very late, and it was enormous. I had been about to give up." The big peak was active, and seemed to be one compound, tryptanthrine, a unique, ringed structure never before observed in mammals and an excellent candidate for a pheromone. But eventually she noticed the tiny blip preceding tryptanthrine on her graph. "It was so close, and so small, we couldn't really detect it." But it was this little blip just before tryptanthrine that turned out to be important. "It was active!"

Another big question still faced Bets. Was the synthetic form of her compound active? Because the compound is an important insect pheromone, Sigma, the big St. Louis chemical company, stocked it. Bets bought some and tested it on three bulls—Packy, Hugo, and Rama. All responded, but their response required higher concentrations of the chemical than Bets had anticipated, probably because the Sigma synthetic compound was only 99 percent pure, and even a small degree of impurity can reduce activity. She then heard of a second product, being manufactured in Holland and sold to farmers to attract moths. "It cuts down on the need to use pesticides. If you could attract all the moths to one place, you wouldn't have to crop-dust."

The Dutch compound was 100 percent pure. When she added minute amounts of it to acetone, put the mixture in water, and set it out on the elephant patio at Portland's zoo, Packy did nonstop flehmens for the hour-long assay period, and had a huge erection. Hugo and Rama did the same. "I never would have found it if I hadn't made that mistake years ago of leaving my machine on while I went to my son's school."

I understood all this a bit better when we moved on from the OGI to Bets's smaller lab at the zoo, where she showed me a couple of the steel domes she and Rei had designed and now manufacture. The dome fits tightly on top of a flat, round pan, like a cake tin, in which the urine, or another fluid, can be heated in a vacuum—that is to say, with zero air inside the dome.

Once the urine has been vaporized, she can collect the volatiles in the "headspace" and store the stuff indefinitely in stainless-steel bottles at room temperature. She can then pressurize the bottle, squirt, and analyze what comes out. This is what Bets meant when she said, "With these, you can trap a chemical at a moment in time."

She made a gc/ms (gas chromatographical mass spectrograph) of each of the compounds that she could now detect in the volatiles of "hot" female elephant urine, and eventually identified sixteen key compounds, of which number sixteen, the very, very late eluting (separating out) and least abundant of them all, turned out to be what she was after—the elephant pheromone (Z)-7-Dodecenyl Acetate. Now she can find it easily; she knows what she is looking for. When females are not in estrus, she can see that the compound is not there. When estrus is just starting, she can see that. When it peaks, she can see that.

Moreover, these pressurized samples can be sprayed back to the elephants and their responses noted. Today she can do the same thing with blood, or temporal-gland secretion, or any other bodily fluid. When her student, Tom Perrin, played back *musth* male temporal-gland secretion to the females, some were clearly afraid of it. The reason, Bets believes, is that it served as a warning that males were nearby, which could be dangerous to mothers with small calves. "It's just amazing to open that tiny stopcock and see the elephant retreat."

She uses the same technique for trapping elephant breath, and has trained Portland's elephants to "blow"—that is, give her a good breath sample—on command. She sticks the valve end of her collecting can up the trunk and "just tell[s] them to blow." If she is working with Africans, untrained to blow but possessed of a "two-fingered" trunk-tip, she closes one "nostril" manually. "I pinch the trunk-tip with my fingers, so they can't exhale, and when I let go they have to blow." Already she can determine by elephant breath alone whether or not a bull is in *musth*.

In short—which may be the only way for a non-chemist to understand Bets's remarkable achievement—she managed to collect samples of all the volatile compounds exhaled by female elephants in estrus. She then employed a variety of sophisticated lab techniques—mass spectrometry, gas chromatography, and nuclear magnetic resonance spectroscopy—to analyze each volatile and identify its chemical components. Eventually she identified a chemical known as (Z)-7-Dodecenyl Acetate (or Z7-12:Ac in chemists' shorthand), which proved to be her long-sought-for snowflake. Then she taught herself to synthesize it artificially. To confirm her findings she sent a sample to a leading authority on pheromones, Dr. Wendell L. Roelofs at Cornell University. Two days later, Roelofs telephoned and said that the compound Bets had extracted from the urine of estrus elephants was indeed a pheromone. What's more, it was identical to the pheromone secreted by more than a hundred species of insects, including the turnip moth, the sugarcane stalk borer, the tomato looper, and the dingy cutworm.

Upon hearing this, Bets mixed up another batch and brought it with her to Florida to test on the six breeding bulls at the Ringling Brothers Center for Elephant Conservation. Result: flehmens galore! She moved on to Busch Gardens, in Tampa, and then to the Dickerson Park Zoo, in Springfield, Missouri, and Burnet Park, in Syracuse, New York. All the animals responded positively. But to validate her work fully, Bets would require an untested population of Asian bulls in the wild. Through Dr. Mike Schmidt, arrangements were made for Bets to visit to Dr. Daw Khyne U Mar's facility in Myanmar.

Bets Rasmussen can fairly be described as a woman without fear. But in Yangon, for the first time in her life, she found herself trembling with anxiety. "What if I get up into those lumber camps two hundred miles north of here and my stuff doesn't work?"

Although severely hampered by dysentery, she managed to make it to her first village, and found three *musth* bulls and their eager *oozies* awaiting her. She mixed a few drops of (Z)-7-Dodecenyl Acetate with distilled water and poured it out onto the grass. One by one, the bulls were brought up to sniff it. All three flehmened, and one had an erection. At the next village she again found three waiting bulls. This time Number One responded, Number Two appeared indifferent, and Number Three backed off. She hoped this meant that numbers Two and Three were simply intimidated by the presence of Number One, the dominant bull. But she couldn't be sure.

"Then I had a bit of luck." The next morning, the Number Three *oozie* came to see her, grinning broadly. He had been very upset the previous day when his bull had "failed the test," he confessed. After midnight, he and his animal had sneaked back alone to the same patch of damp grass. Although it was raining, and Bets's sample was by then more than twelve hours old, Number Three's flehmen and erection had been instantaneous.

CHAPTER 12

SILENT THUNDER

ONCE IN THE wilds of Tanzania, I climbed a small rise and came up close behind a herd of elephants quietly munching. All had their backs to me, thirty huge gray rumps standing knee-deep in a meadow of purple wildflowers and drifts of white butterflies. Then, as if on cue, their trunks rose up in the air and for a moment remained motionless. Next, at some signal I couldn't detect, the entire herd began moving off, and as they ambled away I spotted six or eight baby elephants half hidden in the retreating forest of legs.

A year earlier, unbeknownst to me, Katharine Payne, an acoustic biologist from Cornell University, had made a discovery in Portland, Oregon, that would eventually explain my experience in Tanzania. She had been out on the West Coast doing some lecturing and consulting when she heard that three elephants at the Portland zoo had new calves. Having a bit of leisure to herself for the first time in ages, Payne impulsively decided to give herself the gift of one week's uninterrupted elephant-watching. She had spent much of the previous twelve years camped on a wild beach in Argentina with her biologist husband and their four children, studying and recording the sounds and behaviors of southern right whales. Ever since, she had been eager to learn more about communication among elephants, the land mammal most akin to whales.

For seven days in May 1984, Katy Payne sat on a camp chair in the narrow aisle between the bars and the glass in the Portland zoo's elephant house, observing and listening intently to its six resident mothers and calves. Unknowingly, she had chosen the same spot where Doc Maberry had unrolled his sleeping bag in 1962 to keep an eye on pregnant Belle. Katy has a rare ability to concentrate fully on the subject at hand. Indeed, her modus operandi, perfected during her years of whale study, is to alternate intense concentration in the field with periods of long and careful brooding. At the zoo, she did not leave her post except to return to her motel at night. Nor did she spend time with any of the zoo's other animals. A strange sort of holiday, one might think, especially for a recently separated woman in her forties whose youngest child has just gone off to college. But Katy Payne is a Quaker, well-endowed with that sect's peculiar blend of the mild and the stern, of delicate sensibility and stubborn resolve. And, brooding on her week with Portland's elephants, she gradually became aware of something that would change the world's understanding of elephant life, and change her own life as well.

Late one afternoon the three females and their offspring were together inside the eighty-foot, glass-walled concrete enclosure. Packy was out on his new patio catching a few last rays of sun, and two other bulls were in their separate indoor quarters. It was past closing time, and the elephant house was empty of people save for Katy and two keepers. Gradually, she became aware of a strange, faint throbbing in the air. She didn't give it much thought until the next day on the plane home to Ithaca, New York. Eyes closed, concentrating intensely on memories of the zoo, lulled by the thrum of the jets, her mind flashed back thirty years, to a moment when she was thirteen, singing Bach's *St. Matthew Passion* alongside her mother in the Cornell University Chorale. They stood in the organ loft, next to the biggest pipes. "As the sounds get lower and lower, you lose your sense of pitch," she told me when we met. "You only feel a sort of throbbing." The memory, with its association between powerful, low-pitched sound and a physical sensation, led her to speculate that elephants might call to one another using infrasound—sound below the range of human hearing.

That elephants have exceptionally acute hearing has long been known. Early in the nineteenth century, the celebrated London surgeon Sir Everard Home trundled a piano, and piano tuner, to the city menagerie—"that I might know the effect of acute and grave sounds upon the ears of a full-grown elephant. The acute sounds seemed hardly to attract his notice; but as soon as the grave notes were struck, he became all attention, brought forward the large external ear, tried to discover where the sounds came from, remained in the attitude of listening, and after some time made noises by no means of dissatisfaction."

What Katy's experience in Portland suggested was that elephants may communicate not only with the high-pitched squeals and low-pitched rumbles we all know and love, but also in ultra-low frequencies that humans cannot hear, in the slow vibrations we call infrasound. What humans perceive, if anything, is less a noise than a kind of pulsation in the atmosphere. Katy hadn't so much heard the sound as *felt* it.

Elephants have the best low-frequency hearing of all land mammals tested to date, and the cochlea of an elephant's inner ear appears to be especially well adapted for hearing such sounds. While it is exciting to learn that there is a dimension of elephant communication that people hadn't realized, the main significance of infrasonic communication, Katy believes today, is probably that powerful, low-frequency sound travels much farther than high-pitched sound of the same strength. High sounds lose much energy to "ground reflection, topography, vegetative attenuation, reverberance, masking, wind noise, turbulent scattering, relaxation attenuation by oxygen, nitrogen, and water, and refraction due to vertical wind and temperature gradients, [all of these interacting with] source and receiver height, call strength, hearing threshold, and frequency signature."

Payne and her colleagues later determined that most of the energy in the calls of African elephants is concentrated at or below the lower limit for human hearing, which is around 20 Hz. The higher frequency components of some of these calls are audible to humans as low, soft rumbles. The rumbles, like the large variety of richly audible snorts, growls, trumpetings, barks, and other noises elephants make, originate in the larynx. But elephant anatomy is such that during a powerful call, a close observer can see, and feel, a vibration in the flat, triangular portion of the elephant's forehead where the nasal passage lies between trunk and skull just under the surface. This vibration, first pointed out to Payne by one of the Portland keepers, is evidence that an elephant is calling even when the call is inaudible to us.

Payne returned to Portland as soon as possible, this time equipped with a borrowed infrasound-capable tape recorder and microphones, and accompanied by two colleagues: Dr. William R. Langbauer, Jr., a research associate in the Cornell Bioacoustics Research Program, whose prior work had focused on animal behavior; and Katy's longtime friend Elizabeth Marshall Thomas, author of *The Harmless People* and *The Hidden Life of Dogs*, chosen for her unique abilities as, in Katy's words, "a truly *great* observer!" For a month the three visitors taped almost continuously, whether or not they heard anything. Katy and Liz Thomas sometimes felt throbbing in the air when rumbles were not audible; Langbauer confessed he could not. To preserve battery life, and save time, none of them reviewed any of the tapes until after they had returned home.

At her first opportunity, Katy brought her tapes to the Cornell University lab of Dr. Carl Hopkins, the esteemed acoustic biologist who had loaned her the recording equipment. Hopkins is best known for having figured out the communication system of electric fish. It was Thanksgiving eve. Hopkins rigged Katy's tape recorder to a machine that translates sounds into flickering dots of light on a screen that can then be printed out as a sound picture, or spectrogram. The first tape they chose had been made a moment after Katy and Liz saw Rosy leave the other mothers and infants and walk to the far end of the big concrete enclosure, facing the thick wall between the enclosure and the outdoor patio. "I feel it!" Liz had suddenly whispered, and raced outside to the patio, where she found the big bull Tunga standing within a few feet of the same wall. Remove the wall, and the two animals would be standing face to face.

On the tape, they heard the expected barks, snorts, ear-flappings, and a whirring electric fan high in one corner of the indoor enclosure— nothing unusual. But when they replayed the tapes, this time speeding them up to ten times the normal rate, the pitch was high enough to make infrasound calls clearly audible.

The rumbles were key. Whereas elephants can hear them well, most humans cannot. A normal fifteen-year-old—one who has not listened to too much rock music, that is—has about a ten-octave hearing range. An African elephant can readily hear another octave below that. Moreover, sounds at this low frequency, unlike higher-pitched sounds, pass easily and without distortion through forests and grasslands, enabling wild elephants to communicate over distances of 2.5 miles or more.

What most amazed me about Katy's story was that not only had Shakespeare's famous Pyramus and Thisbe love scene been reenacted by two elephants, but that very night, Payne had a significant midsummer night's dream of her own. As she describes the episode in her book, *Silent Thunder: In the Presence of Elephants:*

> I went home and tumbled into bed. Immediately I received a dream. I was lying in a deep, damp, warm, grassy sward in the faint light of predawn. . . . Looming over me was a swaying, silent circle of elephants . . . several were reaching out with their trunks to sniff me. . . . They swayed hugely, breathing over me for a long time, and then the largest female spoke. . . . "We did not reveal this to you so you would tell other people."

Later Payne offered me this interpretation of the matriarch's statement: "We did not reveal this to you so you would write about it. This is not to make you rich and famous. It is to bring us all into one family."

The dream so haunted her that very early the next morning, at a silent Quaker meeting held to welcome the Thanksgiving dawn, Katy was amazed to find herself on her feet, testifying about it. "The gathered Friends listened as people do when sound comes out of deep silence," she wrote. "Inside me the dream was drumming on my heart. . . . I did not hear my own voice, but in the gray light now entering the room through the clear glass of tall windows, I saw tears running down the cheeks of a woman I did not know."

The researchers published their findings, including their speculation that infrasonic communication enables elephants to coordinate their social behavior over long distances, in a scientific journal.* They heard immediately from the Douglas-Hamiltons and from Cynthia Moss and Joyce Poole, all of whom had ob-

*Zoologist Judith K. Berg of the San Diego Wild Animal Park had earlier reported some very-low-frequency African-elephant vocalizations in a 1983 scientific paper.

served striking examples of inexplicably coordinated elephant behavior. All the members of a herd sometimes stopped or turned together, like a flock of birds. At other times, all herd members on the march would "freeze" simultaneously. "Two to 100 individuals suddenly hold still in their tracks, as if a motion picture frame had stuck in the projector," as Payne described it.

Katy now needed to study elephant communication in the wild, and leaped at Joyce Poole's invitation to visit Amboseli. There she and Joyce became fast friends. Joyce was particularly intrigued by how *musth* males and estrous females manage to find one another, given that they move independently across large areas, and that, generally speaking, a female can be bred successfully only during a brief forty-eight- to seventy-two-hour period.

"But they do find one another," as Katy later emphasized in a *National Geographic* article. "The female is no sooner in estrus than she is surrounded by males that gather from all directions."

For a long time Joyce and Cynthia had been speculating about the meanings of the many different elephant sounds they *could* hear, "especially during reproduction, which is always very noisy." Cynthia and Joyce had broken them down into thirty-three individual categories, each with a specific meaning. Now Joyce and Katy spent two short dry seasons in the bush, recording among the same elephants, and learned that for every call they could hear, they recorded two that were below their range of hearing.

One of the most interesting calls was the "Let's go!" rumble, a series of long, low-pitched, soft calls that is probably what I'd "heard" in Tanzania. It tells herd members busy eating, drinking, dusting, or mud-bathing that it's time to get going again, and the herd moves off as a group. Nearby elephants belonging to another group do not respond. Another common call was the "suckle protest," the sound a nursing calf gives its mother, who always rumbles her acknowledgment, using a distinctly different sound from the "reassuring response rumble" she gives her newborn calf. "Contact calls" enable two herds to move on parallel courses a couple of miles apart and stay in touch, even though they remain at a distance sufficient to insure adequate forage for each. The unique, pulsating "*musth* rumble" of a lone male is preceded, and followed, by a period of "intense listening, standing utterly motionless, head high, ears wide." Poole likens this rumble to "water gurgling through a deep tunnel."

As for the calls that attract males to females, Payne describes "a unique sequence of intense, low-frequency calls that a receptive female makes during estrus. This sequence always has the same form and thus technically may be called a song."

Someone with Katy Payne's focus does not use the word "song" lightly. If elephants disappear from the earth, she has written, gone too will be "the long, urgent songs of fertile females, and the stillness of the night as elephants [freeze] in their tracks to listen."

From Amboseli, Payne moved 3,000 miles southwest to Etosha, a semidesert park in Namibia near the Skeleton Coast. Here she worked again with Bill Langbauer and Liz Thomas. (Joyce remained with Moss at Amboseli, continuing their work and extending their data.) Payne suspects that adult mothers and matriarchs may use a slightly different rumble to address each member of their family. She also suspects there may be a special rumble developed during the centuries in which elephants and human beings have lived side by side, a rumble that says: "Take care! People are nearby."

One population of elephants lives in extreme desert conditions in western Namibia. There elephants may travel seventy kilometers a day as they move between food and water, and can go up to four days without drinking. Acute thirst sometimes causes them to arrive at a water hole at a dead run. In Damaraland, west of Etosha, and other areas where rivers and creeks flow below ground level for most of the year, elephants excavate tiny wells with their trunk tips, no wider in circumference than the trunks themselves, to reach the invisible water they know is twelve to twenty-four inches down. If the calves cannot get to it with their minuscule trunks, mothers and aunts suck up the water and squirt it down the youngsters' throats. The elephant-dug wells also enable the region's myriad other wildlife—from large mammals to the smallest insects—to survive.

One aspect of elephants' lives that currently interests Payne is the way their calls are influenced by the *structure* of the atmosphere. An hour or two after sunset, "low wind speeds and a strong temperature inversion are the norm, and these factors enhance sound propagation," Payne says. At night, the distance traveled by sounds that have the power and depth of elephant calls can increase as much as fivefold over their daytime range, and the area they fill can increase tenfold! A sound that is audible to elephants over an area of thirty square kilometers at midday is audible over an area of 300 square kilometers. In short, the night is continually a-roar, a-tweet, a-rumble, a-whistle, and a-bellow with sounds of animal communication.

In Namibia's bleak landscape, with no jungle to interfere with sightings, elephants can be observed from distances of half a mile or so. But the distance over which elephants respond to one another's calls may be much greater—how does one measure that? Katy and her team built a twenty-foot tower with unimpeded views of one-half square mile of desert, and surrounded it with microphones. The work was always difficult and often frustrating because "you can't always tell *who's* calling, and you can't always locate the responder, who may be miles away, over the horizon. And I thought it would be *easy,* switching from whales to elephants!"

Payne's solution: an "artificial elephant"—a van with a loudspeaker mounted on its roof—would drive to a preselected location a measured distance from the tower and broadcast prerecorded elephant calls while the people on the tower videotaped the behavior of local elephants.

For three months the researchers took turns atop the tower in blistering heat videotaping the behavior of elephants visible from the tower. In one experiment, Katy trained her telescope on a couple of huge bulls more than a mile distant, well beyond her hearing range, that stood alongside a water hole, drying off after bathing. Two scouts invisible to the elephants were parked in the van nearby. By walkie-talkie, Katy instructed them to choose and play one of their recorded elephant calls—sounds never before heard by these elephants—at a pre-ordained volume. Katy did not know which call her scouts would select, nor precisely what time it would commence.

Silence. Dazzling sun. She squinted into the eyepiece. Suddenly she saw first one bull and then the other raise his head, stiffen, and spread his ears wide. In unison both bulls swung their heads to the left, back to center, then to the right and back to center.

By now she knew the recording had ended; no tape was longer than forty seconds. Both bulls had turned around and set off in the direction of the van. Neither animal paused even for water, unheard of in this desert heat. Katy tracked their march. Every so often, one bull or the other stopped to scan the horizon and listen again. They froze for up to thirty seconds before plodding on.

Fifteen minutes later they passed the van, but kept right on going, trunks and tails swaying slightly, until they disappeared, gray on gray, into the scrub brush shimmering on the horizon.

Only later would Katy learn which tape the bulls had been responding to: her scouts had played the estrous song of Zita, a female in the Amboseli herd more than two thousand miles to the northeast.

• • •

Katy Payne's love for sound is evident in her life at home as well as in the field. The day I first visited her little stone house near Ithaca, New York, in the spring of 1998, she was feeling "exultant, if a bit exhausted" after a full-dress performance of the Brahms *Requiem* the night before. This morning her clear blue eyes were intensified by a handsome smock from Oaxaca, embroidered with blue and orange birds and animals, a gift from a daughter who is married to a Mexican ecologist. Three of her children are wildlife biologists, and the youngest is an acrobat with the Cirque du Soleil.

Katy wanted me to hear some tapes of her elephant calls, and suggested we start with the same conversation between Rosy and Tunga that she'd played for Carl Hopkins. Rosy was standing near a heating fan, Katy warned me, and I should not confuse her calls with the fan noise, nor with the flapping sounds of Rosy's ears. We would also hear an occasional loud WHUMPF! That would be Rosy blowing out her trunk.

Katy pushed the play button. I heard the fan and the ear-flapping, loud and clear. After a moment came a WHUMPF!

"Now I'll rewind and speed it up," Katy said, and then pushed play again. The fan was a lot squeakier now, and the ear-flapping sounded like a series of rapid clicks. But in between them, I heard clearly a low and mellow "m-m-m-huh . . . m-m-m-huh . . . m-m-m-huh . . ." It sounded to me like the moaning of ghosts.

Having just finished writing *Silent Thunder*, her first book intended for a nonacademic audience, Katy was planning a trip with an old friend to India to observe wild Asian elephants for the first time, to determine whether her Portland zoo findings also held true in the jungles of India. (They do.) In the Mudamalai Forest Reserve, the friends visited Theppakadu, a small community centered on an elephant riding stable with twenty-eight trained animals, each with its own mahout. They remained there for two weeks, exploring the jungle on elephant-back in blissful near-solitude, the bandits and poachers having frightened away other tourists. Because this elephant camp occupied both sides of a wide river, a great deal of long-distance conversation seemed likely. The elephants' saddles were padded with six-inch-thick straw mattresses, and "Five minutes after saddling up, I felt as well as heard the first call. Amazing! You feel it through the seat of your pants!"

The visit was an irresistible opportunity to answer a question Katy had long speculated on: How do elephants and their mahouts understand one another? Mahouts such as these spend their entire adult lives living, eating, and sleeping with the same elephant, and no one knows the animal better. Every single one of them was excited to hear about Payne's studies of elephant communication and told many stories of mysterious simultaneous behavior of separated elephants that could now be explained by infrasound.

There is no question in Katy's mind but that the elephants in this camp were happy creatures. Their mahouts spent as much time as possible making them happy, scrubbing them so thoroughly for two or three hours at the riverbank that they had literally pink ears and trunks. Afterward, the men kneaded millet, rice, and raw sugar into volley-ball-sized spheres and hand-fed them.

Katy once told me another story involving happy elephants. A few years back, she had attended an elegant dinner party given by Christine (Mrs. Roger) Stevens, chair of the Animal Welfare Institute in Washington, D.C. The cellist Mstislav Rostropovich had become interested in elephant conservation and was happy to volunteer his services. He told the guests that night that after searching the literature, he'd found only one piece that seemed to have been written for or about elephants—Camille Saint-Saëns's

Carnival of the Animals. Since the elephant section was written for double bass, Rostropovich explained, he had loosened the strings of his cello and tuned them down a fifth. Katy played me a tape of the occasion. The music sounded loopy and ponderous but infectiously jolly.

When it ended, Rostropovich spoke a few words. "At the time Saint-Saëns wrote his piece . . . elephants were plentiful. They were happy to be alive, and to have babies. Therefore I think Saint-Saëns wrote the part dedicated to elephants in a major key. . . .

"Now, when the elephants are in danger of extinction, I am sure they know it. So now the music dedicated to them must sound sad, in a minor key. I will try to re-create the state of their souls today," the maestro concluded, and indeed the music that followed, played in a minor key, and at half-speed, sounded ineffably sad, full of tears.

Payne is currently active in efforts to get the full ivory ban restored. True, *Loxodonta africana* finally was added to the CITES list in 1989. But the ban was temporarily lifted only a decade later when Botswana, Namibia, and Zimbabwe were permitted to sell off their massive stockpiles of embargoed ivory to Japan. Preservationists deplored the action, on two levels. First, symbolically it signaled to the world that the African elephant is no longer truly endangered; and second, on the nuts-and-bolts level, it seemed certain to reopen the door to ivory poachers and corrupt traders.

While the Douglas-Hamiltons, Moss, Poole, and Payne all see the vote to lift the ban as a prelude to disaster, they are also aware that in most countries of Africa, wildlife is the major tourist attraction, hence the major source of essential dollars. Their answer is a well-managed, government-run education and tourism program in which wild animals essentially pay for themselves. Still, it is not surprising that most Africans see most wildlife champions as people more concerned with saving wild animals than with saving Africans themselves.

One can see elephants as living beings, or see them as money, Payne once told me, but she personally could not see them as both. She wrote an eloquent editorial deploring the fact that trade is again being permitted despite the lack of any system for monitoring its impact on elephant populations worldwide. Iain, Cynthia, and Joyce were quick to sign the document. The editorial has since been reprinted in newspapers around the world, and in England in *Nature* magazine.

Further evidence of the problem can be found on the Internet, where dozens of big-game safari outfits now advertise—for example: "Come to Tanzania. . . . The very essence of Africa, unspoiled yet spectacular. The 'Big Four'—elephants, lions, leopards, buffalo—are all there. And best of all, you may shoot as much as you please."

Katy says that the most thrilling of her current activities is using a new program to perform a painstaking reanalysis of some of her old data. The program enables her to localize elephants' calls and to attribute them to individual animals and groups as they interact in complex circumstances. It not only automatically makes all sound data visible, producing spectrograms that literally map out the sounds on paper, but to some degree it enables her to match the locations of calls with elephants on her videos, and thus begin making informed guesses about the meanings of some of the calls.

"It's just gorgeous!" Katy trills. "I feel I'm working with the Rosetta Stone."

She dreams of being able one day to census elephants entirely from acoustic data. "We could measure it all—numbers, sexes, activities . . ." Her eyes closed briefly.

Katy was then sixty-two. "Will you ever retire?" I asked, fairly certain I knew her answer.

"Oh, no," she said brightly. "Cynthia and Joyce and I intend to write the first elephant dictionary. We've been collecting material for two decades, and I'm now working on it full time with two assistants at Cornell."

CHAPTER 13

PROBOSCIDEA'S LAST, BEST HOPE

IN 1994, AN 8,000-pound elephant in Louisville, Kentucky, escaped her keeper and seized twenty-eight-year-old Troy Ramsey, a machinist, in her trunk. She attempted a headstand on his chest, then smashed him to the ground and tried to gore him with her tusks. By the time he awakened in the hospital, the man had lost two-thirds of his pancreas and all of his spleen. Upon discovering that he was totally and permanently disabled, Ramsey filed suit against the zoo, the beast, and her handler, charging them with failure to maintain control of a deadly force.

Thus far, the story is routine of its kind. But the machinist spent the time between his injury and his court date reading the latest findings on elephant behavior. To a reporter who interviewed him before trial, Ramsey made a remarkable statement.

"You can't keep an elephant pent up in chains and expect it to be right in the head," he said. "Elephants are intelligent animals and, knowing they are not in their natural environment, don't want to be there. It must be a private hell for them."

Ramsey had given perfect voice to the increasingly vocal and agitated point of view of members of the animals rights movement: that any wild animal held in captivity, but especially something as immense and helpless as an elephant, is a victim of outrageous, inhuman cruelty and must be defended at all costs. If elephants in the wild are the most highly socialized of animal species, then the hardship imposed on a lone elephant in a zoo or circus is monstrous, equivalent to sentencing an individual to solitary confinement for life.

The animal rights movement began early in the nineteenth century in England, and today claims 3,000 British groups dedicated to the preservation of frogs, rodents, turtles, bats, zoo and domestic animals, and pets, indeed all of "our animal brothers and sisters." Extremists among them have gone underground, distributed bomb-making materials and instruction manuals, launched hunger strikes, and even organized ski-masked death squads and hit lists of scientists who use animals in their research. Scotland Yard maintains a special branch to combat "animal rights terrorists" by the same means it employs against the Irish Republican Army.

Some of this new militancy has crossed the water and energized American animal rights groups. By the early 1990s, fringe activists in the United States were girding for action. Some noticed that enslaved zoo and circus pachyderms had been striking back at their oppressors, and asserted that unfortunates like the machinist had only themselves to blame.

The nation had about 600 elephants in captivity, and the animals were managing to kill at least one of their 600 handlers per year. Since 1976, twenty-one Americans, most of them zoo and circus employees, had been stomped, crushed, or gored to death by an elephant, five in the previous eight years. Elephant-keeping remained the most dangerous occupation in America. Something had to be done. By the time Disney's Animal Kingdom opened near Orlando, Florida, early in 1998, a seismic shift in the management of captive elephants had quietly occurred, and Disney's was the model example.

Let us begin with the real estate. In a massive, brilliantly conceived work of imagination, 500 acres of former Florida orange groves and cattle pasture had been transformed utterly into an imaginary section of East Africa—near Amboseli perhaps—with real jungles, swamps, deserts, savannas, racing rivers, spouting geysers, and broad streams in which dozens of crocs dozed. Hundreds, maybe thousands of jewel-colored tropical birds glitter-flitted under an invisible net larger than a basketball court and forty feet high, all underplanted with heliotrope and orchids and flowering vines of sapphire and crimson and burning yellow. Strategically placed windows revealed real veterinarians—there are six on staff, four of them women—in real action. The six staff animal keepers who tend hospitalized sick or injured animals are also women. A colony of tiny mole rats—blind, hairless, almost deaf—live and reproduce deep underground, behind glass, exposed to the wide eyes of children goggling from their strollers, as if they were at a cutaway of an anthill, or a termite mound, or a hippo pool. *Hippo* pool? Yes, with a big hippo family snuggling underwater and looking rather goggle-eyed themselves.

The powerful Disney conservation message is mostly unstated, but omnipresent: "You are seeing a piece of the wild, people, and this is worth saving." Occasionally, it *is* stated, as on the small placards posted in every rest room, "The Scoop on Poop."

Six acres are set aside for elephants. Six young cows and two bulls live there, all of them orphans who started life as culls from Zimbabwe and are now robust and of breeding age. "Welcome to heaven, girls!" their keeper shouted when the first cows were trucked from their temporary home in Tacoma, Washington, and released into this paradise.

Chief of the Kingdom's 231 animal curators, zoological managers, keepers, and support staff is John Lehnhardt. Animal operations manager is his formal title, but he is himself a most informal man. Tanned and toothily good-looking, he has the granitic handshake of Pete Sampras, and the passionate conviction of a Billy Graham that he has the best job in the best of all possible worlds. At fifty-one, he is well-positioned to be one of the few people on earth able to actively save another species from extinction at the hands of humankind. Although the Disney management does not release attendance figures, it is safe to say that Animal Kingdom has at least ten times as many annual visitors as any of our largest zoos. Lehnhardt can reach and educate the public about elephants better from Disney than from anywhere else on the planet.

Lehnhardt has worked around animals all his life, beginning as an unpaid helper at county fairs in rural Iowa. After college—he has a B.A. in biology from the University of Chicago—he worked as a counselor in a children's psychiatric hospital, and as kennel manager of a humane society animal shelter. He was studying rat kidney biochemistry at the University of Chicago Medical School when he decided to take the difficult oral and written exams for an animal keeper's job at Lincoln Park Zoo. Scoring highest among five hundred applicants, he got the job. When the old zoo elephant house was torn down four years later, Lehnhardt became elephant trainer at Canada's Calgary Zoo. Eight years after that, he was hired as large mammal manager at Washington's National Zoo, a division of the Smithsonian Institution. He had been there nine years when Disney made him an offer too good to refuse.

Throughout his zoo career, John Lehnhardt has worked for the betterment of elephants, having heard of and at times witnessed human cruelty and greed with regard to these animals that moved him to tears. He attended and later helped organize weekend "elephant workshops" so that keepers and handlers from around the nation could pool their knowledge for the first time, and address common problems. The workshops evolved into the Elephant Managers Association, a federation with more than 300 members that today publishes journals and newsletters, organizes conferences, and helped develop an American Zoo Association training program for elephant professionals. Lehnhardt was the EMA's first president.

Working on his own, Lehnhardt also compiled the first accurate record of elephant-related deaths. In 1991, he published his paper, "Elephant Handling—A Problem of Risk Management and Resource Allocation," and read his startling findings to the annual convention of zoo owners (the AZAA—American Zoo and Aquarium Association—now the AZA) in San Diego. Three percent of the elephants in the United States and Canada, he announced, had been involved in one or more human deaths. His presentation was a deliberate, in-your-face attempt to awaken the zoo community to the dangers in their lackadaisical approach to elephant management. "I intended it as a shot across their bow," he told me, "and it worked."

The EMA's efforts have had a significant impact on the welfare of captive elephants, as well as on the safety of their handlers. About 40 percent of North American zoos have switched to a system of "protected contact only," meaning that no elephant is ever in direct contact with its keeper. Sturdy bars or rails separate them, but do not interfere with daily scrubs, foot care, the taking of blood samples, or other necessities of captive elephant life. Other zoos feel that protected contact compromises care and have retained their "free contact" systems, though vastly improved, thanks to prodding and the distribution of educational materials by the EMA.

At Disney today, John Lehnhardt stomps his vast turf and buildings wearing a khaki hat with an ear piece that keeps him hooked up by radio-phone to the rest of his animal-husbandry staff—keepers, managers, curators, and so on. He can also switch to frequencies used by veterinarians, scientists, horticulturalists, and park operations. Early one rainy, misty morning, John escorted me on a tour of his model elephant habitat. Already his animals were out of their barns and foraging. Such was their appetite that it had been necessary to totally replant their acreage even before the park opened. "Horticulture is in total conflict with elephants," John said ruefully, meaning "they will eat *anything*." I remembered the gnawed-off handles of Morgan Berry's wheelbarrow. Fortunately, Disney horticulturalists found one shrub, *Arundo donax*, that is equivalent to elephant candy, and stocked up.

When we first met, John had spoken frankly of how difficult it is to do sustained research while entirely dependent on federal funding, as at National Zoo. He has found Disney's profit-making orientation far preferable, though in his early days there he had to spend a good deal of time educating Disney management about his needs. "To us, animal care is serious business, and we collaborate with other zoos all the time," he told me. "But Disney, like any big corporation, does not like to collaborate or share its secrets with other entertainment giants." Then John made the interesting discovery that Walt Disney himself had been a nature lover whose very first film—long before Mickey Mouse—was titled *Plants and Animals*. John brought this fact to the attention of management, adding, "We need to get this company back to its roots."

The diet of most zoo elephants is 80 percent hay. But the Disney herd can forage among sixty-six species of living native African plants. Their home is unique among wild-animal parks in that "No one else allows the animals to eat their habitat." Possibly no one else can afford it. But freedom to forage is an important part of natural elephant behavior, and may be critical for maintaining the animals' natural birthrate. Each animal also gets a daily allotment of one hundred pounds of "browse"—mixed forage, like the truck-size pile of young bamboo prunings I noticed piled up at the back door of the modern, heated, hosed, immaculate elephant house. The six elephant acres the public sees include one mud wallow, two big bathing pools, a place for the "dust baths" elephants love, and big rocks and dead trees on which to scratch themselves. To preserve the "natural" look, Disney ground crews have been obliged to invent and install electrified "grass," in reality green-painted sprigs of wire that border certain planted areas to keep the elephants out. The new product, called Ele-fence, is fabricated on the premises. In areas unseen by the public, Disney also uses standard electrified cattle fencing.

Lehnhardt's objective at Disney has always been very clear in his mind: first, establish a natural social group of elephants living in natural situations, as if in the wild. And indeed, under his watchful, benevolent eye, the eight young elephants swiftly melded into a normal elephant family. Second, once breeding begins, all calves will remain with their mothers until puberty, and the females will live with their mothers all their lives. "This means we're committed in perpetuity to any elephant that is born here," he told me.

Third, he is intent on establishing a "normal social structure," by which he means an all-female herd. "Elephants are the best mothers in the world. If we don't provide an opportunity for them to experience motherhood, and child-rearing, then they don't lead a full elephant life. To deny a female elephant an opportunity to fulfill her fundamental nature—to breed and bring up her babies—is a criminal act."

"Protected contact only" management means not only that keepers are protected, but also that animals act *by choice* only. At twilight, a keeper bangs a drum to signal that the herd may now return from field and jungle to their immaculate, indoor, purple-painted quarters, where they occupy individual stalls, and are monitored by twenty-four hour TV cameras, and spend their nights in tranquil slumber. Or they may choose to linger a while and pluck a last sprig of delectable *Arundo donax* before retiring.

"We use no aversive persuasion," John told me, meaning no cattle prods and no elephant hooks. "They understand the drum's message perfectly—'come home'—and can hear it from a half-mile off. Calling them in is just like whistling for a dog."

Disney's crush is motorized and so powerful it can be rotated to any position needed while performing surgery on an anaesthetized elephant. The animals are habituated to it because they must exit through it each morning, after their daily weigh-in. Thus, in a medical emergency, there will be "no surprises."

In the past, the primary problem in exhibiting wild animals to the public has been that it forced the animals to lead an unnatural, cruel, deprived existence. Lehnhardt recognizes that in order to develop normally and fully, and to breed readily, his elephants need a variety of experience and a variety of stimulation, as well as of forage, and he is pledged to give them such a life.

"But how will all this help preserve the species, so that your grandchildren may know elephants?" I asked.

"The growing human population is what's destroying elephant habitat," John replied. So, "There aren't elephant problems. There are people problems, which affect elephants."

Long before coming to Disney, Lehnhardt had wanted to develop a breeding program. But he had always lacked funds, and a staff person with the necessary research background. Then he found Nancy Pratt. She is a pretty, fresh-faced, and quiet-spoken young woman with thick, shoulder-length brown hair who looks like Andy Hardy's girlfriend. In fact, she is a highly trained reproductive physiologist who today works alongside her mentor Lehnhardt, and is one of three at Disney's Animal Kingdom to hold the title Curator of Mammals.

Elephants have not always been Nancy's specialty. Her Ph.D. thesis investigated the effects of stress on the fertility of the female hamster, a much more convenient mammal to work with than the elephant, as it has a four-day rather than a four-month cycle, and a gestation period of sixteen days, not twenty-two months. And indeed, when hamsters are stressed out, just as when elephants, or human beings, for that matter, are stressed out, their birth rate drops precipitously.

Raised in Huntington, Long Island, Nancy graduated cum laude in biology and English literature from Colgate University, got her Ph.D. in biology and neuroscience from Princeton University, and worked five years at the San Diego Zoo, while earning a couple of postdoctoral fellowships, before being brought to the National Zoo, in Washington, in 1994 as a curatorial intern.

The first person Nancy Pratt and John Lehnhardt reached out to for information was Dr. Michael Schmidt, in Portland, the only person who had ever attempted to breed captive elephants via A-I, and who over the years had published several papers on the subject. But Schmidt did not reply to their calls or letters. Over time, Doctors Hildebrandt and Göritz from Berlin, Debbie Olson from Indianapolis, and Dr. Dennis Schmitt from Springfield, Missouri, also approached Dr. Schmidt, all to no avail.

Lehnhardt, Pratt, and their cohorts have built on Schmidt's work, however, and learned to pinpoint the precise timing of elephant ovulation through the combined use of hormonal assay and ultrasound, which was not available when Dr. Schmidt began his research. Today's elephant researchers use ultrasound to observe the huge ovarian follicle as it ripens. They can follow it as it develops and finally bursts out of the ovary to travel down the ovarian duct. Frequent hormone assays of the cow's blood can determine the brief forty-eight-hour period within which a female is most likely to conceive. For a long time, the biggest problem was the semen. It could not be frozen and still remain potent. "When thawed, it is mobile, but infertile."

The year following Nancy Pratt's arrival in Washington, the internationally known German veterinary scientist Dr. Thomas R. Hildebrandt came to town to do a six-month externship in pathology at the Smithsonian. At thirty-three, Hildebrandt headed the Department of Reproductive Management at the Institute for Zoo Biology and Wildlife Research in Berlin, and he is the primary developer of the successful elephant artificial insemination technique now in use. Before coming to Washington, he and his associate, Dr. Frank Göritz, had made six two-week visits to South Africa at the invitation of the government and, working in the wild, had employed ultrasound to check sixty-six elephants for pregnancies. It is difficult to chalk up that kind of experience. Hildebrandt's elephant studies had begun in 1992, when he was writing his Ph.D. thesis on utilizing ultrasound in domestic animals, and learned that there was very limited anatomical information available on wild animals, and that no wild-animal field manuals existed for veterinary use.

Kruger National Park, like other wildlife reserves in South Africa and elsewhere, practiced annual culling of its elephant herds, for population control. Teams of sharpshooters in helicopters equipped with dart guns fired lethal drugs that paralyze the respiratory system, essentially suffocating the wide-awake animals. The practice was stopped in 1995, due to heavy pressure and contributions from humane societies around the world. But while the policy was still in effect, Hildebrandt obtained government permission to dissect the freshly killed animals at the abattoir, before they were cut up and their meat sold for human consumption. For six years he and Göritz studied the hitherto unknown or misperceived morphology (form and structure) of the reproductive systems of elephants, both male and female. The culling policy allowed the two veterinarians to dissect scores of newly dead animals, then verify their gross anatomical findings with ultrasound exploration, and vice versa. That is, they could wield scalpel and sound probe simultaneously, using each technique to verify the other.

Briefest glossary: *Ultrasound* is sound composed of acoustic frequencies above about 20,000 Hz, which are inaudible to the human ear. An *ultrasonogram,* or sonogram, is the picture made when ultrasound waves are reflected off an internal organ or structure and displayed as an image on a TV monitor. The sound waves are produced by a *transducer* and directed and focused by its attached *probe*. Crudely put, the device reads soft tissue the way an X-ray reads bone structure, and today is in common use for many diagnostic purposes. To visualize a human baby in embryo, for example, the probe is placed on the mother's belly along with a dab of neutral gel to aid in transmitting the waves through her skin. But in an unexplored species, when the examiner doesn't fully know what he is looking at, nor for, the density of the tissue makes it hard to know what one is seeing. Furthermore, an elephant's skin is too thick in most places for the sound waves readily to pass through it.

Transrectal ultrasound begins with the insertion of a specially designed elephant probe deeply into the thin-skinned rectum. It is an entirely noninvasive procedure, but gives the examiner about a five-foot lead over what would otherwise be his starting point.

An *endoscope*, in common medical use today, is essentially a photosensitive microchip on the end of a fiber-optic cable used to examine visually the inside of a body cavity. The picture appears brightly lit, and in vivid color, on a portable scope. But in an elephant endoscope, the cable must be more than six feet long.

Hildebrandt has designed, manufactured, and patented a special device he calls "the swan-neck-shaped probe," which conforms to the animal's unique reproductive anatomy. Its distinguishing feature is a bend in the shaft enabling it to reach over the elephant's high pelvic rim and descend the other side to gain a clear view of vagina and cervix. It is about the size of a bent clarinet, and the doctor carries it around from zoo to zoo in a padded aluminum trunk, along with a load of batteries, special elephant-sized endoscopes, and other tools of his trade.

• • •

The National Zoo had no bulls at the time John and Nancy worked there. To get its first baby elephant, the zoo had to detach one of its females from her home and herd and billet her for two years at the zoo in Syracuse, New York. This was Shanthi, and she came back pregnant. When her healthy calf, Kumari, was born in 1993, shortly before Christmas, jubilation spread throughout Washington, D.C.

Sixteen months after Kumari's birth, a tragic event occurred that redirected Nancy Pratt's career. She had played with Kumari daily, and was present on the fateful Monday afternoon when the little elephant suddenly collapsed. It refused to eat, and by Friday it was dead, of causes unknown. A team of twenty doctors and technicians performed a six-hour autopsy, to no avail. Tissue samples from Kumari's heart eventually revealed the cause of death, a highly infectious, previously unknown elephant herpes virus. A review of the stud book data identified six similar prior deaths. Indeed, the virus was responsible for nearly all (87 percent) of the deaths of U.S.-born Asian elephants during their first ten years of life.

By the time the virus was identified, early in 1999 (by Dr. Laura Richman of the Johns Hopkins School of Medicine and Dr. Richard Montali of National Zoo), nearly a dozen North American zoo elephants, all but two of them zoo-bred young Asians, had succumbed to the fatal hemorrhaging. The virus apparently jumps from African elephants to the Asian species. Kumari was the "index case," the first animal to be definitively identified as having the virus. Other cases were subsequently diagnosed in Florida, California, Missouri, and elsewhere. When a second Missouri elephant, Chandra, appeared to be coming down with the disease, the very experienced Dr. Dennis Schmitt, suspecting a viral infection, injected famciclovir, a known antiviral drug. Chandra recovered, as did a second stricken animal.

To determine whether the deadly virus exists in the wild, the U.S. team worked with scientists in South Africa and Zimbabwe to collect and compare blood and tissue samples. Conclusion: the virus exists in, but is nonlethal to, wild African elephants, and probably is transmitted by them to Asian elephants in zoos. If the disease is diagnosed in time, antiviral drugs are lifesaving. A blood test for the virus is being developed. Meanwhile, the only certain preventive is to keep the two species completely separate. The major health threats to captive elephants today are the herpes virus and tuberculosis.

After Kumari's death, morale plummeted at the National Zoo, no one's more so than Nancy Pratt's. "Seeing that baby die made me vow to do something to help captive elephants reproduce and insure the species' survival." National Zoo still had no resident male, however, and the nation's few proven breeding males were booked for some time to come. Moreover, John and Nancy feared that the stress on Shanthi caused by removing her yet again from her social group for an extended period could put her into the same state of stress-related infertility as Nancy's hamsters.

Solving the remaining riddles of A-I was now imperative. The numbers of African and Asian elephants in the wild were declining so drastically that, in the long view, the survival of both species was in doubt—a portent biologists and zoo people had been aware of for a decade. Nor could captive cows and bulls be expected to reverse the decline by natural means. Far too few animals were available, and the expenses and attendant difficulties of keeping them together long enough for courtship and breeding to occur were insurmountable. Kumari's sudden, swift, mysterious death had underlined the urgency of developing a full-fledged A-I program as quickly as possible. Lehnhardt set out to find the money, and directed Pratt to organize and write the grant proposal that would be needed to secure approval from the Smithsonian.

A few months after Kumari's death, Nancy Pratt had submitted her proposal to the Smithsonian and Lehnhardt had lined up the initial funding. Three weeks later, on August 15, 1995, an agreement to proceed was signed by the Smithsonian and by Thomas Hildebrandt's Institute in Berlin. Attached to the proposal and agreement is a grainy photograph showing one of the team's first ultrasound attempts. The elephant is Shanthi. The bizarre image of a hooded human figure standing on a ladder behind an elephant, surrounded by other people in hospital garb, backed up by a tangle of odd-looking lab equipment, reminded me of old photographs of nineteenth-century surgical operations.

John laughed when I told him this. "Actually, the stuff is very high-tech. But it does look a little tacky."

"I'd like to see the procedure myself one day."

"By all means."

CHAPTER 14

BRAVE NEW ELEPHANT WORLD

"WE'VE BEEN COLLECTING MacLean every weekend for about a year now," Nancy Pratt said. "If you want to see how we do it, come on down. We'd be happy to put you up."

"Collecting," I knew, meant collecting sperm. The fourteen-year-old MacLean, an African elephant, was still too immature, and too small, to breed naturally. But his sperm, obtained by palpation, was superb, distinguished by world-class vigor, motility, and sheer numbers. Under the microscope, it resembled a dense tangle of wriggling earthworms, and the energetic teenager was already a proven sire.

In the spring of 1999 I flew back to Disney's Animal Kingdom to see Nancy collect MacLean. A few weeks later I would go to the National Zoo in Washington to observe Hildebrandt and Göritz attempt to inseminate twenty-three-year-old Shanthi, an Asian elephant. Although previous A-I attempts on her had failed, her health and temperament were perfect, and the zoologists' faith in her unshaken. Three recent A-I attempts on other elephants had succeeded, and three healthy fetuses were confirmed by ultrasound. The first to be born, shortly before the new millennium, would be the offspring of an Asian elephant at the Dickerson Park Zoo in Springfield, Missouri. Shortly thereafter, the Indianapolis Zoo expected two baby African elephants, one the following February or March, and the next—sired by MacLean—in August 2000.

Nancy met me at the Orlando airport and drove me to the breezy, flower-filled new home she shared with her husband, Paul Hawkes, a Disney animal man with special expertise in invertebrates. "If Kumari had lived, A-I might never have happened," Nancy said. "But her death occurred in a place which had the talent and money to follow up. It's ironic. Her death was more advantageous to A-I than if she had lived. She saved us at least five years."

The pioneering research in A-I today is in the hands of a new generation of scientists. They range in age from thirty-five to fifty. They have better training, better equipment, and a wiser approach than their predecessors. They subscribe wholeheartedly to Nancy Pratt's dictum that "The female elephant has to be very comfortable with everything going on," and they are passionately committed to "making it a positive experience for the animal"—which, God knows, is more than can be said of most practitioners of human gynecology.

Speaking of which, let us pause for a brief review of the reproductive structures of the order Proboscidea. The preeminent authority here is Dr. Susan K. Mikota of the Audubon Park Zoo in New Orleans. Dr. Mikota is the principal author of the 1994 textbook *Medical Management of the Elephant* and is the acknowledged Dr. Spock of elephants. She writes that the species' reproductive anatomy "is similar to that of other mammals with the exception of the long urogenital canal of the female, and the intra-abdominal testes of the male." But these are two big exceptions. The canal is more than five feet long. The exterior opening under the belly leads into the "vestibule," an internal cavity more than a yard long that has openings to the vagina, bladder, and rectum. Visualize it as an uninflated dirigible, though not quite so large. Nancy Pratt refers to it as "the sperm lobby." Whatever you call it, the thing is unique to elephants; no other animal has one.

At the far end of the thirty-nine-inch vestibule lies the entrance to the twelve-to-fourteen-inch-long vagina, which has an opening smaller than a dime, and a diameter no wider than a pencil. The opening is bracketed by two blind pouches, and the entry to the bladder is adjacent.

The vagina terminates at the cervix—the opening to the uterus—which lies at least fifty inches down within her dark declivities. Until and unless the spermatozoa reach this point, conception cannot occur. What's more, the canal is not a straight shot. It crosses over a sharp rise of bone, called the "pelvic rim," before tilting down again to the vagina and cervix, so for a part of its journey, the sperm must defy gravity and swim uphill.

The male elephant, too, is exceptional. He lacks a scrotum. His testicles are interior, near his kidneys, suspended, like bats, from the ventral surface of his spine. In natural elephant mating, the tip of the penis presses directly onto the tiny opening of the vagina, causing a contraction, and the sperm is "sucked in." But this happens only at the hormonal high point of the female cycle.

• • •

Propagation of an elephant by artificial insemination is a long and costly three-stage procedure requiring the focused cooperation of two dozen individuals—reproductive physiologists, hormone assayists, ultrasound technicians, biologists, keepers, and sweepers. Step One is precise timing of the female's estrous cycle. Step Two is collecting and shipping viable spermatozoa to her at the optimum moment. Step Three is the correct placement of the semen in her reproductive tract.

Hildebrandt's anatomical studies indicated that Mike Schmidt had always misunderstood—that is, mis-visualized—the internal structure of the female elephant. He evidently assumed that the entry to the uterus was at the end of the vestibule. Hence, what he had been doing all those years, in Lehnhardt's words, was "splashing not-good semen on the *outside* of the female's reproductive tract." It is even possible that Schmidt was depositing semen into one of the pouches, or the bladder, with attendant risks of infection. To put it another way, Schmidt had gotten Step One right, "But he was stuck, or failing, on Step Two, and he was out in left field so far as Step Three was concerned." Having misunderstood the anatomy, the unfortunate man had spent years placing nonviable sperm, floating in the wrong extender, in the wrong spot. An extender, commonly used in horse breeding, is a pH-balanced chemical broth of vitamins, nutrients, and antibiotics that prolongs spermatozoal life and vigor during shipment. But there are several kinds of extenders. The wrong one will shorten the sperm's life, and the one Schmidt was using was wrong.

To begin work on Step Two, said Nancy, "We needed some really good semen." She and John got in touch with Dr. Dennis Schmitt at the Dickerson Park Zoo in Springfield, Missouri. Schmitt was independently interested in elephant A-I, and had for thirteen years been collecting sperm from his Asian bull, Onyx, and publishing his results. Instead of the original Portland A-V (artificial vagina) technique, similar to the standard procedure in horse breeding, Dennis Schmitt makes a "condom" by tying a knot in one end of a standard veterinary palpation sleeve. This fits over the shaft of the penis, allowing him to collect clean samples and to separate the ejaculates as they are collected. Ejaculation is stimulated by rectal massage, and the elephant requires little or no training.

Nancy's biggest problem would be getting fresh, live sperm back to Washington in time to use it, without freezing it. The window of opportunity was only twenty-four to forty-eight hours.

After that, semen becomes stale and motility drops. She flew to Springfield to do an on-the-spot analysis, and took a room at the Day's Inn motel. There, in the bathroom, she set up a lab—microscope, water bath, and a variety of extenders—and for shipping, used an Equitainer, a small, insulated cooler normally used to transport horse semen. It maintains its contents at 40°F, about the temperature of a home refrigerator, thus slowing down the spermatozoa's metabolism and prolonging their life.

By this time, "We were very, very happy with Shanthi's cycles. We could predict ovulation within forty-eight hours." Two different female hormones were involved. The first was progesterone, secreted in the ovary. It proved difficult to detect, as its concentration in elephant blood is very low, only 1/1000 the level found in human blood. "Just another thing that's unique to the elephant's biochemistry," John told me. "No one knows why. But Dr. Mike Schmidt did the original progesterone measurements, and they were accurate."

The second female hormone is the luteinizing hormone, referred to as LH. It is released into the bloodstream by the brain's pituitary gland, and acts on the ovary to trigger ovulation. This sequence is true in all mammals, humans included. But only elephants have *two* LH peaks, and in this fortunate fact lay the key to precise mapping of the female elephant's cycle. The peaks always occur exactly twenty days apart; and it is the second peak only that triggers ovulation. Again, "Nobody knows why."

Lehnhardt was the first person to tell me, early in 1998, that Mike Schmidt had quietly left the Portland Zoo after a twenty-five year reign, his long-running quest for A-I never achieved. "He got left behind. There's no question that his work on ovulation opened the door. But his take on artificial insemination could never have worked." Without ultrasound, Schmidt "could never verify where he was in the reproductive tract." The fact remains, "He was probably showering dead sperm, in the wrong extender, on the wrong place."

His successor is the very capable and experienced Mike Keele, who had come to Portland fresh out of high school in 1971 as a part-time cage cleaner for rats and armadillos. He began working with elephants four years later, and in 1980 he was made foreman of animal keepers. Five years after that, the AZA named him keeper of the Asian Elephant Studbook for North America. In 1996, the AZA made him coordinator of the North American Elephant Species Survival Program, a hundred-year, long-range commitment by the zoo community; and the following year Portland appointed forty-four-year-old Mike Keele its top animal man and Mike Schmidt's boss. Schmidt now works full-time with his wife on their horse-breeding project, and has done some valuable consulting in Myanmar. From time to time he also gives presentations in shopping malls on "How to Care for Your Pet."

• • •

The Disney management goes to great lengths to maintain the illusion that visitors *are really in* East Africa. All employees are taught to think of themselves as "cast members," always "on stage," and they must "stay in character" at all times when visible to the public. Labs, offices, and other necessary workplaces are deemed "backstage," and must remain invisible. Hence it was difficult for me to obtain permission to view MacLean's collecting, and the taking of photographs was strictly *verboten.* We began backstage, in the animal hospital, where a staff veterinary technician helped Nancy get prepared. She took a vial of extender from the lab refrigerator and submerged it in a warm-water bath to gradually bring it up to elephant body temperature, then packed it in an insulated container. One of the technician's duties is to assist Nancy in sperm assessment. She checks every sample under the microscope, and notes sperm concentration, motility, and any of fourteen possible abnormalities she may find, ranging from "microcephalic head" to "terminally coiled tail."

I was not permitted to see MacLean until he had been securely enclosed in the purple-painted steel hugger out behind the elephant house. This device—a form of crush—is made from two heavily barred steel grates joined at the bottom in a V-formation, like an old-fashioned toaster. Small sections of the grates swing open so that workers can reach inside to handle the part of the elephant needed. A Disney PR lady stood beside me to be sure I did not sneak any photographs. But there was really very little to see. Inside the well-armored hugger, MacLean was almost invisible. Nancy, however, had told me what to expect. Collecting the male requires two teams of technicians working in tandem. After the animal has been assiduously hosed out and everyone thoroughly disinfected, two strong, well-muscled men palpate the bull's accessory glands through the rectal wall, while two young women crouch under his belly and stimulate his three-to-four-foot penis by massage. When he reaches the point of ejaculation, which may take up to thirty minutes' stimulation by both teams, the girls will be ready to catch his ejaculate in a long, narrow bag of clear plastic.

A young woman keeper stood at one end of the hugger with a bushel basket of sliced fruits and carrots, and reached inside to feed MacLean a steady stream of treats throughout the procedure. Two more young women knelt on the concrete just forward of his hind legs and swung open a two-by-four-foot door in the grate. Beside them were stacks of turkish towels and lengths of plastic sleeving knotted at one end. Nancy, the PR woman, and I stood behind them. Two burly young men and a lithe, athletic-looking young woman were stationed at the tail. All attendants wore short-sleeved green scrub suits like operating-room personnel. While the girl at the rear held MacLean's tail out of the way, the men scooped out armloads of feces and trundled it off in a wheelbarrow. This was followed by a thorough enema from a warm water hose.

Work began. In all, three male and seven female zookeepers worked on MacLean over the next half-hour, shouting encouragement, slapping his rump or trunk with their hands, and exhorting, "Come on, Mackie!" As his erection became manifest, the male attendants shouted encouragement. "Good boy, Mackie!" His black penis, five or six inches in diameter, protruded from his black foreskin like the hoof of a black horse. The girls were silent, working hard.

Ejaculation by palpation (which appears to be a nice word for masturbation, but I believe is a common practice in animal husbandry) is the collecting method used by both the Disney people and Dr. Dennis Schmitt. The technique requires manual massage of the prostate and accessory glands, done through the floor of the rectum, and it is a strenuous workout. Nancy lacks both the inclination and the shoulder strength, so two young male keepers, both built like Olympic swimmers, alternated. Each in turn stood on a foot-high platform, planted his feet firmly on its wet, slippery surface, inserted one stiff arm into the rectum up to the elbow and rotated his fist as hard and fast as he could. I was reminded of the spin cycle on a heavy-duty washing machine. With the other arm he maintained an iron grip on the bars. The workout was vigorous, causing the man to grit his teeth, grimace, pant, and grunt. Soon he had to change arms. Then the second man relieved him. At one point, when both men were exhausted, one of the female keepers stepped in temporarily. Ejaculation occurs in two to thirty minutes, I'd been told. Unfortunately, ours was a thirty-minute day. After a while, the shouting stopped, and the only sound was the men's panting grunts, and an occasional trunk-snuffle, or gargle, of possible pleasure from Mackie.

The bulls quickly get used to the procedure, said Nancy, and indeed, fourteen-year-old MacLean, who is routinely collected every weekend, "loves it, and comes running." Usually they collect 300 milliliters, about three-quarters of a cup. "But five milliliters is enough to use, if it's sufficiently concentrated." Alas, today's collection, after thirty minutes' exhausting work by all hands, yielded mostly urine and fluid, very few spermatozoa.

Nonetheless, routine procedure called for it to be examined under the microscope and its abnormalities logged. "Then we throw it away."

One reason bulls don't mind the experience: "It's enriching for them. They get attention, company, treats," said Nancy. "I've never known an elephant, male or female, who didn't enjoy these procedures." Palpation is the preferred method of collection, she added, because electroejaculation requires anaesthesia, and yields poorer-quality semen.

"It's best to work hard, then give him a break," said Jeff, the head keeper. "Often, when you resume, it comes immediately."

"What do you feel in there?" I asked.

"There's a lump, on the bottom, ventral surface. As you go over and over it, you feel a sort of ball starting to firm up. Then—for a moment—he is very still. Then his right leg kicks out."

Only then did I understand that Mackie's other three legs had been stoutly chained to the floor of the hugger during the entire procedure.

• • •

A few weeks later, on a rainy Sunday morning in Washington, D.C., large crowds of visitors, many with children in strollers, shuffled through the tropical air of the National Zoo's palm-decked, skylighted, ninety-foot elephant house. The elephants and a couple of rhinos were ranged along one side in big, barred cages. Opposite were pygmy hippos and a colony of golden tamarin monkeys. A pool of hippos was at the far end, and the other end, where Shanthi's A-I would take place, was overlooked by a pair of fourteen-foot giraffes.

Doctors Hildebrandt and Göritz had set up shop in a cluttered basement room down a short flight of steps, in a warren of coats, parkas, half-eaten bags of chips and Coke cans. The visiting Germans were fit, tan, fair-haired and handsome in their short-sleeved green scrubs. They looked like Alpinists, which, in a way, they are. Arm-long rubber gloves and knee-high rubber boots would complete their outfits. The crowded basement corridor was a tangle of spare electric cables, discarded junk-food wrappers, empty bottles, ladders, brooms, and hoses. A powerful smell of bananas cut through the overwhelming, fetid fug-smell that pervades all elephant houses.

But upstairs, all was immaculate. A bunch of the attractive, scrubbed young women one always finds hanging around elephants—assistant keepers, graduate students, interns—had been sweeping, cleaning, and mopping since dawn. They were now pouring huge jugs of disinfectant over the floors and gutters of the empty stall adjacent to the giraffes that had been designated the "operating room." Across a six-foot alley from the OR was the visitors' gallery, a raised, railed, thatched platform with a fine, unimpeded view. At right angles, under the giraffes, a makeshift counter held microscopes and slides. On the back wall, a forlorn poster still invited people to the zoo's birthday party for the ill-fated Kumari, and alongside it was a display of condolence letters and drawings from schoolchildren. High above us, the gentle giraffe faces, more richly eyelashed than Minnie Mouse, swiveled like giant cranes, following the action.

In charge today was Dr. Janine Brown, hormone assayist from the Smithsonian's Conservation and Research Center in Front Royal, Virginia. She was a pretty woman with a long braid down her back and gold-rimmed glasses. In preparation for today's insemination, Janine had been taking weekly and, for the past few days, daily blood samples to check Shanthi's hormone levels. "The female has to have a very, very high level of trust with her keepers," she told me. "Otherwise this procedure is much too dangerous, for people and animals." A sterile field inside the elephant herself must also be maintained, lest her cervix or other organs be contaminated by fecal matter. All instruments, catheters, and attendant paraphernalia were first soaked and washed in Nolvasan, a standard veterinary disinfectant. All persons who might touch her reproductive tract would wear surgical masks and gowns, and double sets of latex gloves. The team members scrubbed up and helped one another suit up in a manner familiar to viewers of TV hospital dramas.

The arrival of two sperm specimens had been expected by now. But as often happens, the sperm was a problem. The quality of MacLean's semen had declined of late, so today's two designated donors were Onyx, in Springfield, Missouri, and Calvin, in Calgary, Ontario. But surprisingly, Onyx's sample had been so poor last night that the zoo had not even bothered to ship it, and Calvin's contribution was tied up in Canadian Customs where agents were taking their time clearing a shipment of elephant sperm, urine, feces, and temporal gland secretion. Shanthi's devoted, lifelong keeper, Marie Galloway, had rushed off to the airport to try to move things along.

"Why do so many women do this type of work?" I asked Janine.

"It's an emotional thing for us. For men, the animals are a means to an end. They are interested in *results*. But I want to do more than just discover something in the lab. For us, the elephants are important in themselves. And not a *means*, not by any stretch. If something goes wrong with the elephants, I can get so saddened. If things go well, I'm so pumped. My husband can always tell."

Thomas Hildebrandt had come up from the basement. "Women are interested in *behavior.* Men need *success*," he said.

"Why bother doing this A-I today, if the sperm is of such poor quality?"

"Because we know so little," Janine said. "The sperm may be only immobile, not dead. Or perhaps some fluid in the female will activate immobile sperm."

Marie dashed in with the Canadian shipment, gave it to Janine's assistant at the microscope, then led Shanthi into the OR from her adjoining stall. Elephant and keeper had been together every day since Shanthi arrived at the zoo, and no crush nor other restraints were needed; she had been trained to stand perfectly still throughout the procedure. Marie would remain at her head with a bucket of treats, all the while cooing and whispering endearments, keeping her calm.

No time today for regular meals. The bevy of zoo girls noshed on health-food snacks between bouts of shoveling, scraping, disinfecting, and scrubbing. Lucy, the zoo vet, arrived with a flashlight to check out Shanthi's condition, and a hypodermic to take blood from an ear vein. "Foot!" Marie commanded. Then, "Leg!" At each instruction, Shanthi presented for Lucy's examination the called-for body part.

Frank Göritz joined Thomas, and they began checking over their equipment. "Welcome to the bunker!" someone cried. Junk food had piled up on the microscope table. People were too busy to eat. The ultrasound and A-I equipment was laid out on wheeled carts along one wall of the OR.

A tall young man in top-to-toe yellow slicker and boots appeared, and the girls got him into three pairs of shoulder-high plastic gloves, each taped to the armpits of his slicker. He would strip these off, pair by pair, as he worked. He scooped up a couple of handfuls of a lubricating jelly. A jolly, devil-may-care spirit prevailed, rather *M*A*S*H*-like, as these preparations were being made. But as soon as he put his arm in Shanthi up to the shoulder, to begin the cleaning-out—a ten-minute procedure, abetted by a warmed high-pressure hose—everyone fell silent.

Shanthi stood facing away from us. Thomas was behind her, four feet off the ground on a plywood platform balanced across the backs of four chairs—a risky-looking perch. The cart with the vivid color ultrasound screen was to Shanthi's right, elevated, and readily visible to us, to Thomas, and to Frank, crouching low and partially underneath Shanthi's rear legs. The black-and-white monitor showing what the probe sees was on a cart to Shanthi's left. The first few times they had done this, Hildebrandt removed his shirt, smeared his chest and arm with sterile gel, climbed a ladder and donned the black hood, like an old-time photographer's. The hood contained a microphone and a tiny TV screen so Thomas could work and communicate with his colleagues without needing to turn his head. He simply gripped his probe in the Bengal Lancer position, waited while someone held the tail out of the way, and plunged his arm into the animal up to his shoulder. Recent refinements had obviated the necessity for the ladder and hood.

Thomas would guide the transrectal ultrasound probe until it could "see" the vagina and cervix. We would watch on the monitor. But first, before any other instruments were inserted, Dr. Göritz would carefully position a "balloon catheter" in the vestibule, then inflate it with a tiny, hand-operated pump so that it expanded into a semirigid, ten-inch-wide cylinder that prevented the vestibule walls from collapsing in on the equipment. Next the endoscope would slowly ascend the reproductive tract, lighting its way through vulva and vestibule to the vagina and, finally, to the tiny, four-millimeter cervix.

It had taken time to get all this assorted plumbing and tubing properly hooked up. Thirty minutes had passed. Shanthi had remained motionless. In the corner, at a long table below the giraffe enclosure, Janine's assistant, a girl with sublime red hair, bent low over her microscope, focusing with her right hand and clicking a counter in her left, counting the Canadian sperm. Another girl was warming the first sperm vial in its tepid water bath very slowly, to avoid any violent temperature shock.

Then the zoo's electricity failed, plunging the entire building into semidarkness. Somebody at length found the zoo electrician, who ambled in, showing no more surprise at the bizarre goings-on than Shanthi herself, still nibbling Marie's tidbits. Eventually, Shanthi's enclosure was properly spotlighted, and the rest of the elephant house and its strange collection of animals, even the giraffes, were in shadow. The zoo's house camerawoman moved around confidently. The public had long since been shunted out. The profiles of the volunteer and staff girls, leaning forward on the railings of the raised pavilion to gain a better view, were side-lit like a row of gothic angels. The room had grown quiet.

Frank introduced the endoscope: six feet of minuscule-bore tubing passed through the balloon catheter and on up the reproductive canal. Its fiber optics provided a very sharp color picture. Socn we could actually see the bright pink cervix, glowing and trembling on the monitor. But only Thomas, watching for wrong turns and blind alleys, fully understood the geography of what we were watching. Suddenly Frank's catheter had started up the urethra toward the bladder. Thomas spotted the error, told Frank to withdraw forty centimeters, then try again. Frank now had a butterfly catheter in hand, essentially a needle with wings for guidance in its placement. He made fine corrections in the placement of the catheter-tip with a handheld device bearing two dials, one controling the up-down motions of the tip, the other the left-right corrections.

"Gut?" he finally asked.

"Gut." Thomas replied.

Shanthi would have to stand absolutely still for the next twenty minutes. Janine loaded eighty milligrams of warmed semen into a standard hypodermic syringe and handed it to Frank. The needle just fitted the exterior end of the catheter, and capillary action, aided by gentle pressure from the hypo, gradually moved the semen along to the cervix, almost five feet inside the animal's pitch-dark interior. Thomas watched for air bubbles that might interfere with the passage of the semen.

"We try to leave all the equipment in place and motionless for twenty minutes," Nancy had told me. "If we withdraw the catheter sooner, the sperm might all gush out, too." We waited in silence. The elephant's cervix was much swollen and full of ridges and traps, due to her level of hormones, and these ridges and traps also helped prevent back-flow. Perhaps fifty minutes had passed since introduction of the balloon catheter. All subsequent movements had been swift, deft, practiced, and precise. It was important to place as little stress as possible on ever-patient Shanthi, and to avoid excess irritation of her reproductive tract.

After one of their earlier attempts, Nancy had had a bit of semen left over and she poured it out onto the floor in front of Shanti. The elephant immediately rumbled, then flehmened, and her ears flapped wildly. Her response prompted Nancy in future to "try to mimic nature more," and for subsequent A-Is, she asked donors to ship samples of the bull's feces, urine, and temporal-gland secretion along with his spermatozoa. The added stimulus worked even better than anticipated. "You could actually *see* the pelvic contractions. I don't mean see them by ultrasound, I mean you could see her sides rippling!"

Today's semen had come from Calvin of Canada, which sounds like, but is not, a high-fashion fragrance. Calvin was thirteen. Janine had earlier pronounced his semen "Great!" meaning a concentration of one-half-billion spermatozoa per milliliter. In all, 100 cc of extended sperm had been used. Shanthi seemed particularly happy. Also, she had "good mucus" in her reproductive tract, another indication that her uterus was properly prepared. The mucus was also thought to aid somewhat in sperm transport. Her temporal-gland drainage was also "good," but Janine cautioned that "We don't really know *what* this means. It seems to denote excitement, either good or bad."

Janine poured Calvin's excess semen on ground, then placed bowls of urine, feces, and temporal-gland secretion alongside, as if making an offering to propitiate the gods of elephant fertility. Shanthi sniffed it and instantly flehmened. One could see muscle contractions along her flanks. It would be a mistake, however, to refer to these as "orgasm"; the correct term is "reproductive response." Shanthi flehmened again; the drama was over.

As soon as the equipment was removed, the elephant was free to move about. A few people burst into applause. I felt utterly wiped out. Dr. Brown would continue her regular hormone assays in the coming months. If Shanthi's blood and urine progesterone levels remained elevated for ten weeks, the animal was probably pregnant. But the team could not be absolutely certain until four months had passed and the presence of another hormone, prolactin, told them that milk production had begun.

Most of the scientists' time today had been devoted to readying their equipment. The elephant's time, from enema to end, was about an hour and a half.

As I left the zoo, the rain stopped. The gardens shimmered in the spring sunlight. I thought again of something Mike Schmidt had told me. "When venturing into the biological unknown, one expects to make many false starts."

Although we couldn't be certain yet about the outcome of today's events, we already knew that three females—and perhaps several more—were in a fairly advanced state of pregnancy. Indeed the wait was not long. The first elephant ever born as a consequence of artificial insemination finally made his appearance on the Sunday after Thanksgiving, November 28, 1999, in the reinforced concrete "family stall" of the Dickerson Park Zoo in Springfield, Missouri. The mother was an eighteen-year-old Asian elephant, aptly named Moola, who during her confinement was continually soothed and encouraged by two older, experienced "auntie" cows in an adjoining stall.

With Moola in her stall were three men she knew well, two keepers and the unflappable Dr. Schmitt. As Moola's labor began in earnest, Schmitt was asked for comment on his historic achievement. "This work is highly labor intensive," he said. "It was really our whole team that did it."

Thirty-four hours later, Moola gave a final grunt, and her healthy, hairy, 378-pound son tumbled into the straw. The team voted to name him Haji, Arabic for one who has completed the holy pilgrimage to Mecca, and the honorific seemed entirely fitting for such an important little fellow.

ACKNOWLEDGMENTS

The long list of people I want to thank for helping me to write this book begins with Dr. Matthew "Doc" Maberry, veterinarian at the Oregon Zoo at the time of Packy's birth, and Doc's buddy Morgan Berry, the extraordinary Seattle-based wildlife lover and professional wild-animal importer.

Over the years, the list has grown to include a prizewinning array of zoologists, biologists, field explorers, geneticists, anatomists, chemists, archivists, and other scientists and laypersons with the wisdom and nerve to devote their lives to the oversized mysteries of the elephant.

At the Oregon Zoo: Former Director Michael J. Schmidt, D.V.M., retired senior elephant keeper Roger Hennous, and most especially Michael Keele, assistant director/curator of the Oregon Zoo since 1997, keeper of the Asian Elephant Studbook for North America, and chief of the American Zoological and Aquarium Association's Elephant Species Survival Program.

At Disney's Animal Kingdom: Animal Operations Manager John Lehnhardt, and Nancy Pratt, Ph.D., mammal curator.

At the National Zoo, Washington, D.C.: public relations director Robert Hoag and head keeper Marie Galloway.

At Wildlife Preservation Trust International (WPTI): Dr. Mary Pearl and Dr. Raman Sukumar, D.V.M.

At Dickerson Park Zoo, Springfield, Missouri: Dr. Dennis L. Schmitt, D.V.M., Ph.D.

At the Elephant Interest Group, Wayne State University: Dr. Jeheskel Shoshani, Ph.D., and Sandra Shoshani.

At the Institute for Zoo Biology and Wildlife Research in Berlin, Germany: Dr. Thomas Hildebrandt, D.V.M., director of the Department of Reproductive Management, and Dr. Frank Göritz, D.V.M.

I want to express my special thanks to the executives and staff of the Ringling Bros., Barnum & Bailey Center for Elephant Conservation, in Florida, a private research facility, for inviting me to visit.

I am also indebted to a remarkable group of independent scientists and researchers, including Dr. Iain and Oria Douglas-Hamilton, Dr. Cynthia Moss, Dr. Joyce Poole, Dr. L.E.L. (Bets) Rasmussen, Dr. Randall J. Moore, Katy Payne, Dr. Janine L. Brown, and Debbie Olson.

For countless hours of precious research, I thank archivists and historians Stuart Thayer, Fred Pfening, Jr., and Fred Dahlinger, Jr., director of Circus World Museum, and his able staff; and most especially, I thank my own librarian and researcher nonpareil, Elizabeth Burns.

Some individuals were the more valuable for utterly defying categorization. Among them: Corky Christiani Bowes, Dr. Teresa Howard-Carter, Charles McCarry, and Robert F. Levine.

In addition, I am eternally grateful to a special group of people who excel in the long-term nurture of struggling writers: Robert Treuhaft and his late wife, Jessica Mitford; my sister friends Dr. Maya Angelou and Laurel Bentley; my wise and generous neighbor friends Peter and Maria Matthiessen, Mr. and Mrs. John R. Hearst, and Tee Addams; the poet who inspired me most, Walker Gibson; and my beloved Laurence Z. Rubenstein, M.D.

Finally, I want to thank once again my impeccable editor and dear friend, Robert D. Loomis. His enthusiasm for this project has been steadfast, and more than anyone else he has helped to make my dream of a book a reality.

SOURCES FOR MORE INFORMATION ABOUT ELEPHANTS

African Wildlife Foundation, 1400 Sixteenth St., N.W., Suite 120, Washington, D.C. 20036

Disney's Animal Kingdom, P.O. Box 10,000, Lake Buena Vista, Florida 32830-1000

Portland Zoo, 4001 S.W. Canyon Road, Portland, Oregon 97221

Save the Elephants Foundation, P.O. Box 54667, Nairobi, Kenya

Elephant Interest Group: Dr. Jeheskel Shoshani, 106 East Hickory Grove Road, Bloomfield, MI 48304

Wildlife Preservation Trust International, 1520 Locust Street, Suite 704, Philadelphia, PA 19102

BIBLIOGRAPHY

Books

Adams, Dr. Jack. *Wild Elephants in Captivity.* Carson, CA: Center for the Study of Elephants, 1981.

Agee, James. *Letters of James Agee to Father Flye.* Boston: Houghton Mifflin Company, 1971.

Allen, F. Edward, and F. Beverly Kelley. *Fun by the Ton.* New York: Hastings House, 1951.

Aristotle. *Historia Animalium. The Works of Aristotle,* translated into English under the editorship of J. A. Smith, M.A., and W. D. Ross, M.A. London: Oxford University Press, 1949.

———. *The Works of Aristotle, Vol II.* Encyclopedia Britannica, Inc., 1952.

Bakeless, John. *The Eyes of Discovery.* New York: J. B. Lippincott, 1950.

Barnum, P. T. *Barnum's Own Story: The Autobiography of P. T. Barnum.* Gloucester, MA. Combined & condensed from the various editions published during his lifetime by Waldo R. Browne and P. Smith, 1972.

Beard, Peter. *The End of the Game.* New York: Doubleday, 1965.

Bedini, Silvio A. *The Pope's Elephant.* Manchester, England: Carcanet, 1997.

Benedict, Francis G. *The Physiology of the Elephant.* Publisher unknown, 1936.

Bonner, Ray. *At the Hand of Man.* New York: Vintage Books, 1994.

Campbell, Joseph. *The Mythic Image.* Princeton: Princeton University Press, Bollingen Series C, 1974.

Carrington, Richard. *Mermaids and Mastodons.* New York: Rinehart & Co., Inc., 1957.

———. *Elephants: A Short Account of Their Natural History, Evolution, and Influence on Mankind.* New York: Basic Books, 1958.

Chadwick, Douglas H. *The Fate of the Elephant.* San Francisco: Sierra Club, 1992.

Clark, Kenneth. *Civilization.* New York: Harper & Row, 1969.

Culhane, John. *The American Circus.* New York: Henry Holt, 1990.

De Beer, Sir Gavin, *Alps and Elephants.* New York: Dutton, 1956.

Delort, Robert. *The Life and Lore of the Elephant.* Trieste: Gallimard, 1990; English translation, for New York: Harry N. Abrams, Inc., 1992

DiSilvestro, Roger L. *The African Elephant: Twilight in Eden.* New York: John Wiley & Sons, Inc., 1991.

Douglas-Hamilton, Iain and Oria. *Among the Elephants.* London: Collins & Harvill Press, 1975.

———. *Battle for the Elephants.* New York: Viking, 1992.

Drummond, W. H. *The Large Game and Natural History of South and*

South-East Africa. Edinburgh: 1875. (*Note:* Another source/listing gives this as "from the journals of the Hon. W. H. Drummond, Salisbury, Rhodesia, The Pioneer Head, 1972.)

Eckley, Wilton. *The American Circus*. Boston: Twayne Publishers, 1984

Edgerton, Franklin. *The Elephant Lore of Hindus*. Translated from the Sanskrit by F. E. Salisbury. Delhi, Motilal Banarsidass, Varanasi, Patna, Madras, 1985.

Ellwood, Robert S., Jr. *Many People, Many Faiths*. Pub. unknown.

Eltringham, S. K. *Elephants and Man*. Dorset, England: Blandford Press, 1982.

Gale, U Toke. *Burmese Timber Elephant*. Rangoon, Myanmar: Trade Corporation, 1974.

Gowdy, Barbara. *The White Bone*. New York: Metropolitan Books, 1998.

Halliburton, Richard. *The Famous Adventures of Richard Halliburton*. New York: Bobbs Merrill, 1940.

Hammarstrom, David Lewis. *Behind the Big Top*. South Brunswick, NJ, A. S. Barnes and Company, 1980.

Heard, Gerald. *The Human Venture*. New York: Harper & Brothers, 1955.

Helfer, Ralph. *Modoc*. New York: HarperCollins, 1997.

Hochchild, Adam. *King Leopold's Ghost*. Boston: Houghton Mifflin, 1998.

Hoh LaVahn G., and William H. Rough. *Step Right Up!* White Hall, VA: Betterway Publications, Inc., 1990.

Innes, Hammond. *The Big Footprints*. New York: Alfred A. Knopf, Inc., 1977.

Ives, Richard. *Of Tigers and Men: Entering the Age of Extinction*. New York: Nan A. Talese, Doubleday, 1996.

Jurmain, Suzanne. *From Trunk to Tail: Elephants Legendary and Real*. New York: Harcourt, Brace, Jovanovich, 1978

Keele, Michael N., Norie Dimeo-Ediger and Laurie Bingaman Lackey. *Asian Elephant Regional Studbook: 1 April 1994–1 July 1997*. Portland, OR: Metro Washington Park Zoo, 1992.

Kelley, F. Beverly. *It Was Better Than Work*. Gerald, MO: The Patrice Press, 1982.

Kunhardt, Philip B., Jr., Philip B. Kunhardt III, and Peter W. Kunhardt. *P. T. Barnum: America's Greatest Showman*. New York: Alfred A. Knopf, 1995.

Kunkel, Reinhard. *Elephants*. Translated from the German by Ursula Korneitchouk. New York: Harry N. Abrams, 1982.

Langley, Myrtle. *A Book of Beliefs*. Lion Publishing, England, 1981.

The Larousse Encyclopedia of Mythology. Batchworth Press, Ltd., 1959.

Lawrence, D. H. *The Complete Poems of D. H. Lawrence*. Collected & edited with an introduction and notes by Vivian De Sola Pinto and F. Warren Roberts. New York: Viking Press, 1964.

Lewis, George "Slim" and Fish, Byron. *I Loved Rogues: The Life of an Elephant Tramp*. Seattle: Superior Publishing Co., 1978.

Livy. *The War with Hannibal*. Middlesex, England: Penguin Books, Ltd., 1965.

MacNeice, Louis. *The Collected Poems of Louis MacNeice*. London: Faber & Faber, 1966.

Masson, Jeffrey Moussaieff, and Susan McCarthy. *When Elephants Weep*. New York: Delacorte Press, 1995.

Matthiessen, Peter. *The Tree Where Man Was Born*. New York: E. P. Dutton, 1972.

May, Earl Chapin. *The Circus—From Rome to Ringling*. Duffield & Green, 1932.

Mikota, Susan K., D.V.M.; Eva Lee Sargent, Ph.D.; and G. S. Ranglack, D.V.M., Ph.D. *Medical Management of the Elephant*. West Bloomfield, MI: Indira Publishing House, 1994.

Moore, Marianne. *The Complete Poems of Marianne Moore*. New York: The Macmillan Company/The Viking Press, 1967.

Moore, Randall Jay, with Christopher Munnion. *Back to Africa*. Johannesburg: Southern Book Publishers, 1989.

Moss, Cynthia. *Elephant Memories: 13 Years in the Life of an Elephant Family*. New York: William Morrow, 1988.

Murray, Neil. *The Love of Elephants*. London: Octopus Books Ltd., 1976.

Orr, Gertrude. *Here Come the Elephants*. Caldwell, ID: The Caxton Printers, Ltd., 1943.

Parker, Dorothy. *Death and Taxes*. New York: The Viking Press, 1931.

Payne, Katharine. *Elephants Calling*. New York: Crown, 1992.

Payne, Katy. *Silent Thunder: In the Presence of Elephants*. New York: Simon & Schuster, 1998.

Pliny [Plenius Secundus]. *Natural History*. Vol. III. Boston: Loeb Classical Library, Harvard University Press, 1940.

Poole, Joyce. *Coming of Age with Elephants*. New York: Hyperion, 1996.

———. *Elephants*. Stillwater, MN: Voyageur Press, 1997.

Price, Charles Edwin. *The Day They Hung the Elephant*. Johnson City, TN: The Overmountain Press, 1992.

Pringle, Lawrence. *Elephant Woman: Cynthia Moss Explores the World of Elephants*. New York: Athenaeum, 1997.

Redmond, Ian. *Elephant*. New York: Alfred A. Knopf, 1993.

Sanderson, Ivan T. *The Dynasty of Abu: A History and Natural History of the Elephants and Their Relatives Past and Present*. New York: Alfred A. Knopf, 1962.

Sanderson, G. P. *Thirteen Years Among the Wild Beasts of India . . . With an Account of the Modes of Capturing and Taming Elephants*. London: W. H. Allen & Co., 1882.

Scullard, H. H. *The Elephant in the Greek and Roman World*. London: Thames & Hudson, 1974.

Shand, Mark. *Queen of the Elephants*. London: Jonathan Cape, 1995.

———. *Travels on My Elephant*. London: Jonathan Cape, 1991.

Shoshani, Jeheskel, Ph.D., consulting editor. *Elephants: Majestic Creatures of the Wild*. Emmaus, PA: Rodale Press, 1992.

Sillar, F. C., and R. M. Meyler. *Elephants Ancient and Modern*. New York: Viking Press, 1968.

Singer, Peter. *Animal Liberation: New, Revised Edition*. New York: Avon Books, 1990.

Speaight, George. *A History of the Circus*. London: The Tantivy Press; San Diego and New York: A. S. Barnes and Company, 1980.

Sukumar, Raman. *Elephant Days and Nights*. London: Oxford University Press, 1994.

Sutton, Felix. *The Big Show*. New York: Doubleday, 1971.

Thayer, Stuart. *Annals of the American Circus: 1830–1847, (Vols. I–II–III)*. Seattle: Dauven & Thayer, 1992.

Thornton, Allan, and Dave Currey. *To Save an Elephant*. London: Transword, 1991.

Toynbee, J.M.C. *Animals in Roman Life and Art*. Ithaca, NY: Cornell University Press, 1973.

Tsuchiya, Yukio. *Faithful Elephants*. Boston: Houghton Mifflin, 1988.

Wallace, Irving. *The Fabulous Showman: The Life and Times of P. T. Barnum*. New York: Alfred A. Knopf, 1959.

Weill, Kurt, and Lotte Lenya. *Speak Low (When You Speak Love): The Letters of Kurt Weill and Lotte Lenya*. Berkeley and Los Angeles: University of California Press, 1996.

Western, David. *In the Dust of Kilimanjaro*. Washington, DC, and Covelo, CA: Island Press/Shearwater Books, 1997.

Williams, Lt.-Col. J. H., O.B.E. *Elephant Bill*. New York: Doubleday, 1950.

Winfrey, Laurie Platt. *The Unforgettable Elephant*. New York: Walker & Co., 1980.

Magazines, Newspapers, and Scientific Journals

Alexander, Shana. "Big Blessed Event: 22 Pounds and All Elephant." *Life*, May 11, 1962.

———. "For the Love of Elephants." *Life*, March 1980.

Alispaw, Fred C. "The First Recorded American Bred Baby Elephant." *The White Tops*, published by Circus Fans of America, five articles, in issues dated October 1931, December 1931, January 1932, March 1932, June 1932.

Asbury, Edith Evans. "Zoo Destroys a Sick Elephant that Attacked Keeper." *The New York Times*, December 16, 1976.

Ben-Ari, Elia T. "A Throbbing in the Air." *Bioscience*, May 1999.

Burton, Professor Thomas G. "The Hanging of Mary, a Circus Elephant." *Tennessee Folklore Society Bulletin*, October 3, 1970.

Chadwick, Douglas. "Elephants." *The National Geographic*, May 1991.

Chester, Lewis. "Sex and the Single Elephant." London *Sunday Times*, *Spectrum* section, December 23, 1972.

Crews, Harry. "A Walk in the Country." *Playboy*, February 1975.

Gary, Romain. "Dear Elephant, Sir." *Life*, December 22, 1967.

Hess, David L., Anne M. Schmidt, and Michael J. Schmidt. "Reproductive Cycle of the Asian Elephant *(Elephas Maximus)* in Captivity." *Biology of Reproduction*, 1983.

Hildebrandt, Thomas B., D.V.M.; Frank Göritz, D.V.M.; Nancy C. Pratt, Ph.D.; Dennis L. Schmitt, D.V.M., Ph.D.; Sybille Quandt, D.V.M.;

Jacobus Raath, D.V.M.; and Reinhold R. Hofmann, D.V.M., Ph.D. "Reproductive Assessments of Male Elephants *(Loxodonta Africana* and *Elephas Maximus)* by Ultrasonography." *Journal of Zoo and Wildlife Medicine* 29(2): 114–128, 1998.

Hornaday, William T. "The Elephant in Jungle, Zoo and Circus." *Mentor,* Vol. 12, No. 5, June 1924.

Larom, David, Michael Garstang, Katharine Payne, Richard Raspet, and Malan Lindque. "The Influence of Surface Atmospherical Conditions on the Range and Area Reached by Animal Vocalizations." *The Journal of Experimental Biology 200,* 1997.

Mar, Daw Khyne U., B.V.S., F.R.V.C.S. "Development of Artificial Insemination in Myanmar Elephants [*Elephus maximus*]," Forestry Science Research Paper, Union of Myanmar Ministry of Forestry, Forest Department, 1992.

Mydans, Seth. "Bangkok Journal: Hungry and Jobless, Elephants Wander the Streets." *The New York Times,* November 4, 1996.

Payne, Katharine T. "Elephant Talk." *The National Geographic,* August 1989.

Sahagun, Louis. "Elephants Pose Giant Dangers." *Los Angeles Times,* October 11, 1994.

Santiapillai, Charles and Peter Jackson. "The Asian Elephant: An Action Plan for Its Conservation." Gland, Switzerland. Brochure, published by International Union for Conservation of Nature and Natural Resources, 1990.

Schmidt, M. J. "Studies on Asian Elephant Reproduction at the Washington Park Zoo." *Zoo Biology 1,* 1982.

Shoshani, Dr. Jeheskel. "Understanding Proboscidean Evolution: A Formidable Task." *TREE,* January 1999.

Terborgh, John. "Trouble in Paradise." *The New York Review of Books,* February 18, 1999.

Tisdale, Sallie. "The Only Harmless Great Thing." *The New Yorker,* January 23, 1989.

Zora, Lucia. "The Bravest Woman in the World." *The Ladies Home Journal,* Vol. 41, June 1924.

"The Elephant Species Survival Plan." *Science,* Vol. 265, September 9, 1994.

"World Press Review." *Der Spiegel.* August 1996.

"Science and Technology." *The Economist,* May 15, 1999.

INDEX

ABOUT THE AUTHOR

SHANA ALEXANDER was educated at Vassar College, and trained as an anthropologist. She has spent her life writing and talking about people—in newspapers, magazines, and books, and on radio, television, and the lecture circuit. This book, more than thirty-five years in the making, marks her first foray into the animal kingdom, and has introduced her to an entirely new world of beings and wonders.

Alexander was born in Manhattan, and now shares a cottage on a pond on Long Island with two poodles, Zinny and Zombo.

ABOUT THE TYPE

This book was set in Caslon, a typeface first designed in 1722 by William Caslon. Its widespread use by most English printers in the early eighteenth century soon supplanted the Dutch typefaces that had formerly prevailed. The roman is considered a "workhorse" typeface due to its pleasant, open appearance, while the italic is exceedingly decorative.

BALLARD JR-SR HIGH IMC
T 17742